AIRWAR: VOLUME I

AIRWAR: VOLUME I

TERROR FROM THE SKY

EDWARD JABLONSKI

DOUBLEDAY & COMPANY, INC., GARDEN CITY, NEW YORK

1971

For my friends,
CLAIRE and PETER CLAY
once of the hospitable "George II,"
Luton, Bedfordshire, and now
of the "Coach and Horses," Rickmansworth,
Hertfordshire, England.

Man, have pity on man.
Rain from the outraged sky
drowned the innocent earth
yet the seed did not die.
Flowering from that rebirth,
man, have pity on man
as you hold the fire in your hand
that can destroy mankind
and desolate every land.
If the power and the glory is this,
a flame that burns to the bone,
what shall be left to grow
when you and your fires have gone?
What maimed and desolate few
shall recover life's full span
from among the ashes of time?
Man, have pity on man.
                Ursula Vaughan Williams

Preface

THIS is the first of four volumes collectively entitled *Airwar*. Originally the intention was to produce a reasonably comprehensive one-volume history of aerial warfare as it evolved during the historically brief but crucial period of the Second World War. The finished work, despite certain omissions and some short shrifting, proved to be a rather large tome indeed.

The practical solution (achieved with a nimble editorial brain and a deft editorial hand) was to break it down into what seemed to be natural divisions and to issue the book as a multivolumed set over a period of time. Each book would be complete in itself and yet a part of a continuing larger narrative. A decided advantage of this solution was that the illustrations could be larger and the individual volumes easier to handle and, hopefully even if only because of a generous type size, to read.

If there is a major theme of *Airwar* it is that evolution of air power already mentioned against the human background. War does not make war, men do. Men also fashion weapons under stress with a fiendish ingenuity (taken for granted at the time) which after the urgency has passed are recognized as appalling expediencies. But once fashioned the weapons cannot be forgotten nor wished out of existence. So it was with the development of airwar

during 1939–45. Certain technical advances occurred during these years, while men endured terrible stresses, suffered misgivings and pain, and many —too many—died. It was a time of unquestioning (at least prevalently) valor and great deeds that contributed to the accomplishment of a weapon of greater potency than anyone concerned had imagined.

This volume, *Terror from the Sky,* is devoted to beginnings: with the rise of the German Luftwaffe, with the eruption of the Second World War (a war that can be attributed to the sickness inside Nazi Germany more than is generally done). The narrative carries the story through the decisive (though little understood) Battle of Britain and what beleaguered Londoners called "the blitz." These beginnings were more tentative than they appeared to be at the time. The Stuka dive bomber, that winged terror, seemed to be the ultimate air weapon; at the same time the early fighting in France was little more than a sequel to the aerial jousting of the First World War—and equally decisive (which was practically nil).

It was not until the Luftwaffe's rebuff in the Battle of Britain and its ineffectual bombing of British cities which followed that a certain pattern began to emerge. For one thing, despite the old dictum, the bomber did *not* always get through. Also, when it did, great numbers of non-combatant civilians were injured or died—and their dying did not inevitably lead to pleas for peace. Humankind, while capable of devising infinite methods of extinguishing (one is tempted to use "extincting") itself, can also draw upon tragically inexhaustible reserves of courage and a capacity for sacrifice. This was equally true, during 1939–45, of airmen, foot soldiers, seamen, civilians, of friend and enemy. It is on this note that this first volume closes, but it is a subtheme that must thread through the entire work.

The second volume, *Tragic Victories,* is an account of groping, of a search for a method of wielding a weapon not fully understood. Its telling is a tale of loss, of great triumphs that were not triumphs at all. The Flying Tigers were abused and sacrificed for a nation only half-concerned with the ethics of the war; the famous Doolittle raid accomplished little militarily and Midway was, we know now, one of America's most poignant victories. The early attempts at reaching the industrial heart of Germany with British and American bombers are sorrowing in terms of great dedication and sacrifice—and scant fulfillment. The volume opens with the most tragic victory of all, Japan's attack on Pearl Harbor, which inexorably led to Japan's own searing destruction.

Outraged Skies, the third volume, is devoted entirely to that orphaned theater of war, the Pacific. It was an infuriating secondhand kind of war in which those who fought had to learn how to make do until they could be supplied with needed equipment, matériel, and men. It was not official policy to deprive these men of necessities, of course, but the ultimate effect was that it just as well might have been. And some of those who fought believed it was. Thus their feats were no mean accomplishments. They fought against natural enemies—the sea and jungle—and a human enemy whose psychology and philosophy of death were incredible to them. But they persevered, despite dispiriting handicaps, and eventually turned the tide of battle. Still there were times, in their darker moments, when all who fought in the Pacific—Allies as well as Japanese—wondered just who their enemies were, not the least of whom seemed to be some angry aerial deity who implacably and without favoritism sought to destroy them all.

Finally, *Wings of Fire,* the last volume, relates how the air weapon came of age in those last hectic months of the war. Although the Second World War, especially in Europe, was decided on the ground (primarily because its high commanders were traditional ground men), the ultimate victory owed much to air power. If unleashed it could have been *the* decisive weapon—but at a cost to mankind that might have been too frightful to consider. As it was, the fiery endings in both Germany and Japan were devastating enough. It would be best that they never be repeated; nor should it be forgotten that those weapons, now refined but yet the same weapons, are poised—hopefully in limbo. But they are poised.

A last general word: My appreciation to all those who contributed to the preparation of this work and a long bibliography appear in the concluding volume, number 4, of *Airwar.* It might be noted, too, that the word "airwar" was not coined by me; it was a term used widely during the Second World War, although as two words. Eliminating the space took no great ingenuity, but the single word, I feel, capsulizes a concept, a type of warfare that is capable of striking anywhere, anytime, and everyone.

EDWARD JABLONSKI

New York, N.Y.
June 1970

Contents

Foreword

MILITARY aviation attained dreadful maturity during the Second World War—actually the first war of truly world-wide dimension. Whether or not this coming of age in technology and strategy was in fact a blessing (read: "deterrent") or a scourge remains for history to determine. Or rather, for men to determine in the course of history. This history—from the club to the intercontinental ballistic missile—is a long one, but the major innovation, the air weapon, is peculiar to the twentieth century.

As we all know, the "flying machine" or "aeroplane" was metamorphosed from a sportsman's plaything into a weapon of war during the early months of the Great War of 1914–18. Despite an exceptionally favorable press, a flood of pulp literature, cinematic fatuities, and a latter-day cult (nurtured by young innocents who never suffered a single experience of war), the "aeroplane" contributed very little to the outcome of that war.

The embryo air weapon, however, gave birth to the myth of the "ace," the high-scoring pursuit, later fighter, pilot, the twentieth-century equivalent of the medieval knight in a curiously anachronistic reversion. So much attention was focused upon these gentlemen jousters, their dainty craft, and their in-conclusive "dogfights" that the more deadly transition of the toy turned weapon was scarcely noticed.

There were inklings and intimations. The Germans introduced, with their abortive Zeppelin depredations, the terror bombings upon cities. With the advent of the giant bombers—the Gothas, Staaken, and others—the German war leaders skirted along the edge of the idea of strategic bombardment: the elimination of an enemy's means of making war far from the battle fronts. But this was not systematically pursued and the Giants, like the Zeppelins, were more assiduously employed at destroying civilians than war industries.

Germany was spared by the Armistice the horrors of mass bombings in the Great War. It was a near thing, actually. Two astute airmen, England's Hugh Trenchard and America's William Mitchell, had grasped the potential of aircraft as a weapon and how it might be used in terms of that potential. Had Germany not surrendered, its cities would have been bombed by huge fleets of large aircraft and its industries laid waste. It very well may have changed the course of history.

Between the wars, especially because of a general revulsion to things military in the democracies, the development of air power was minimal. However, Trenchard managed to keep his RAF out from under the thumbs of the established services and thus encouraged the doctrine of the independent air force. Mitchell, dishonored prophet in his own country, also campaigned for an air force free of Army and Navy control with especial emphasis upon the heavy bomber designed to strike at the enemy behind the lines. About the same time also, Giulio Douhet, in Italy, expounded his concept of "Command of the Air," which was based upon the big bomber. Neither Douhet nor Mitchell were popular among their more conservative military peers, who continued to view war through nineteenth-century eyes. Mitchell, in fact, propheted himself into a court-martial because of his outspoken views on the U. S. Navy's attitude toward aviation.

A not very subtle change in military thinking was obvious in the generally realistic theories of Mitchell and Douhet. For centuries the civilian had been permitted to "enjoy" war at a distance. Unless, of course, he happened to live in the path of armies; if he were swept aside, his home and fields destroyed, himself even killed, it was accepted as the "fortunes of war." It was merely bad luck; no one deliberately set out to kill him.

The introduction of the doctrine of strategic bombardment changed all that. The once flimsy, harmless little flying machine brought this change about. It was suggested during the Great War, lay dormant through the between-the-wars period, and came to full bloom during the Second World War. Curiously, the idea of strategic bombardment was nurtured in the peace-loving democracies, England and, to a greater extent, the United States. Mitchell's ideas, for all their unpopularity, were sustained and understood by his young disciples Henry H. Arnold, Carl A. Spaatz, and Ira C. Eaker, among others.

These men were not devoted to killing civilians—the thought was repellent to them—but to the idea of the destruction of enemy war industries by what came to be called "high-altitude, daylight, precision bombing." Their argument lay in the truth that if you eradicate the enemy's means of making war, he will stop fighting. This could be done, they contended, only if targets could actually be seen (this was before the advent of radar) and efficiently struck: that is, virtually erased off the map. Such bombing could be done in daylight with extremely

accurate bombsights in powerful high-flying, self-defending aircraft. This plane was produced by the Boeing Company in 1935 and became celebrated as the B-17 Flying Fortress. That it was not in fact a flying fortress was proved in combat, but that was beside the point; it was the first flying proof of the efficacy of the strategic bomber.

Over this same period, interestingly, there was no parallel development in Germany, Italy, or Japan —nor France, for that matter. All three of the aggressor nations of the Second World War evolved mighty and potent air forces, but they were invariably subordinate to ground command. This was especially true of Germany. Japan depended upon a formidable navy with its major force being the carriers equipped with an outstanding aircraft, the then unknown Zero.

Germany plunged into war with the most powerful air force in the world at the time. Modern-day apologists claim it was not as powerful as was imagined at the time. Perhaps its strength was overestimated by the Allies (and even the Germans themselves) and some of its sweeping impact could be attributed to shock as much as to superior tactics. But like the carrier-based Japanese naval air forces, it was a fearful instrument of destruction.

Because these great forces were subservient to thinking predominated by surface tactics, they were ultimately wasted. As for Germany and Japan— and Italy and France—such thinking lost them the war.

The Second World War opened and closed with aerial attacks: Dirschau Bridge in Poland by a *Kette* of Stukas and Nagasaki in the Pacific by a lone B-29. And yet the war was not a pure air war. It was throughout, to some extent, and especially in Europe, tied to (and often tied down by) ground strategy.

The role of air power, however, was anything but minor in 1939–45: it was decisive. It is a dangerous delusion to pretend that the bombings of Germany did not contribute heavily to the Nazi collapse. That all was not perfection in the strategic bombardment program is true; how could it have been otherwise? The Germans were not cooperating in its prosecution. But without air power it is unlikely that Allied ground forces would have set foot upon the beaches of Normandy when they did, or quite so firmly. It would have been possible to have bombed Germany into submission without an invasion at all; several responsible airmen believed this. Given the B-29 and the atomic bomb, had the war lasted some months longer in Europe, this would have been inevitable.

The aircraft in operation at the beginning of the war and those at its close were quite different. Those nations whose aircraft development stagnated (partially because they were bombed into stagnation) were defeated. Germany, it is true, developed the first operational jet- and rocket-powered fighters, but fortunately they came too late to have an effect upon the war—thanks to that great military philosopher, Hitler, and to Allied bombardment. There was a wide range of development in the progression from the B-17 to the B-29 and from the P-40 to the P-51. There is an even greater one from the early general-purpose bombs to such refinements as the missile and the atomic bomb.

Aircraft, their weaponry and ordnance, contributed to the war's outcome; immeasurably when compared to their contribution in the First World War. This can be attributed partly to mere technical improvement, but even more to application, to *how* the air weapon was employed. The war opened as a kind of sequel to the Great War and, excepting the innovational doctrine of the German blitzkrieg (the tank plus aircraft team), seemed fated to repeating the inconclusive dogfighting of the previous war. The Battle of Britain changed all that and revealed that German bombardment theory was all but ineffectual in a strategic sense.

It was when the British and Americans, for all their doctrinal wrangling, combined to destroy German industry that the fuller implications of modern air war became a tragic realization. The Japanese, though they initiated the lesson at Pearl Harbor, learned the full lesson themselves at Midway. The aircraft had truly revolutionized war, though few were anxious to acknowledge it.

Air war meant that the day of the civilian noncombatant was over. The cozy concept of leaving war to "guilty" soldiers and sparing "innocent" civilians was dead. That millions of innocent civilians were slaughtered cannot be denied, but war being now what it is, neither can it be avoided.

Remember that.

And it should not be forgotten that the air weapons developed during the Second World War (and

refined since) make practically every pin point on the globe vulnerable to attack.

In effect, the evolution of air war during 1939–45 also marked the end of land warfare in the future. It also sank the battleship forever.

The Second World War was the last large-scale war out of which individuals, personalities, emerged. As the war progressed, individual exploits were lost in the emphasis upon "formations." It was the last war of the aces. That last rugged individualist, the fighter pilot, became part of a team whose function was not to *joust* but to escort a load of explosives to a specified target. The lone fighter pilot who went into combat with a "daredevil aces" complex did not last.

But as always, alas, wartime was a time of heroes, of incredible sacrifice—of wasteful sacrifice, of pointless sacrifice—for man has an infinite capacity for such deeds. Courage in war is not a rare or exclusive commodity: all people have it and draw upon it when they must. What makes the heroism of airmen so much more romantically fascinating is the otherworldly element in which they perform: the cloud-laden, cerulean, vasty skies. And when the airman "bought it," his going was spectacular to witness; experiencing it was another matter. Still, there seemed something so clean and pure about falling five miles before ramming into the earth in a splash of flame. Perhaps, but no one has ever been able to communicate his thoughts, feelings, and pain during that remarkable final plunge. Nor would anyone who had seen the interior of a stricken aircraft which managed to return from a rough mission forget the experience: flak and flame produced anything but purity and cleanliness.

There seemed something impersonal, too, about loosing bombs into what appeared to be a toy city; certainly it was inconceivable that full-sized humans lived there. But the horror and misery of those bombed cities have been set down and, when war becomes less objective, it becomes more questionable.

The Second World War was inevitable. The German leaders rationalized sufficiently for themselves and their people good reasons for going to war. The Japanese felt justified in attacking Pearl Harbor. Once the stunned Allies found themselves embroiled, the only recourse was to fight back with all they had—and, as time went by, they had more than the enemy. Neither the Germans nor the Japanese had planned on a long war; they had hoped for short, swift victories and timorous opponents. It did not go, simply, according to plan.

The man who maintains that there is such a thing as a science, or art, of war is, no matter who he is, a fool. In the abstract, as a game, where there is true control and when blood is not the argument, perhaps there is a kind of science or art. But not in real war. It is ultimately a form of international murder and now that air war has placed the nearly ultimate weapon at man's disposal and aircraft have so shrunk the earth, all wars are virtually civil wars of extinction.

It was Walt Whitman who chanted:

> *Word over all, beautiful as the sky,*
> *Beautiful that war and all its deeds of car-*
> *nage must in time be utterly lost . . .*

There must be, as the poet pleads, a reconciliation between enemies. The Second World War provided an overwhelming number of "deeds of carnage" which should be forgiven but never forgotten. Many of these deeds, excepting those committed in Nazi extermination camps, were done by air-

craft: Warsaw, Rotterdam, London, Coventry, Hamburg, Dresden, Berlin, Tokyo, Hiroshima. Such deeds were not exclusive to either side; atrocities were committed by all warring nations; war itself is an atrocity. It is not a matter of which nation perpetrated this or that outrage, but the fact that man is capable of such acts, no matter how just or evil his cause.

This history attempts to trace the evolution of air war and the men and aircraft contributing to it. But I hope, too, that it serves as a warning and a reminder. We must not forget the deeds of courage any more than the deeds of carnage. The development of jet aircraft, the missile, and the atomic bomb—all products of the Second World War—make any future world war unthinkable. Imagine a war with few survivors, without heroes, without victors. What consolation lies in knowing that when "we" go, "they" will go too?

There is scant comfort in the knowledge that there will never be a World War IV. What we all know now can prevent the third.

E.J.

New York, N.Y.

TERROR FROM
THE SKY

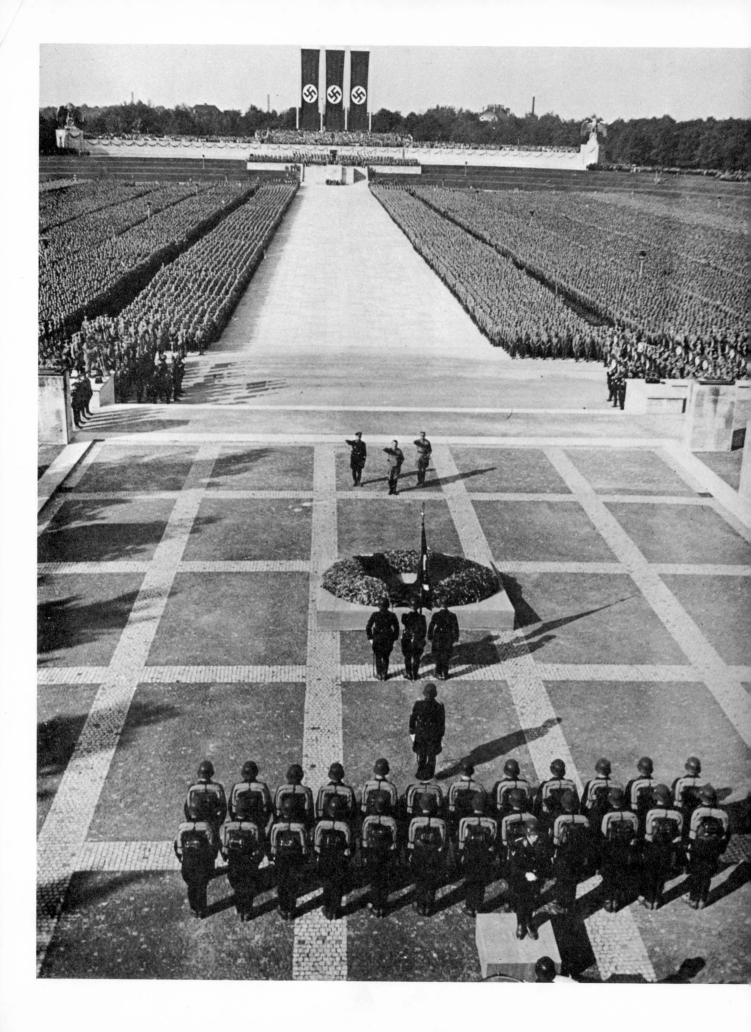

Prologue

PAX GERMANICA

To posterity it will appear like a fairy tale!

—ADOLF HITLER

I

A NATION OF FLIERS

THE BATTLE OF BRITAIN, and perhaps the outcome of the European phase of the Second World War, was predetermined on June 3, 1936, in the smoldering wreckage of a single aircraft near Dresden, Germany. In later years Dresden would acquire immortality as the site of a more dreadful tragedy than the deaths of one German general and his sergeant-mechanic. But the smaller tragedy and the greater one would one day be linked by the inexorable, blind dynamics of history.

The accident that summer day in a world relatively at peace was not impressive enough to make world headlines. The New York *Times* reported it deep inside the paper, on page fifteen. It noted briefly that, during an inspection tour of military bases, Generalleutnant Walther Wever, Chief of Staff of the Luftwaffe, had crashed in a takeoff while piloting his personal plane, a Heinkel He-70, the sleek *Blitz* ("Lightning"). With Wever perished his concept of air power, a concept which, four years later, might have spelled victory for his Luftwaffe in its struggle with the Royal Air Force.

To many an American reader wrapped up in postwar isolation, involved with his own Depression-inspired anxieties and eager to shun Europe's cyclic paroxysms, it came as a surprising revelation that Germany had an air force at all.

The *Times* noted that when "the German Air Ministry was created under the Hitler regime he [Wever] was transferred to that branch of the Army with the rank of major general. He became chief of Section 2 in the Ministry in charge of statistics, with the special task of studying the air forces of foreign powers. It was on his latest assignment as Chief of Air Staff that he was promoted to the rank of lieutenant general."

In 1936 the name of Adolf Hitler meant little to most Americans and the name of Walther Wever even less. Wever had served in the infantry during the First World War and in the Reichswehr (German Armed Forces) until Hitler had come into power. Youthful, dynamic, Wever was an advocate of very modern application of air power.

Had the American scanned the page on which the death of Wever was reported, he would have found little there to disconcert him, although the eventual impact of those events were to alter his life greatly within a few years. Two full columns were devoted to a study of "war rumors" in China which the leaders of that country stigmatized as "a plot." A subhead was terse: "Tokyo Doubtful of War." Another more compact article announced: "Peace Aims Snag on Reich Arming." An attempt to frame an air pact between Germany and Britain had failed. With one wary eye focused upon Moscow, Hitler boasted that his Luftwaffe was superior in quality as well as quantity to the Royal Air Force.

He referred to aircraft and numbers, not men: he was unaware of the fact that with the loss of Wever, much of the quality had already been lost.

II

In 1936 not even Hitler, for all his saber rattling, would have predicted another great war within three years. A master of the big bluff, he was fated, like the Kaiser before him, to blunder into catastrophe, taking millions of victims with him.

There are not any simple causes for war, but the summation of countless variables. But if one single element was required to ignite the Second World War that element was Adolf Hitler. In 1936 Imperial Japan was already on the march in the Far East, but without Hitler's Germany it is unlikely that Japan would have attacked Pearl Harbor. Without its Nazi ally Japan would not have been able to challenge the United States and Great Britain in the Pacific. A Second World War without Hitlerian Germany, therefore, is inconceivable.

An easy rationalization for what occurred in Germany during the two fateful decades 1919–39 has been the hard peace imposed upon Germany by the Treaty of Versailles. The terms of the treaty, however malevolent, did not create the mood and setting for the war to come, they merely supplied the later justifications. The implementation for the next war was set in motion on November 9, 1918—two days before the Armistice was signed, ending four of the most wasteful years in man's history.

This implementation was a secret mutual protection agreement between the newly proclaimed German Republic and the newly discredited German General Staff. It was brought about by a simple telephone call. On that November 9 the call came to Berlin over the secret wire which connected it with the Supreme Headquarters at the Hôtel Britannique at Spa in southeast Belgium adjacent to the German border. The new President, Friedrich Ebert, found himself speaking with Lieutenant General Wilhelm Groener (not the wily Hindenburg, who wished to disown any responsibility for dealing with either the enemy or the new Republic). The general, speaking for the High Command, offered a proposition.

Obviously the new Republic needed help and with the aid of the Army it might have a chance of survival. Ebert, who had known Groener during the war and trusted him despite his military credentials, was moved to tears by this generously offered hand from an unexpected quarter. The Republic, in turn, Groener then stipulated, must shelter the Army from the Allies. It was agreed, secretly of course.

It was an anomalous *mariage de convenance,* for the democratic Republic was avowedly anti-military and the Army, especially the General Staff, was equally anti-democratic. But they would need each other, they agreed, in the parlous days ahead —the virulent specter of Bolshevism rose like a grimy cloud in the east and vengeance-bent Allies rolled in from the west. This binding of the German government to the military doomed the Reich to a second dance of death—and the old dance was not yet over.

The Allies, hoping to maim Germany's ability to make war again, made the German General Staff one of its chief victims at Versailles. As the repository of Teutonic military philosophy the General Staff was dissolved, along with its fountainhead, the Kriegsakademie (War College). The Army was reduced to a mere hundred thousand men and its instruments of war were seized by the Allies or destroyed. All military aircraft were confiscated and the German Air Force disbanded. How, with all such restrictions, was Hitler in 1936 able to boast of an air force second to none?

The chief architect, the guiding genius, behind the military resurgence of Germany despite the restrictions of the Versailles Treaty and the supervision of the Inter-Allied Commission of Control was the all but unknown Generaloberst Hans von Seeckt. His very anonymity made him acceptable to the Allies to head Germany's token military force; his reputation as a brilliant military thinker delighted the remnants of the General Staff which still remained in the German Army.

What the Allies did not know then hurt them later. Seeckt regarded the so-called Great War as merely the first of a series which Germany might lose. But Germany would rise again, fight again, and ultimately win. Within the limitations of his small army Seeckt began resuscitating the discredited General Staff and building a new, elite,

Hans von Seeckt (1866–1936), brilliant architect of the resurgence of Germany's war machine. Despite the strictures of the Versailles treaty, and with the co-operation of the Soviet Union in the early 1920s, Seeckt created the antecedents of the panzers and the Luftwaffe even before Hitler came to power.

(NATIONAL ARCHIVES)

more modern Reichswehr under the very noses of the Allies. New, unwarlike names were devised for certain departments of the Reichswehr. The "Ministry of Pensions," for example, ostensibly under civilian control, was actually under the direction of "retired" Army officers. The function of the Ministry was in fact the collection of data on Germany's manpower potential for the next war. In the guise of "historical research," Seeckt's staff officers (although not designated as such) kept abreast of the latest military developments in the world.

Seeckt was no conservative; he fully appreciated the importance of mobility in warfare (as opposed to the attritional trench war of 1914–18). As for aircraft, nearly everyone in the previous war had been blind to its potential. Seeckt brought several airmen into the Reichswehr. Beginning with only three officers, the air branch of the Reichswehr quickly expanded to fifteen. Among the younger officers were Hugo Sperrle, Albert Kesselring, Hans-Jürgen Stumpf, and Wolfram von Richthofen, a former civil engineer and cousin of the celebrated "Red Knight of Germany." It was a good name for Seeckt's growing circle; in a few years all the names would stand for something.

But names only meant little in 1920, when Seeckt sought to improvise a German military renaissance. With a monocled eye on the greater objective, he managed to keep himself and his burgeoning little army out of the internal strife that erupted in Germany. His military elite was thus nurtured even while Germany's government and economy boiled and festered. Thanks to the agreement between the government and the Army, Seeckt was able to side-step those official inconveniences that might have interfered with his plans.

If he was able to dominate or hoodwink his own Minister of Defense, Seeckt was even more ingenious in solving the problem of how to revive the German Air Force and replenish the supply of aircraft which Allies so wastefully destroyed. If he could co-operate with his own government, which he detested, then why not take aid from a government he truly hated—the Bolshevik Soviet Russia?

Soviet Russia from about the summer of 1922, when an organization called Gesellschaft zur Förderung gewerblicher Unternehmungen (Company for the Advancement of Industrial Enterprises) was formed, contributed immeasurably to the rise of a newly militarized Germany. Known more familiarly as GEFU, the company was formed by a joint German-Russian group, the German members being trusted friends of Seeckt. The existence and function of GEFU was known also to Reich Chancellor Dr. Joseph Wirth and Foreign Minister Walter Rathenau. Wirth was especially essential to the project, for he was at the same time Reich Finance Minister, and Seeckt required additional financing which was not forthcoming from his stringent military budget.

Among the "industrial enterprises" established by GEFU was a Junkers aircraft factory at Fili, not far from Moscow (for Germans were forbidden to manufacture aircraft—in Germany). Another enterprise was named Bersol-Aktien-Gesellschaft, a Soviet-German operation at Trotsk, in the province of Samara. Bersol was to produce poison gas. Several factories for producing artillery shells were projected, and some built, in other sections of Russia. Finally, in the same spirit of dedication to the welfare of the proletariat, the Russians granted to Krupp, the German industrial empire, a large tract of land on the Manych River, a tributary of the Don, for use as an "experimental farm." This was ostensibly for the testing and demonstration of tractors and other farm equipment. A "large-size tractor," it might be noted, produced at this "farm" mounted a 7.5-centimeter gun.

At the same time training schools were established in Soviet Russia—all of this with the blessing of the saintly Lenin—where Germans and Russians could exchange the latest developments in the "art of war."

By 1923 an excellent training ground and tank school was established at Kazan on the Volga; there tactics were devised, vehicles developed, and leaders trained for Seeckt's new army. The seeds of Kazan reached full flower when German panzers smashed across the Polish frontier to open the Second World War and, later, Lenin's legacy to his workers came home too as Hitler's Operation Barbarossa.

The "air weapon," the other element essential to Seeckt's mobility concept, was reforged at the German Air Force Center at Vivupal, near Lipesk about 250 miles southeast of Moscow. The so-called "4th Squadron" stationed there was supplied from Germany through the free port of Stettin, where German customs officials winked when necessary. Military materials of embarrassing bulk were slipped across the Baltic under cover of night. German officers sent to Russia for training were first discharged from the Army. Should anything happen to them while in training, it would happen to a civilian, not a German soldier.

Among the early trainees graduated from the aviation school at Lipesk was Hans Jeschonnek, who would one day serve as Chief of Staff of the future Luftwaffe. Thus were hundreds of airmen trained in Russia during the late twenties—the nucleus of an incipient air weapon. At the same time new—and, according to the treaty, prohibited—aircraft were developed and tested in Russia and other countries.

Inevitable training accidents posed special problems, for there was no simple explanation for the shipment of German bodies from Soviet Russia. The Inter-Allied Commission of Control could not be blind to everything. But the solution was efficiently simple. The bodies of young airmen killed while training at Lipesk were returned to their families in Germany in crates stamped: "Machinery—Spare Parts."

To Seeckt none of this sub rosa activity appeared illicit, nor did it cross his mind that he was disloyal to Germany. He did, of course, scorn the so-called Weimar Republic with all its democratic, anti-military avowals. It was merely the instrument —a temporary one he was certain—for his own ambition to fashion a truly formidable German Army. "The Army," he said, "should become a state within a state . . ." which, under his administration, it certainly was, with its own laws and aims free of internal and international law. "But," Seeckt added, the Army "should be merged in the state through service; in fact it should become the purest image of the state." Thus a state dedicated to the art of war. To Seeckt the excuse of the Versailles Treaty was not necessary; he had begun making his plans long before there was such a treaty. All he needed was a lost war.

"We must become powerful," he declared, "and, as soon as we have power, we will naturally take back everything we have lost."

Meanwhile, civil Germany had become a political cesspool—also attributed to the Treaty of Versailles. Political factions, some of them quasi-military, proliferated as Germany itself sank into economic depression. The central hotbed of German reactionary movements was Bavaria, where the disgruntled gathered to voice their disgust with their government and to curse the treaty. It was in Bavaria's capital, Munich, that Seeckt met with the young leader of one of the more clamorous political groups, the German National Socialist Workers' Party. Seeckt was at the time hoping to put the party's own private army, the Sturmabteilungen, to his own use should he require additional hands to rid the Ruhr of the occupying armies of the Allies.

Seeckt was most impressed with the party's fanatical, ranting leader, who seemed capable of haranguing for hours on a subject dear to the general's heart: the criminality of the Versailles Treaty, the ineptitude of the Weimar Republic, and the eventual emergence of a mighty Reich. The party leader was, of course, Adolf Hitler. "We were one in our aims," Seeckt later said of Hitler, "only our paths were different."

Hitler had no intention of placing his Storm Troopers at Seeckt's disposal—as Seeckt had been misled to believe—for he had other plans for his bully boys. This was revealed in the abortive Bürgerbrau Keller fiasco in a Munich beer hall the following November when Seeckt actually permitted his troops to fire upon the National Socialists. Among them was no less than war hero Field Marshal Erich Ludendorff, with dreams of glory of his own. Hoping to ride into the role of military dictator of Germany on Hitler's coattails, Ludendorff merely strode through Seeckt's firing line— miraculously unhurt—and out of history forever. Sixteen party members lay dead in the street; one party member, second only to Hitler, the ex-fighter ace Hermann Göring, was seriously wounded, and Hitler fled the scene in a thoroughly unmilitary style.

With his rivals out of the way—for Hitler was imprisoned for a while: long enough to dictate *Mein Kampf*—Seeckt could turn his attention to his own plans for a *Putsch* and his own dream of a military dictatorship. But within three years Seeckt himself would fall. Not, ironically, for his remarkable building up of a new German military structure or his all but inexplicable dealings with Soviet Russia—instead Seeckt provided comparatively trivial indiscretions which served as well.

For example, he issued an order entitled "The Proper Conduct of Duels Between Officers," which resulted in a small flurry in the press. Such arrant Prussianism at a time when the Germans were concerned with diminishing that wart in the profile of the national stereotype. With characteristic disdain, Seeckt chose to ignore the criticisms. Whereupon he committed another *gaffe*. During the autumn 1926 maneuvers of the 9th Infantry Regiment Seeckt gave permission to Prince Wilhelm, son of the former Crown Prince, to participate in the exercises. The Prince, as one of the deposed Hohenzollerns, was anathema to the sincere democrats and especially to the vociferous Left. The Socialist paper, *Vorwärts,* declared that Prince Wilhelm's presence, in full resplendent uniform, was "not simply a question of whether parliament or the military shall be the predominant factor in Germany; it is a question of democracy or militarism!"

With the world only recently made safe for democracy, it was obvious that Seeckt would have to go. But what few realized at the time was that by then Seeckt had already succeeded in making Germany safe for militarism. And to some extent his accomplishments were known to insiders. His "military genius," as historian John Wheeler-Bennett has written, was a unique combination: "the precision and accuracy of the soldier" and "the vision and imagination of the creative artist. For such he was, an artist in making bricks without straw, in beating ploughshares into swords, in fashioning a military machine which, though nominally within the restrictions of the Peace Treaty, struck admiration and awe into every General Staff in Europe."

By the time Seeckt made his exit, in October 1926, the presidency of the Republic had been filled by the great hero of the First World War, Field Marshal Paul von Beneckendorff und Hindenburg. Bitter because Hindenburg had not lifted a finger to help him, Seeckt permitted the formation of yet another political party around him, the Deutsche Volkspartei. When he realized, after little success, that his future did not lay in politics, Seeckt diverted whatever power his party had to the party he believed had the most promising future: Hitler's resuscitated Nazis. Seeckt died in 1936, never to know what he had done for that party's ultimate destiny.

Hitler, who had in 1923 appeared to be little more than a loudmouthed incompetent revolution-

ary, had within a decade worked his way into the Hindenburg government as Chancellor. Although the senilescent Hindenburg detested the lowly "Bohemian corporal," he was forced eventually to recognize the power of the Nazis. Hitler—by virtue of verbose spellbinding, blackmail, threat, cajolery, murder, and the aid from German big business, bankers, political conservatives, industrialists, Junkers landowners, and an enormous majority of the German people (who found Hitler's anti-Semitism, anti-communism, and anti-Versailles spoutings very good listening)—had made himself politically inevitable.

So it was that when Adolf Hitler became Chancellor of Germany on Monday, January 30, 1933, he was placed in a position to take over the government of Germany, thanks to Field Marshal Hindenburg. And thanks to General Seeckt he had the superb beginnings of a great war machine. Never before had a mere corporal owed so much to a field marshal and a general, particularly to the latter with his dream of the next war.

"The whole future of warfare," Seeckt had observed, "appears to me to be in the employment of mobile armies, relatively small but of high quality, and rendered distinctly more effective by the addition of aircraft. . . ." Although the term had not yet been coined, Seeckt in the early twenties had already visualized the concept of blitzkrieg.

III

There was no Luftwaffe as such when Hitler became Chancellor of the Reich. Significantly, his first important address, made on the very next day, January 31, 1933, was to the troops of the Berlin garrison. He charmed them all.

As for the Air Force, Seeckt and others had done well by Hitler. In 1926—when Seeckt was forced to resign—the German Air Force consisted of two fighter squadrons, a single bomber squadron, and an auxiliary bomber squadron. By 1931 there were four fighter squadrons, three bombardment squadrons, and eight observation squadrons. While the figures might not have been impressive—and they were not supposed to be—they contained within them hundreds of future air leaders, most of them trained in Soviet Russia.

There were other even less obvious developments. In 1926 also the Deutsche Lufthansa Aktiengesellschaft was created as a joint private and governmental enterprise. Lufthansa combined two of Germany's successful though financially unstable airlines, Deutsche Aero-Lloyd and Junkers Luftverkehr. This consolidation came about under pressure from the German Ministry of Air Transport, supposedly a civil agency, headed by a trusted Seecktian, Captain Ernst von Brandenburg. The captain had attained wartime immortality as the leader of the famed Bomber Squadron No. 3, the *England-geschwader,* which had flown the giant Gotha bombers to attack London from the air. One of Brandenburg's functions was to arrange for the training of future military (obviously bomber) pilots in special sections of Lufthansa's Deutsche Luftverkehrschule. In time there were four of these flying schools turning out civil pilots who could double as bomber pilots.

Board chairman of Lufthansa was Erhard Milch, an ex-German Air Force pilot who had been a salesman for Junkers. Milch was an astute, sharp-dealing, well-organized administrator. As an ex-World War aviator he naturally came into the sphere of Hermann Göring, who had found politics more profitable than postwar aviation in Germany. The gregarious, bluff, gross, and well-liked Göring loved to meet with other ex-war fliers and relive the beautiful days of the war. Those were the best years of their lives, when men were men and they fought like knights in single combat in the clean air miles above the trenches.

But when Milch sought out Göring in 1928 it was not to talk about the splendid days of the Great War. No romantic, Milch was concerned with more practical matters. Lufthansa was in trouble and needed government backing to survive. Göring with his reputation as an air advocate was the most likely representative in the Reichstag to approach on this matter. The two old fliers struck up a warm friendship and Göring, though he represented a minor party, did all he could to advance the fortunes of Lufthansa. He boasted to Milch that one day the little Nazi party would run Germany and when it did, Milch would have an important

role to play in the new German Air Force. Milch with his shrewd practical mind could hardly take *der Dicke* ("the Fat One") very seriously; and he did not make any effort to join the party.

When the Nazis did come into power Milch was asked by Hitler himself to serve as Göring's deputy Air Reichskommissar. Milch accepted on the condition that he remain Lufthansa's chairman. By April 1933 Göring was Air Minister and Milch Secretary of State for Air; in effect this signified the convergence of German civil and military aviation. Milch was efficient, ruthless, and ambitious; he obviously would fit into the scheme of things very well. There was, however, one slight hitch. His father had the taint of "Jewish blood" and an important platform of the Nazi party was a virulent anti-Semitism. This was easily remedied considering Milch's aspirations and abilities: his mother simply signed a statement in which she swore she had committed adultery. Milch was, it turned out, a pure Aryan bastard.

The advent of Hitler began to entwine the various strands of German society which had been unraveling since the Armistice. The masses as well as big business were behind him. Seeckt had prepared a military machine for him and Hindenburg put him in power. In truth, however, when Hitler became Chancellor, he had no real social program for Germany beyond a determination to "call to account the November Criminals of 1918" and his own ill-defined power lust. Nor, unlike Seeckt, did he have a military program.

In fact, Hitler, the eternal enlisted man, had little respect for the Officer Corps. On its part, the Officer Corps remained aloof from politics as Seeckt had insisted, smugly content with its privileged lot. Their only concern with Hitler was how they might use him to further their fortunes. Militarily Hitler, the leader of a rabble and such roisterers as the Storm Troopers and his private protective guard, the Schutzstaffel, was an amateur; he would be no great war lord. An intuitionist, Hitler was no practitioner of classic strategies.

But he proved more than the match of the Officer Corps as a tactician. He wooed them with respectful references to their honored traditions and to their important role in the state. He bided his time, as the officers preened, and then he ravaged all of

*Adolf Hitler, leader of the New Germany, and Her-
mann Göring, leader of the newly spawned Luftwaffe,
in an early happy hour greeting their admirers, the
German people. Two men less capable of planning and* *executing an aerial war could not be imagined: Hitler
neither trusted nor liked aircraft and Göring did not
understand them as a weapon of military strategy. This
was their major combined contribution to the outcome
of the Second World War.* (NATIONAL ARCHIVES)

them: Hitler transformed the famed German General Staff into an ensemble of lackeys. They were
masters of nothing.

IV

The Luftwaffe was Hitler's pet; its leader was
Hermann Göring, a good friend and number two
Nazi. Beyond the Open Cockpit and Flames in the
Sky mystique which Göring advocated, there was
no long history, no accumulation of tradition and

privilege for Hitler to contend with, as with the
Army. And there too was the proficient Milch, to
set a new air force on a sound organizational and
administrative basis.

The new Air Ministry, under Milch's direction,
was formed from the old Commissariat for Air and
the Transport Ministry. This last would naturally
include Captain Brandenburg's flying schools for
bomber pilots. Among those holding high office in
the new Ministry were Oberst Walther Wever, who
had been transferred from the Defense Ministry,
Albert Kesselring, and Hans-Jürgen Stumpf. Gö-

ring, faithful to old comrades and to the glorious days of the Great War, saw to it that posts were found for two of his friends of the old days: Bruno Loerzer and Karl Bodenschatz. Youthful flying personnel were available in limited numbers from the school in Russia and in greater numbers from Deutscher Luftsportsverband, where flying enthusiasts learned the art of gliding under Kurt Student, a member of the Reichswehr Air Technical Branch. The most promising of these sporting pilots were sent to Lufthansa's schools for training on powered aircraft. Among those trained in the schools was Adolf Galland. Although ostensibly prepared for civil aviation Galland and other young German pilots received training also in combat flying, aerobatics, and gunnery.

By the beginning of 1934 Milch had projected an expansion of the aircraft industry and the German Air Force which would require more than four thousand planes. During 1933 the prototypes of the Heinkel 111 and the Dornier 17 were in the planning stage; though little known then these aircraft were to become notorious during the Battle of Britain. Milch's plans called for six bomber, six fighter, and six reconnaissance *Geschwader*. The *Geschwader* was comprised of from ninety to a hundred aircraft as compared to the *Staffel*'s nine. In 1931 the German Air Force was reckoned in *Staffels* (roughly equivalent to squadrons in the American Air Force); three years later Milch quite realistically thought in terms of *Geschwader*. Because Hitler was not yet ready to show his hand, such work was of necessity accomplished in secret.

Not so secret was the growth, under governmental encouragement, of "air-mindedness" among Germany's youth of both sexes. Göring fostered this enthusiasm by initiating annual competitions for civil pilots. On March 8, 1934, following a cross-country contest, he made the awards with characteristic verve. He was aware of Milch's planning and Hitler's dreams for the future, but he could not resist invoking the past in speaking of "the spirit of German aviation." It was a curious point to make: that the individual should become subservient to the state, considering that the fighter pilot of the First World War was an archindividualist.

Göring spoke glowingly of "the spirit that in four years of heroic life proved so successful and singled

out German aviation during the war—the team spirit among the crews.

"My comrades! We must admit that after the dissolution of the old German air service it was impossible to carry on the old spirit of comradeship in disciplined form. Most of us were uprooted from our work and the air service remained only a dream. The terrible longing for flying nevertheless remained in all of you." His next statement revealed a hint of the future. "The new Reich," Göring shouted, "has ordained that flying—even in forms other than sport and civil flying—shall rise again!"

This stirred the audience and Göring told them how they, the youth of the new Reich—one year having passed in Hitler's projected Thousand Year Reich—would contribute. "The young Germany," Göring promised them, "shall be brought up in a passion for flying in order that the German nation shall become a nation of fliers!"

He returned to the subject of the spirit of German aviation. "It is your duty to keep this spirit alive," he told them. "You have this duty to the sacrifices that your comrades have made in the greatest struggle of all times. We have the right to honor our heroes and to hold them up as models to our German youth. In no treaty is there a clause demanding the destruction of this spirit, but the cowards who have made our people unhappy for the last decade and a half have tried to break this spirit."

Göring could not close without a tribute to the Führer, from whom all these blessings came. The young aviators had dropped roses on Hitler's retreat, Haus Wachenfeld, near Berchtesgaden, at the close of the competition. In this luxurious villa Hitler too was able to enjoy some of his blessings among the magnificent vistas of the Bavarian Alps. From his terrace he could observe the young German fliers dropping roses, of which Göring said, "This compliment is the natural thanks. . . .

"For without Adolf Hitler, where would German pilots and German air transport be today? Where would have gone our dream—our longing—if he had not created the new Germany? Therefore, comrades," Göring concluded on a hushed note, "before I award the prizes, we will stand and think a moment in silent respect for our leader—our beloved leader—our people's chancellor!"

A year later, almost to the day that Göring summoned a "nation of fliers," the Führer officially announced to the world—on March 9, 1935—the existence of the Luftwaffe. Hermann Göring was named Commander in Chief, Erhard Milch was Secretary of State for Air, and Walther Wever was Chief of Staff. Within a week Hitler repudiated the Versailles Treaty with the declaration of a German Army of no less than thirty-six divisions (this would require some 550,000 men) and the reintroduction of conscription. The Reichswehr, the Officer Corps, and the underground General Staff were elated. At last they could operate in the open, Germany would once again take her place in the sun.

V

The "Bohemian corporal" was not such a bad fellow, after all. He had, in fact, behaved himself commendably so far as the military was concerned. Even the grisly Blood Purge of June 30, 1934 had certain points to the Army's advantage. The slaughter of Ernst Röhm and some of his unwholesome associates eradicated a serious threat to Army authority by curbing the Storm Troopers. If the Army lost two of its own in the contrived conspiracy, it was but the fortunes of war. But neither General von Schleicher, who had been Hitler's immediate predecessor as Chancellor, nor Kurt von Bredow was involved seriously with Röhm. The power of the Storm Troopers was smashed, however, and the military could make allowance for zeal. Hindenburg even sent congratulatory telegrams to Hitler and Göring, commending them for having "saved the German nation from serious danger." Even so, the Storm Troopers were merely superseded by the SS and Göring's private Geheime Staatspolizei (the "Gestapo"). Estimates of the murders, many of them settling intraparty feuds, ran as high as a thousand, although Hitler admitted to only seventy-seven.

That he and Göring succeeded in such mass slaughter without Army interference attested to the internal impotence of the Reichswehr. Irresolute, self-centered, and indifferent to all except their own small world, the Army had already been trapped by Hitler. This snare was further strengthened when he required them to take the new oath he had devised. It contained no pledge to sustain the German Constitution, nor to protect the German government. It did not even swear allegiance to the Reich. Instead, it was a personal oath of loyalty to the corporal himself:

I swear before God to give my unconditional obedience to Adolf Hitler, Führer of the Reich and of the German People, Supreme Commander of the Wehrmacht, and I pledge my word as a brave soldier to observe this oath always, even at peril of my life.

The Reichswehr was no more, supplanted by the Wehrmacht, of which Hitler assumed command. That the oath neglected both patriotism and legality did not concern the German generals; they were too preoccupied building up a thirty-six-division Army.

Even the Luftwaffe had grown considerably. Toward the end of March 1935 Hitler boasted to Sir John Simon, the English Foreign Minister, and Anthony Eden that his Air Force had already reached parity with the Royal Air Force. This was not true, but it had its effect. It was a diplomatic victory for Hitler in dealing with England and France. It also confirmed the fears of Winston Churchill, whose lone voice had been raised in warning against the rise of the Luftwaffe. Hitler's vain boast roused the British government enough to begin expansion of the Royal Air Force and to concentrate upon the single-seater fighter aircraft as outlined in Air Ministry Specification F5/34. Among the aircraft this inspired were the Hawker Hurricane and the Supermarine Spitfire.

Having come out into the open with his military plans, Hitler could proudly announce the opening of the Air Warfare Academy at Berlin-Gatow on November 1, 1935. The principal address of the day was given by the Chief of Staff, Generalleutnant Walther Wever, already widely respected and recognized as a leading exponent of the strategic concept of aerial warfare and a disciple of the Italian military theorist General Giulio Douhet. Greatly influenced, as were other military thinkers in Europe, England, and the United States, by Douhet's ideas, especially as expounded in *The Command of the Air* (1921), Wever was a proponent of the independent air force and of the heavy bomber. As such he was not in tune with Göring's Open Cockpit romanticism. Wever was a realist and a powerful, highly regarded officer whose impact upon the growing German air weapon was bound to be an important one.

He opened his remarks with an allusion to 1918 and the Versailles Treaty when "a leaderless nation collapsed internally and dashed the weapons from the hands of the gallant Army." It was the old refrain, The Legend of the German Defeat, still alive late in 1935.

"How will it be in the future now that a new weapon—the Luftwaffe—has appeared?" Wever asked. "Only in a war of the future will it reach full development. The Air Force, which came into existence hardly twenty-five years ago, found its great military origin in the Great War, from which glorious traditions have been handed down to the Air Force of today. Its greatest heroes are shining examples for us; Manfred von Richthofen—its proudest name. . . ."

Popular First World War ace and between-the-wars stunt flier, Ernst Udet. A dashing, ebullient personality, Udet was a superb pilot but had little conception of the meaning of air power in war. He was the advocate in Germany of the dive bomber (an idea picked up in the United States), which resulted in the Stuka concept. (NATIONAL ARCHIVES)

But, Wever emphasized, the air heroes of the Great War strove for something which only Hitler's National Socialism was making possible: ". . . a strong Air Force with independent status in the services." Wever, however, not wanting to slight the Army, was quick to indicate that an independent Air Force could co-operate with the ground forces where necessary, but he visualized a time when it would be possible to avoid "the positional warfare of massed armies," meaning, of course, the wasteful trench warfare of the Great War.

Wever then made his major point: "Never forget that the bomber is the decisive factor in aerial warfare. Only the nation with strong bomber forces at its disposal can expect decisive action by its Air Force."

Under Wever's direction specifications were drawn up for long-range, four-engined bombers. The result was the Dornier 19 and the Junkers 89, prototypes of which were ready for flight trials late in 1936.

Before this took place, however, Walther Wever died at Dresden in the summer of 1936. With him died the development of the heavy bombers. His successor, Albert Kesselring, canceled the Do-19 and Ju-89 to concentrate on medium bombers and the dive bomber, such aircraft as the Heinkel 111, the Dornier 17, and the Junkers 88 in the former category, and in the latter, the Junkers 87, the "Stuka."

In the reshuffling of the Luftwaffe's command following Wever's death another old Great War fighter pilot, Ernst Udet, was placed at the head of the Air Ministry's Technical Branch. The likable, good-humored, dashing Udet was a fine flier but not gifted with organizational or political skills. With his sunny personality Udet was too wholesome for the company he kept. As Germany's number one living Great War ace (with sixty-two "kills" to his credit), Udet's voice meant something to the amateurs in charge of the Luftwaffe after the death of Wever. Unwittingly Udet did them a disservice with his enthusiastic expertise.

In 1933 Udet visited the United States, one of his stops being the Cleveland Air Races. He was most impressed with the performance of the Curtiss-Wright BFC-2, the "Hawk." As the Curtiss Hawk II, the dive bomber was released for export and Udet, with Göring's help, was able to purchase two

The Junkers 52, all-metal commercial transport which was converted into a troop transport and bomber. As a military plane it first was used in the Spanish Civil War in 1936. (LUFTHANSA PHOTO)

A Junkers 87B Stuka of the Condor Legion over Spain. The Ju-87 proved most effective against ill-defended Spanish installations and received more credit than it actually deserved. (NATIONAL ARCHIVES)

of them in October 1933. The German government authorized payment of $11,500 each. In December Udet demonstrated the Hawk at the Luftwaffe's test center at Rechlin. He delighted in kicking the plane into a screaming dive and pointing it vertically at a pin-point target and then whipping it out of the trajectory dangerously close to the ground. Even so, the High Command was not awed by the performance. Major Wolfram Freiherr von Richthofen was especially unimpressed and resisted Udet's proposals for the development of such a plane (a curious sidelight, for Richthofen later commanded a Stuka unit).

Udet did not advance his cause any when in the summer of 1934 he lost the tail of one of the Hawks while stunting over Tempelhof and had to take to his parachute. But despite Richthofen's objections, by January 1935 development contracts for dive bombers were placed with Arado, Blohm and Voss, Heinkel, and Junkers. The designation for this class of aircraft was "Sturzkampfflugzeug," from which the popular term "Stuka" was derived. Although this referred to all dive bombers, it was the Junkers 87 which became widely known as the Stuka. The Ju-87 was selected over its competitor, the Heinkel 118, which Udet had managed to crash during a test because of his unfamiliarity with a small technical detail. Now head of the Technical Branch, Udet was able to proceed with his Stuka campaign.

Around this same time a new fighter, the Messerschmitt Bf-109, was undergoing tests at Rechlin. The Heinkel 111 had already been displayed at Tempelhof as a "commercial" aircraft with ten seats for passengers and a smoking compartment in the bomb bay. Less susceptible of simulation was the Dornier 17, which was rejected as a mail carrier and taken over by the Air Ministry as a bomber and nicknamed "the Flying Pencil." The first Junkers 88 took off on its test flight on December 21, 1936; it too was a medium bomber. Thus was the character of the Luftwaffe established by the close of 1936—a character much different from that envisioned by Wever in his speech at the Air Warfare Academy.

VI

In the summer of 1936 the new Luftwaffe and its young pilots and aircraft were supplied with a testing arena for their theories in Spain. That hapless country soon became an ideological battleground for the forces of the Left and the Right. Russia sent advisers, technicians, and equipment to the "Loyalists," the Popular Front Republican Government of President Manuel Azaña y Diaz. When the "Insurgents," led by General José Sanjurjo Sacanell (who was killed in the early fighting) and General Francisco Franco, sent out a call for aid from the fascist nations, both Mussolini and Hitler responded in his favor. Göring urged Hitler to intervene "firstly, to prevent the further spread of communism; secondly, to test my young Luftwaffe in this or that technical aspect."

Within a week men and equipment were en route to Morocco, where the fighting had begun, and to Cádiz. Among the aircraft were the Junkers 52, the Lufthansa transport converted to a bomber transport, and Heinkel 52s, obsolescent biplane fighters. By November 1936 the "Condor Legion" under command of Hugo Sperrle and with Wolfram von Richthofen as his Chief of Staff was formed. One of the fighter *Staffels* was commanded by the young "civil" pilot Adolf Galland.

Under Richthofen's direction the technique of close support was developed. Thus was Germany's supposedly independent Air Force wedded to the ground forces. That this was a violation of Wever's early plans went unnoticed in the success of the tactics in Spain. By the summer of 1937 more modern aircraft were dispatched to the Condor Legion.

The Messerschmitt 109B-2 began to replace the He-51s. It marked the end of the biplane fighter era. New tactics, particularly as developed by the youthful Werner Mölders (who replaced Galland as *Staffel* leader in the Jasta 88), proved most effective. The old Great War V-formations were abandoned in favor of the *Rotte,* a two-plane unit of great flexibility. (Two *Rotte* made up a *Schwarm* and three *Schwarms* a *Staffel.*) It was learned that in the old close formations the pilots spent a good deal of time avoiding collision and not enough scanning the sky. The lack of radio communications between aircraft, too, was found to be a serious handicap. The *Rotte* technique was eventually used by most air forces during the Second World War in the leader and wingman combination.

Richthofen, in time commander of the Condor Legion, found that the Stuka Ju-87, of which he had not approved originally, was a most terrifying and useful weapon in his close-support tactics. The ugly, bent-winged dive bomber, with the shrieking sirens attached to the landing gear, was hailed as a scourge of the battlefield. Only a few Stukas were sent to Spain, but these were widely used by alternating

Heinkel 111s approaching a Spanish town. When the He-111 was first introduced in 1936 it was passed off as a ten-passenger commercial aircraft. By late 1937 it was functioning as a bomber in Kampfgruppe 88 in Spain. (NATIONAL ARCHIVES)

A Condor Legion He-111 releasing bombs upon a Spanish town. The success of the missions without escort convinced the Germans that the bomber was impervious to fighter opposition. As with the Stuka, this misconception would come to roost during the Battle of Britain. (NATIONAL ARCHIVES)

Guernica: April 26, 1937. The bells in this burning church rang out to warn of the approach of bombers, a warning which was ignored by the people in the village, unaccustomed to air raids. By nightfall more than sixteen hundred lay dead in Guernica's burning streets. (NATIONAL ARCHIVES)

crews and proved most effective in attacks on such port cities as Valencia, Barcelona, and Tarragona. The Stukas also disrupted communications, destroyed bridges, bombed roads, and harassed troops with frightening invulnerability. Franco's Nationalists had by late 1937 achieved air superiority—thanks to the Germans and Italians—which enabled the Stukas to perform most successfully. It was the same also with the medium bombers which had preceded the Stuka to Spain, the He-111s and the Do-17s. Because they were superior to most of the aircraft of the Republican forces, the German planes gained a reputation beyond reality. The most formidable opponent encountered by the Condor Legion was the Russian Polikarpov I-16, the stubby, rugged little fighter—the fastest of its time. The early Condor Legion fighters, the Heinkel 51s, were no match for the I-16; not until the Messerschmitts

arrived in Spain did the *Ratas* ("Rats") meet a better contender.

The Spanish experience taught the Luftwaffe advanced fighter tactics, as well as the use of radio communications in combat, but the seeming invincibility of the bomber formations encouraged overconfidence, for which a dear price would be paid over England. Also the tradition of ground support as the major Luftwaffe function would take its toll in the future.

Still another tradition was established in Spain. On Monday—market day—April 26, 1937, at four-thirty in the afternoon church bells rang out a warning of approaching aircraft in the vicinity of the Basque village of Guernica. Nestling among the gentle hills of the Vizcaya province nearly twenty miles behind the front lines, Guernica had never been bombed although there had been raids in the area

Guernica burns after bombing by German aircraft. History's first senseless terror bombing.

(NATIONAL ARCHIVES)

before. The alarm conveyed by the church bells meant little to the villagers and the farmers gathered in the market place. Ten minutes after the peal of the bells a formation of Heinkel 111s appeared over Guernica. Small, longish objects began to drop from the bellies of the aircraft; within seconds explosions erupted in the crowded streets of Guernica. Their bombs disgorged, the planes descended to low level and strafed the streets. In another twenty minutes Junkers 52s flew over to pour incendiaries upon the smoking terror of Guernica. These lumbering planes too came down to machine-gun the refugees attempting to flee the village. And so it continued, in flaming, dust-embroiled waves, for three hours until Guernica lay shattered and scorched. In the streets, in the broken cottages and houses, there were 1654 dead and 889 wounded—of a population of 7000.

Guernica was only the first name in history to stand for the fiery desolation from the air; others would follow: Warsaw, Rotterdam, Coventry, London. A nation of fliers had found its wings. Guernica symbolized its potent invincibility.

Only history, in the phrase of John Wheeler-Bennett in its "incalculable variations in the tempo of events," would endow it with fuller tragic significance.

BOOK I
Blitzkrieg

Whoever lights the torch of war in Europe can wish for nothing but chaos.

—ADOLF HITLER

2

SCHRECKLICHKEIT

Hardly thirty feet above the fog-enshrouded ground the *Kette* of three Junkers 87B Stukas roared through the slumbrous countryside. Their engines resonating through the river valley, they looked like three ugly predatory birds with gaping jawlike radiators, contorted, splayed wings, and taloned undercarriages. Dangerously close to the earth because of the fog, the *Kette,* led by Oberleutnant Bruno Dilley of Stuka Geschwader 1, sought out its target.

Only minutes before they had taken off from their advance base at Elbing to find the bridges over the Vistula River at Dirschau. They were not, as they had in Spain, to destroy the bridges. Instead they were to keep them open to enable the German Third Army in East Prussia to join with the Fourth Army moving in from the west through the Polish Corridor. The bridges were a crucial supply and transportation link and, it was known, they had been mined by the Poles in the event of a German attack. Once the alarm was given the bridges would be blown and the fine timetable of conquest would be upset.

Dilley's problem was to sever the wires which lay in the left embankment of the Vistula at Dirschau. The fog and the darkness, for it was barely dawn of Friday, September 1, 1939, did not make the mission an easy one. There were trees to skirt and landmarks to seek which disconcertingly slipped past or disappeared in a patch of fog before they could be properly identified. At least the river was in the right place. For an instant Dilley saw the indistinct forms of the bridges emerging from the mist. Snapping his head from left to right, he noted that the others had seen the bridges also. He kicked the rudder and leveled at the left embankment. It would be a low-level attack, not the classic Stuka peel-off and screeching dive, as Dilley, followed by the other two pilots, plunged at the riverbank, released his bombs, and pulled up in as steep a climb as possible. The engine whined in near protest and that sound was coupled with the explosions. The rear gunners in the Stukas watched as the earth shook and erupted in a gush of smoke and dust.

Dilley glanced at his wristwatch: four thirty-four.

They had begun the Second World War eleven minutes ahead of schedule. It was a portent of things to come. Further: although they had hit their target and had, indeed, snapped the wires leading to the explosive charges on the bridges, the Poles had succeeded, by six-thirty, in blowing one of the spans which sagged into the Vistula. By then the war had officially begun.

The "incident" which had justified the unleashing of *Fall Weiss* ("Case White," the code term for the attack on Poland) had already been staged. On August 31 Hitler issued his "Directive No. 1 for the Conduct of War." Classified as "Most Secret," it read (in part):

1. Now that all political possibilities of disposing by peaceful means of a situation on the Eastern Frontier which is intolerable for Germany are exhausted, I have determined on a solution by force.

2. The attack on Poland is to be carried out in accordance with the preparations made for *Fall Weiss,* with the alterations which result, where the Army is concerned, from the fact that it has, in the meantime, almost completed its dispositions. Allotment of tasks and the operational target remain unchanged.

The date of attack: 1 September 1939.
Time of attack: 04:45 [written in red pencil]. This time also applies to the operation at Gdynia, Bay of Danzig, and the Dirschau Bridge.

3. In the west it is important that the responsibility for the opening of hostilities should rest unequivocally with England and France. At first, purely local action should be taken against insignificant frontier violations.

—Adolf Hitler

Harbinger of war: three—a Ketté—Stukas such as began the Second World War in the early morning of September 1, 1939. (U. S. AIR FORCE)

Terror of the battlefield: with engine whining and propeller screeching, the very sound of the Stuka was frightening as it dived to release its bombs.

(U. S. AIR FORCE)

In his proclamation to the Armed Forces issued on the following day, Hitler stated that "Several acts of frontier violation, which cannot be tolerated by a great power, show that Poland is no longer prepared to respect the Reich's frontiers. To put an end to this madness, I can see no other way but from now on to meet force with force."

He was right about the madness. At the German city of Gleiwitz, for example, Polish troops attacked the radio station in the early evening of August 31. An excited voice interrupted the broadcast and shouted over the air that the time had come for war between Poland and Germany. The sound of shots could be heard also. When the foreign press members were taken to Gleiwitz the next morning they saw about a dozen bodies strewn about the area of the radio station—all in Polish Army uniforms.

They were, of course, dead Germans, condemned criminals who had been promised freedom if they participated in the "incident" and escaped. But even that possibility had been considered: all of the Germans had been fatally injected before the attack on the radio station. The SS leader of the operation, Alfred Naujocks, saw to it that those men who fell unconscious from the lethal drug rather than to gunfire were properly inflicted with gunshot wounds for the visiting newsmen. The entire operation had been planned under the direction of Hitler and Heinrich Himmler, leader of the SS. Polish uniforms and small arms had been supplied through the efforts of General Wilhelm Keitel, Chief of the Armed Forces, and Admiral Wilhelm Canaris, head of German Intelligence. While neither approved, neither did they object to Hitler's plans—which were known to them early in August.

II

Hitler's chief military aide, Field Marshal Wilhelm Keitel, whose major function was to agree with Hitler's contributions to the military art. His own final contribution to the war was being present at the surrender ceremonies when the war was over; later he was hanged for his role in the war.

(U. S. OFFICE OF WAR INFORMATION)

It was not to the professional minds of Keitel and Canaris an honorable means of making war, but all this was overlooked in the spectacular thrust of the German blitzkrieg into Poland. It was a kind of war which neither understood—just as neither understood Hitler. Canaris, however, was not the toady that Keitel was (a subservient sycophancy earned him the nickname among his fellow officers of *Lakaitel,* "Lackey"). In fact, Canaris was one of the earliest of the German conspirators who hoped to rid the Reich of Hitler. His conspiracies eventually cost him his life; but on the morning of September 1 Canaris visualized an even greater price when, with tears in his eyes, he said, "This means the end of Germany."

It was a characteristic exclamation, for the professional soldiers had little faith in the war that Hitler had unleashed against their better military judgment. But when Hitler ignited "the torch of war in Europe" the stunning advance of the Wehrmacht behind the Panzer divisions and the Luftwaffe's seemingly ubiquitous Stukas heartened the German generals as much as they shocked a breathless world. All along the German-Polish frontier the wheels of the German juggernaut ground into action. Laughing young, blond soldiers snapped the wooden frontier barrier gates—or smashed through in tanks. The Luftwaffe struck at Polish airfields, railroads, and communications lines, crippling aerial defenses from the beginning and rendering troop movements all but impossible.

In Berlin, Hitler watched the blitzkrieg on a massive battle map: the plan, he knew, was foolproof. Two Army Groups were smashing across the Polish plains toward Warsaw. Army Group North, composed of two armies—the Fourth, which flowed eastward from Pomerania across the Polish Corridor and then would turn south for Warsaw; and the Third, which struck westward from East Prussia toward the Polish Corridor, where, it was hoped, on meeting with the Fourth Army, it would race southward to the Polish capital. Attached to Army Group North, under command of General Feder von Bock, was Luftflotte 1, (Air Fleet 1) under Albert Kesselring, who had served as Luftwaffe Chief of Staff immediately after the death of Walther Wever.

Army Group South (Gerd von Rundstedt) was also to push toward Warsaw in a northwesterly direction through Slovakia and Silesia with its three

Hans Jeschonnek, Chief of Staff of the Luftwaffe when the Second World War began. Like many of the Luftwaffe's top echelon, Jeschonnek had been trained at the secret German Air Force center in Russia. A devoted admirer of Hitler, Jeschonnek (who once even begged Hitler to assume command of the Luftwaffe) was unpopular with his immediate chief, Göring.
(NATIONAL ARCHIVES)

armies, the Eighth, Tenth, and Fourteenth. These units were supported by Luftflotte 4 under Alexander Loehr, former commander of the Austrian Air Force, which had been absorbed into the Luftwaffe via Hitler's infamous *Anschluss* in 1938. Chief of Staff of the Luftwaffe was the youthful—forty years old—able Hans Jeschonnek, "graduate" of the school at Lipesk in Soviet Russia, an ardent admirer of Göring, a devotee of Hitler, and an advocate of the high-speed medium bomber and the Stuka.

The two Air Fleets (Luftflotten) were virtually self-sufficient air forces whose components were made up of assorted aircraft types for various assignments as well as antiaircraft batteries (*Flugabwehrkanone*=air defense gun, or more simply *Flak*). The *Geschwader*, the basic tactical unit of the Luftwaffe, took its name from the type of aircraft which

Albert Kesselring, commander of Luftflotte 1 during the Polish blitzkrieg. (H. J. NOWARRA)

The Polish fighter, PZL-11 (for Panstwowe Zaklady Lotnicze-State Aircraft Factory). Designed by Zyg-munt Pulawski in the early 1930s, the PZL-11 represented Poland's first line fighter against the Luftwaffe in 1939. (NATIONAL ARCHIVES)

comprised it. The level bombers, mainly Heinkel 111s and Dornier 17s, and later Junkers 88s, were designated *Kampfflugzeug;* the fighters, the Messerschmitt 109 (later the Focke-Wulf 190s), were assigned to *Jagdflugzeug Geschwader (JG)*; the so-called "destroyer" aircraft, the twin-engined Messerschmitt 110 fighter, were termed *Zerstörerflugzeug.* The Junkers 87, and other dive bombers, which included, in the initial days of the war, the Henschel 123, were assigned to *Sturzkampfflugzeug Geschwader (StG).*

When the war erupted Kesselring's Air Fleet 1 had roughly 800 aircraft with which to support Army Group North (500 level bombers, 180 dive bombers, and 120 fighters). In the south Loehr's Air Fleet 4 had slightly less than 600 planes (310 bombers, 160 dive bombers, and 120 fighters). The Luftflotten total in the east was about 1390 planes (excluding reconnaissance and transport aircraft), which is considerably less than the number generally given as the Luftwaffe strength at the time. In brief, the Luftwaffe was a good close-support air force for

the short war Hitler had in mind; he was hoping too that the French and English would permit him to settle "the Polish question" as they had all the other demands since the *Anschluss,* with little interference.

Compared to the less than second-rate Polish Air Force, the Luftwaffe was indeed a powerful Goliath. The total number of planes in the entire Polish Air Force was slightly over five hundred, of which less than half could be called modern. Even that figure tended toward excessive optimism. There were only thirty-six first-rank bombers, the PZL-37, the *Los* ("Elk"), available to combat squadrons on September 1, 1939. These were used to bomb advancing German armored divisions. The Elk was effective, and the Poles attacked with ferocious courage, but the small band was easily overwhelmed by both numbers and the superior performance of the German fighters.

The backbone of the Polish aerial defense force was the attractive gull-winged PZL-11c—the *Jedenastka* (the "Eleventh"). A product of the State

The Messerschmitt 109E, formidable opponent of the Polish Air Force in 1939. This plane was that of Adolf Galland, one of Germany's outstanding fighter pilots and air commanders. (H. J. NOWARRA)

Contrary to legend, the Polish Air Force was not destroyed on the ground in the opening days of the war. PZLs were dispersed to emergency airfields and camouflaged; Polish pilots succeeded in destroying about sixty German aircraft before the Polish Air Force was wiped out, most of it in air fighting with the superior Me-109s.

(EMBASSY OF THE POLISH PEOPLE'S REPUBLIC)

A Polish road after the Stukas had finished with it. (EMBASSY OF THE POLISH PEOPLE'S REPUBLIC)

Aircraft Factory (Panstwowe Zaklady Lotnicze, whence the PZL), the P-11, with its fixed landing gear, high wing, struts, and inferior top speed (about 240 miles per hour as compared with the Me-109's 300), was all but obsolete when the war began. Nor could the little fighters climb to the German bomber altitudes to intercept. In all there were about 158 first-line fighter planes in the Polish Air Force when the Germans struck. Of these there were 128 P-11s and 30 of the more outdated P-7s. Even if the Luftwaffe did not contain multitudes, it did easily outnumber the Polish Air Force around ten to one.

Contrary to the widely held belief, the Polish Air Force was not wiped out on the ground. Long before the tanks began to roll and the Stukas began swooping down on the airfields, the Polish planes were moved to well-camouflaged emergency airstrips. While serious damage was done to the runways, hangars, and the planes left behind, what there was of the Polish Air Force was generally untouched by the strafing attacks and dive-bombing.

The first German plane to fall in the Second World War was a Ju-87 Stuka brought down by Lieutenant W. Gnys (who would later serve in the Royal Air Force's No. 302, "Polish," Squadron in the Battle of Britain) piloting a P-11 of the Second Air Regiment, based at Krakow. Despite the victories it was a hopeless battle and typical of the Polish defense. On the ground Polish horse cavalry charged German tanks and armored cars with sword and lances. The cavalry was decimated from the air also when the Stukas attacked men and horses in the vicinity of Wielun, leaving behind an unreal devastation of dead and dying, smoke, flame, and futility. These were delaying tactics—for the blitzkrieg did not always plunge ahead inexorably—and they were disturbing. Heinz Guderian, commanding a Panzer corps, tells of how a section of his advance was held up by a Polish bicycle company. But these were fugitive and tragic efforts. On Hitler's large-scale map, safe in Berlin, the blitzkrieg moved ahead with breath-taking speed.

As the Poles were pushed back from the frontier they retreated inward toward Warsaw, creating pockets of potential resistance in the vicinity of Posen, Lodz, Krakow, and Przemysl. The roads were choked with retreating soldiers and fleeing refugees. Swarms of Stukas screamed down to bomb

Stuka fodder: a Polish girl weeps over her dead sister after the Ju-87s have swept by.

and strafe the highways in another Teutonic contribution to "the art of war," *Schrecklichkeit* (frightfulness). The roads disintegrated into a massive chaos of terror. The great Nazi steam roller crushed all before it, Polish mobilization was stopped before it had really begun, and resistance was dissipated haphazardly along the frontier or in encircled pockets. With no reserves to call upon the Polish Army was overrun by the panzers, motorized infantry, and the booted German Wehrmacht.

All roads led to Warsaw, which was the last stronghold and the prime target. Göring had had to cancel Operation Seaside, the full-scale attack on Warsaw scheduled for September 1, because of the fog which interfered with the aerial operations in the Army Group North area. The Warsaw-Okiecie airfield, home of PZL factories, was bombed by a few He-111s despite the early morning mist. By the late afternoon the weather had cleared enough for more intensive attacks by He-111s and Stukas. *Kampfgeschwader* 27, named for the World War I hero Oswald Boelcke, flew nearly five hundred miles from northern German bases for the first really heavy bombardment of Warsaw. Escorting the bombers were the *Zerstörer,* the Messerschmitt 110, the so-called "strategic fighter" or "destroyer." It was

Veteran of the Spanish Civil War and erstwhile passenger plane, the He-111 looses itsbombs on Warsaw.

Destruction on the Bzura River. Luftwaffe bombers spared Warsaw momentarily to smash a counteroffensive by the Polish Posen Army, delaying the blitzkrieg. Luftwaffe close support broke the Polish offensive, with the Stukas wreaking the havoc in this photograph.

(EMBASSY OF THE POLISH PEOPLE'S REPUBLIC)

Warsaw, September 25, 1939, bombed out of the war by the Luftwaffe. An He-111 sweeps in to add its bombs to the already burning city.

(EMBASSY OF THE POLISH PEOPLE'S REPUBLIC)

during these attacks on Warsaw that the first air battles of any size occurred between the Luftwaffe and the Polish Air Force. The Polish P-11s climbed in vain to reach the bombers; the Me-110s dived to intercept, the Polish fighters darted away. In a matter of minutes five of the P-11s had tumbled to the ground. In the few short weeks of fighting a total of 116 Polish fighters were destroyed in combat (of these 11 fell to antiaircraft fire, German as well as Polish). Some PZLs were lost when their pilots, in desperation, rammed the German aircraft to bring them down.

But nothing held up the German advance. Within a week the panzers of Walther von Reichenau's Tenth Army (of Army Group South) approached the outskirts of Warsaw. By this time the Polish Air Force had been all but completely expended; most of the first-line aircraft had been lost in the savage, one-sided dogfights. Almost as devastating was the supply problem, for without replacement parts and fuel the planes could not fly; communications, too, had been so disrupted that all military command broke down. Only a few of the Elk bombers continued to operate for a few days and then those remaining and the operational PZLs were ordered to Rumania. By September 17, 1939, the air war in Poland was over.

On that day the Soviet Army marched from the east to seal the fate of Poland. The Red Army met even weaker resistance than the Germans had; the Poles that had escaped the German envelopments were pushed back into the Nazi pincers or were captured by the Russians. With neither an army nor an air force, Poland was finished as a fighting power. "The German Luftwaffe," the Wehrmacht report stated, "has won undisputed mastery over the whole of Poland."

But Warsaw remained, crowded with refugees and fleeing soldiers whose officers rallied to a last-ditch defense. The encircled city became a honeycomb of trenches and improvised barricades as civilians and troops alike prepared for the German attack. The government had already fled to Lublin, and then into Rumania—and internment. By September 13 Operation Seaside, the aerial devastation of Warsaw, was reinstated. In the train of the onrushing German troops, the Luftwaffe had set up temporary airstrips within easy striking distance of the capital. The first sizable air raid occurred on September

13 when Wolfram von Richthofen ordered an attack on military targets—rail centers, public utilities, military establishments—within the city. Later Richthofen was to say that the "chaos over the target was indescribable." The first major aerial attack of the Second World War was not, by German standards, very worthy of those high standards which they had been demonstrating for the past two weeks to a stunned and frightened world. The bombing timetable went awry and various units came in over Warsaw haphazardly. With more than 180 aircraft converging on the target area there were collisions and confusion. But to the terrorized Poles below it was not confusion of command and timing, but a sky filled with aircraft dropping bombs.

Following this attack, Warsaw was given some respite from the air when the bombers were called off to assist the German Eighth and Tenth Armies under pressure of an offensive suddenly launched by the Polish Posen Army, which had been bypassed during the first week of the war. While the Stukas and He-111s and Me-110s were dealing with the Poles in the Bzura River fighting, the dropping of leaflets pleading for the Poles to surrender began fluttering down upon Nazi-encircled Warsaw. Posters soon appeared upon buildings and trees in Warsaw's outskirts promising those who surrendered food and good treatment. But the pleas went unheeded and all attempts by the Germans to propagandize the Poles into surrendering Warsaw "to prevent useless bloodshed and the destruction of the city" failed. The Poles had already witnessed sufficent German frightfulness along their highways, in the villages and towns, and in some Warsaw suburbs to realize the propaganda promises were delusion. They chose to fight to the end. Those who survived had worse than death in store for them. Behind the Wehrmacht into Poland came Dr. Robert Ley, ex-chemist, alcoholic, and chief of the German Labor Front, who believed that "Germans can never live in the same condition as Poles and Jews." And as he conscripted slaves for German industry, he was as good as his word.

On the day that the Russians began moving upon Poland, September 17, the first real mass attack on Warsaw was canceled when it appeared that the Poles were willing to negotiate for the evacuation of civilians and foreigners. The Polish representative did not appear to negotiate. With the Russians

Warsaw after the air blitzkrieg by Richthofen's bombers. ". . . everything was quiet. Warsaw was a dead city."

swarming in from the east, it was even more important to the Germans that Warsaw fall. For the next several days, until September 24, millions of leaflets rained down upon the beleaguered city promising honorable surrender terms—officers would even be permitted to keep their swords!

At eight o'clock in the morning, September 25, Richthofen unleashed the Luftwaffe upon Warsaw. At his disposal were 8 *Gruppen* (240 aircraft) of the Ju-87 Stukas, some He-111s, and a *Gruppe* of the clumsy Junkers 52 transports. In all Richthofen had about 400 aircraft to deal with Warsaw (the usual accepted number has been 800), not an im-

pressive number once again. But never before in the world's history had 400 planes attacked a single city. Here was the sequel to Guernica modernized, refined, and revised according to the concept of *Schrecklichkeit*. Flying two or three sorties through the day, Richthofen's forces were magnified into a massive destructive weapon.

The Stukas began with their familiar shriek, unleashing their bomb loads into the city. Thirty Ju-52s flew low over Warsaw to deliver the incendiaries into the churning clouds of flame, debris, mortar dust, and smoke. These clumsy craft were not ideally suited for their assignment; the incendiary bombs

General Wolfram von Richthofen (center foreground), cousin of the intrepid Red Baron of the First World War and Stuka specialist of the Second. Although originally cool to the idea of dive bombers, Richthofen learned to use them in Spain and then employed the Stukas with devastating skill in Poland. To his left is General Richard Ruoff, whose V Corps troops Richthofen's dive bombers supported in the conquest of France which came later. (HEINZ J. NOWARRA)

were literally shoveled out of their large side entrances (these were specifically for paratrooper use). The lumbering trimotored aircraft were slow and at least two fell to Polish antiaircraft fire. Also, the method of delivering the bombs did not make for accuracy, for thanks to a strong eastern wind, some of the incendiaries fell among German troops. An

immediate demand was made by Eighth Army headquarters for the cessation of the bombing, but Hitler, who had flown to the battle zone in his own Ju-52, instructed Richthofen to continue over the protests of Brauchitsch.

By late morning Warsaw lay under a pillar of smoke that coiled up thousands of feet into the air. And still the bombers came, although it was practically impossible to find specific targets because of the smoke and destruction. By nightfall five hundred tons of high-explosive bombs and seventy-two tons of incendiaries had been dropped into Warsaw. To this was added the massed artillery which encircled the city. After the planes had left the artillery continued.

The red glare of Warsaw's flames could be seen for miles around, as German and Pole alike stood in awe of what the bloody glow in the sky signified. On the next day Warsaw agreed to surrender; food had all but run out, the water supply was ruptured, and ammunition had been expended. The defenders of Warsaw officially capitulated on September 27, 1939. In less than a month Hitler's blitzkrieg had erased Poland, with the help of the accommodating Soviet Army, from the map.

Walter Schellenberg, a young SS intelligence officer, entered what remained of Warsaw and "was shocked at what had become of the beautiful city I had known—ruined and burnt-out houses, starving and grieving people. The nights were already unpleasantly chilly and a pall of dust and smoke hung over the city, and everywhere there was the sweetish smell of burnt flesh. There was no running water anywhere. In one or two streets isolated resistance was being continued. Elsewhere everything was quiet. Warsaw was a dead city."

Tomorrow the world.

3

"SITZKRIEG"

FORTY-EIGHT HOURS after Hitler had launched his blitzkrieg, Great Britain and France submitted their ultimatums to Berlin. Hitler still had hopes for a swift, tidy German-Polish war to be followed by a breathing spell before he made his next move. But the determined British and the reluctant French had decided to honor their promise to fight if Germany violated the independence of Poland. The policy of appeasement had come to an end and on Sunday afternoon, September 3, 1939, the tired voice of Neville Chamberlain informed the world that Britain had declared war upon Germany to fight against "brute force, bad faith, injustice, oppression and persecution."

When Göring learned of the British ultimatum, delivered at nine in the morning by Nevile Henderson, he exclaimed (echoing the view of Canaris), "If we lose this war, then God help us!"

Hitler's solution to "the Polish question" had now become the Second World War. His partner in the "Pact of Steel," Mussolini, backed down at the last moment and informed Hitler that he could not take part in military operations "in view of the *present* state of Italian war preparations."

If Hitler was unable to count upon Mussolini, he had found a worthy ally in Stalin, with whom he had had the audacious foresight to make a Treaty of Non-Aggression (Nazi-Soviet Pact) before embarking upon the Polish adventure. Thus had Hitler spared his nervous High Command the terrors of

Zweifrontenkrieg (war on two fronts). Thanks to his prescience Hitler had turned this double-front war upon the Poles and the campaign had gone smoothly and at a reasonably small cost. This may have been small comfort to the families of the 13,-981 Germans killed in the Polish invasion and of little strategic import to the 30,322 maimed and wounded. The Polish casualty figures because of the savage fighting, confusion, and destruction may never be known. As for the Luftwaffe, it had lost 734 men and 285 aircraft, over a hundred of which were bombers.

After the partition of Poland by Germany and Russia the period followed which Neville Chamberlain called fittingly a "twilight war" and which many Americans referred to cruelly as the "phony war" (a phrase attributed to the isolationist Senator William E. Borah). Following the devastation of Poland there came a strange pause in the blitzkrieg, a sitting war, or "stitzkrieg," in the press. Along the Western Front it was quiet indeed. Neither the Germans nor the Allies seemed anxious to make the first move. The mood in a still invulnerable America was observed, sadly, by Undersecretary of State Sumner Welles, who found that "many people appeared to feel, like Senator Borah, that the failure of Great Britain and France to undertake the offensive was somehow reprehensible. This feeling was almost sadistic."

Nor were the Germans eager to go on the of-

Hitler and Luftwaffe chief Göring in Poland, September 1939, to survey the results of the blitzkrieg. It was a high moment for both, for Hitler's Fall Weiss *had succeeded in answering "the Polish question" and the Luftwaffe had contributed to the bloody solution.*
(H. J. NOWARRA)

Army. At no time and in no place have I ever acted contrary to British interests." He continued with a statement of his aims by saying that his "chief endeavor has been to rid our relations with France of all trace of ill will . . ." and that he fervently believed "even today that there can only be real peace in Europe and throughout the world if Germany came to an understanding . . ."

But when he came to the crux of their misunderstanding, Hitler took another stance. "Why should this war in the west be fought?" he asked. "For the restoration of Poland? Poland of the Versailles Treaty will never rise again." He reminded his listeners that this was assured by Nazi Germany and Soviet Russia. Despite what German newspapers called "Hitler's Peace Offer," the speech contained nothing upon which negotiations could be initiated. Hitler closed with a veiled warning. "And let those who consider war to be the better solution reject my outstretched hand."

It was, as usual, the iron fist in the velvet glove, for ten days previously he had already instructed

fensive. Just two days before he unleashed *Fall Weiss* Hitler had said, "In two months Poland will be finished and then we shall have a great peace conference with the Western powers." But it had not turned out that way—and besides, the High Command did not feel ready to launch a western offensive. Most seemed to agree with the Commander in Chief of Army Group C (which faced the French opposite the Rhine and the Maginot Line), Wilhelm Ritter von Leeb, who wrote, "The sword does not have the edge which the Führer seems to assume." Leeb had in mind the great number of less than first-rate (older men, ill trained) troops under his command, some of whom were already muttering, "It is the generals who push the war."

But the generals were not pushing the war; even Hitler, speaking is Berlin on October 6, 1939—the day after he had entered a wasted Warsaw—appeared to be pushing peace. "Every German soldier," he told the Reichstag and the world, "has the greatest respect for the feats of the French

A French poilu in the spring of 1940, dug in on the Western Front, during the period described as the "phony war." Writing home, the soldier evokes the stagnation of trench warfare of the First World War. That he does not bother to wear a steel helmet is an indication of the general air of non-belligerence of the time. (U. S. INFORMATION AGENCY)

the Wehrmacht High Command to formulate plans for an early attack in the west, an attack that would strike through neutral Belgium and Holland. The generals were thrown into alarmed opposition. They argued that the steel shortage would seriously affect the outcome of a prolonged war—especially as it concerned the production of aircraft—and that the approaching winter, with its short days and certain fog, would interfere with air support. This argument went on for months between the Army High Command on one side and the Führer on the other during the so-called phony war.

II

During this period, however, there was no phony war at sea, where the German U-boats sank British merchant ships, or where the German pocket battleship *Graf Spee,* after a successful career as the scourge of the south Atlantic, was found by the British Navy and driven into the port of Montevideo, Uruguay, where the German captain scuttled his ship and committed suicide.

Also during the period of Hitler's "command crisis," his partner in war Stalin began activities in the Baltic regions to close off the northern approaches to the Soviet Union. "Treaties" were forced upon Estonia, Latvia, and Lithuania which agreed to the establishment of Russian garrisons, as well as naval and air bases in the Baltic states. Finland, however, refused to be bullied into a treaty. The Russians demanded a strip of the Karelian Isthmus, connecting Finland and the Soviet Union, from which it would be possible to shell Leningrad. In addition, there was the port of Hangö, which the Russians had wanted for thirty years as a naval base. In exchange the Russians would happily cede more than two thousand square miles to Finland along their common frontier. Finland found such demands incompatible with their definition of national sovereignty and neutrality. The predictable ensued: attacks in *Pravda,* broken-off negotiations, and border incidents in which the Finns were cast as villains. On November 30, 1939, Russian bombers attacked Viipuri and Helsinki.

The Winter War of 1939–40 was no blitzkrieg. Although greatly outnumbered, the Finns fought

The Graf Spee, *one of the most formidable of Germany's small battleships which operated in the south Atlantic in the winter of 1939. A float plane is in readiness on a catapult aft of the stack. Damaged in a battle* with British cruisers off South America and unable to escape, the ship was scuttled by its own crew. The captain, Hans Langsdorff, after writing a letter of explanation, committed suicide. (NATIONAL ARCHIVES)

grimly and imaginatively in the cold, heavily forested terrain. Entire Russian divisions were wiped out in the ghostly, white landscapes. But the Russian masses, tanks, and aircraft, and in time, better leadership, made the difference. The Treaty of Moscow was signed on March 12, 1940. The northern approaches to the Soviet Union were secured at great cost: at least 200,000 Russian dead and nearly 25,000 Finnish dead. It was another deadly move in the massive chess game between the two master dictators. Hitler, despite German sympathies for Finland and Mussolini's outspoken criticism of the German-Soviet Pact, needed Russian aid to circumvent the British blockade. It was still a one-front war—even though Russian naval and air bases in the Baltic could only have an eventual, and obvious, function. Stalin trusted Hitler no more than Hitler trusted Stalin.

Hitler, in fact, during these uncertain months of the "twilight war," could hardly have felt much trust in anyone whether ally, friend, or foe. Using the bad weather as justification he continued to postpone the attack in the west while goading his generals to prepare a blueprint for such an attack and to agree to carry it out. By early January it seemed that he would have his way. With clear weather forecast by midmonth, the day of attack was set (for at least the sixth time) for January 17. But then, for even the gods of war have been known to laugh, another hitch in plans came about.

Luftwaffe Major Helmut Reinberger, commander of the paratrooper school at Stendal, was summoned to assist in the planning of air-borne operations in Holland and Belgium. He was on his way to meet with Kurt Student's staff in Cologne but was held up by the congestion in the Ruhr area railways. In Münster he met a Luftwaffe major, Erich Hoenmanns, in the officers' club and explained his problem. Hoenmanns, eager to visit his wife in Cologne, offered to fly Reinberger to his conference the next morning—January 10. Although he was not supposed to fly while carrying highly secret documents, Reinberger was anxious to be on his way.

They took off the next morning in a Messerschmitt 108, the *Taifun* ("Typhoon"), a prewar sportplane converted into a courier and personal transport. The major was familiar with neither the craft nor, apparently, the route. For in the clouds the little monoplane with the two passengers became lost and off

course. In attempting to find his way Hoenmanns inadvertently flicked the wrong switch and turned off the engine.

There was nothing to do but crash-land the *Taifun* near the Rhine River, which Hoenmanns found below the clouds. Except that it was the Meuse, not the Rhine, and they were not in Germany, but in neutral Belgium near Mechelen-sur-Meuse.

When Belgian soldiers arrived at the crash scene they found Reinberger attempting to burn the contents of his briefcase. The fire was stamped out and Reinberger and the hapless Hoenmanns, as well as what remained of the papers, were taken to a nearby army camp. There, too, Reinberger attempted to destroy the papers, which had been placed upon a convenient table, by tossing them into an equally convenient stove. But again the incriminating documents were retrieved from total destruction. Reinberger was certain, as he later reported to Göring, that all that remained were "insignificant fragments, the size of the palm of my hand." He would, naturally, have been most anxious to make that point.

But how much of the papers actually remained? One thing was certain: copies of the fragments which escaped Reinberger's frenetic pyromania were sent to the British and French. There was consternation in all camps. The Germans could not be sure that Reinberger had really succeeded in destroying enough of the evidence. On the other hand, had the Germans, wise war makers that they were, deliberately let the papers fall into the hands of the Belgians? The Allies tended to overestimate the German penchant for adroit skulduggery and leaned toward the latter interpretation. Even the Belgians, who would be among the first to suffer if the plans materialized, did not take the papers seriously enough. Mobilization of the Belgian Army was accelerated, but there was no attempt to unite with the British and French, however, to face the inevitable.

The conferences in Berlin meanwhile were desperate, clouded with doubt and clamorous. Hitler affected an icy calm, always a dangerous sign. Göring, embarrassed by his Luftwaffe, ranted and swore dire retribution. However, it devolved upon Colonel General Alfred Jodl, Chief of the Wehrmacht's Operations Staff, and Hitler's military "adviser" Keitel to determine the next move depending upon how much they thought the Belgians—and the French and British—had learned. The situation was characteristically manic-depressive. One moment all agreed that Reinberger had burned the plans and the next moment they were not so certain. Word had reached Berlin of Belgian troop movements along the frontier. Three days after the incident Jodl noted that a decision had been made: "Order to General Halder [Chief of the Army General Staff] by telephone—All movements to stop."

The Führer was unperturbed (he now had an excuse for another postponement which he could blame on others) as Göring unleashed his vendetta. General Helmuth Felmy, commander of Luftflotte 2, to which Reinberger belonged, and Oberst Josef Kammhuber, his Chief of Staff, were immediately relieved. Felmy, never a Göring favorite, was retired to civil life (though he would later be recalled to serve in Russia) and Kammhuber was sent to Bavaria to command a bomber unit. Kesselring, at the time commanding Luftflotte 1, replaced Felmy.

III

With the attack in the west postponed until the spring (for the weather, too, had turned against the Germans), Hitler turned his eyes northward. The Russians had moved into Finland; it seemed that inevitably the Allies would also invade Scandinavia to cut off that line of approach. Hitler resolved to "save" Norway and Denmark from such a drastic fate. There was the matter, too, of Sweden's supply of iron ore, upon which the German war economy depended so heavily. Equally consequential was the point raised by that stepchild of the Wehrmacht the German Navy. Grossadmiral Erich Raeder insisted that the Imperial Navy could make something of itself if it could operate from bases in Norway, say at Trondheim and Narvik, instead of being bottled up in the North Sea by the Royal Navy.

When Raeder brought up the proposal for a Scandinavian campaign Hitler was in a receptive mood. If he had any fleeting doubts, these were quickly resolved by the doughty and resourceful British.

The auxiliary supply ship *Altmark,* which had been attached to the scuttled *Graf Spee,* had made its way up from the south Atlantic and had slipped through the British blockade into Norwegian waters.

Grand Admiral Erich Raeder, in a prewar portrait. Anxious to make a name for the German Navy, Raeder pressed for an invasion of Norway and Denmark—a move which nearly cost him his fleet. He was later succeeded by Karl Dönitz. (U. S. INFORMATION AGENCY)

The British knew that the *Altmark* carried captured British seamen, survivors of the encounters with the *Graf Spee.* Agents in Norway reported the presence of the *Altmark* and a Lockheed *Hudson* of the RAF's Coastal Command Squadron No. 220 was dispatched to confirm. The *Altmark* was located and soon a British destroyer flotilla converged on the German ship. A Norwegian boarding party inspected the *Altmark* and assured the skeptical British that the German ship was unarmed and carried no prisoners. Winston Churchill, First Lord of the Admiralty, ordered Captain Philip Vian of H.M.S. *Cossack* and commander of the British flotilla, to board the German vessel.

It was night, February 16, 1940, and the *Altmark* had taken refuge in Josing Fiord. With searchlights blazing, the *Cossack,* with Vian aboard, lanced into the narrow inlet. The Norwegian gunboat *Kjell* was first encountered and, with a nod to international law, Captain Vian invited its captain to join him in a search of the *Altmark;* pointedly the British captain made it clear that he intended to board the German ship and release the prisoners he knew were aboard but which the Norwegians apparently could not find. There was no further intervention on the part of the Norwegians.

The *Cossack* then pulled alongside the *Altmark,* which had grounded itself in an escape attempt, the ships were grappled, and a boarding party swarmed over the side. It was like a page out of the career of Francis Drake. There were hand-to-hand combats in which four Germans were killed, several wounded, and a number fled over the side. To the cries of "The Navy's here!" the 299 "non-existent" British seamen were released from locked storerooms and empty oil tanks. In addition to the prisoners Vian also noted several guns, overlooked by

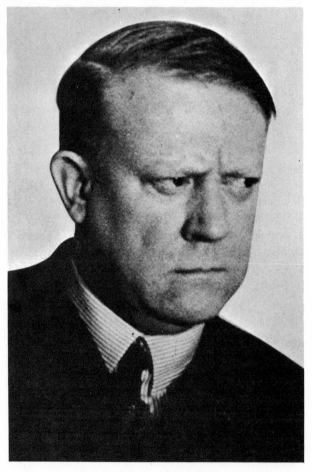

Vidkun Quisling, Norwegian fascist leader, whose name became a synonym for traitor. Quisling assisted the Germans in their invasion of Norway in 1940. Under Nazi occupation Quisling served as premier; after the war he was tried, convicted, and executed for high treason. (NATIONAL ARCHIVES)

the Norwegians, who remained, in the words of Churchill, "passive observers throughout."

Three days later Hitler, who could not remain passive in view of the British resolution, ordered final plans for the "occupation" of Denmark and Norway. "This operation," he stated in a directive dated March 1, 1940, "should prevent British encroachment in Scandinavia and the Baltic. Further it should guarantee our ore bases in Sweden and give our Navy and Air Force a wider starting line against Britain."

Meanwhile the Allies had also been giving serious thought to the strategic importance of Norway and its northern port, Narvik. It was there that Swedish ore was sent via rail for shipment through the North Sea when the Baltic was closed by winter ice. There had even been a plan during the Russo-Finnish War to send troops to help the Finns through Narvik and across Sweden. This raised the question of transit rights across these two neutral countries which the Allies did not actually need to face; the surrender of Finland in March of 1940 made it all academic. Rumors of Allied intentions had already reached Hitler, some through the Norwegian Nazi Vidkun Quisling. Clearly aid to Finland would cut off the Swedish ore, for the English and French would occupy Narvik and the railroad from Narvik to Luleå, Sweden. But the collapse of Finland spoiled Hitler's rationale as well as that of the Allies.

Each side, however, continued with some course of action. Finally, on the morning of April 8, the English began laying mines in Norwegian waters used by German ore ships. What they did not know was that already German warships were under way up the Norwegian coast and troops were ready to move across the border of Denmark. On April 9 Denmark had become a German province and the Luftwaffe had, as Göring insisted, sites for advance fighter bases and air-warning systems. Because the Scandinavian occupation had been prepared in secrecy Göring for possibly the first time had not been informed of *Weserübung* (the code name for the operation) until it had been all but in final form. Göring, whose relations with the other Wehrmacht services had never been good, did not endear himself further by dominating the first meeting he attended on *Weserübung.* The Field Marshal spent most of his time criticizing the already formulated plans, venting "his spleen" as one attendant noted,

A German soldier examines the wreckage of a Norwegian plane, destroyed by Luftwaffe attacks, at Sola. Bombed, strafed, invaded by German paratroops followed by air-borne infantry, the great air base fell into German hands the first day of Hitler's invasion of Scandinavia, April 9, 1940. (NATIONAL ARCHIVES)

Erhard Milch, former board chairman of Lufthansa Airlines, and one of the architects of the Luftwaffe. A shrewd administrator, Milch was a greater asset to the German Air Force than Göring. He was also ruthless in dealing with his rivals; at the close of the war he was a field marshal. (NATIONAL ARCHIVES)

Hans-Jürgen Stumpf, whose Luftflotte 5, operating from Norwegian bases, effectively harassed the British fleet in the North Sea and British ground and air forces that attempted to aid the Norwegians.

(NATIONAL ARCHIVES)

and generally disrupting the conference. As a result some changes were made in the plans, putting heavier responsibilitites on the Army and Navy, as well as ascertaining the bases. All of Denmark was conquered in about five hours. The determinant was the vaunted Luftwaffe, although most of the country was overrun by ground troops. The threatened bombardment in the style of Guernica and Warsaw of Copenhagen ended all Danish resistance.

Norway, also invaded on April 9, was not so readily overcome. The tiny Norwegian Army fought gallantly, but the Germans in a carefully prepared operation succeeded in landing troops in a half-dozen important coastal cities, from Narvik in the north to Christiansand in the south. Within hours the great airfield at Sola, a few miles to the east of the fishing village Stavanger on the southwest

The Focke-Wulf 200 "Condor" as a Lufthansa airliner in the late 1930s and as converted into a Luftwaffe reconnaissance bomber. The Condor was the only long-range aircraft available to the Luftwaffe when war came, and although not designed as a warplane, it was made into one by adding various gun positions and a ventral gondola under the fuselage, which served as a gun position, and eventually a bombardier's position. Though ill suited to its wartime role, with structural weaknesses, and vulnerable to fighter attack, the Condor proved to be surprisingly effective and earned the name of the "Scourge of the Atlantic" after its introduction in the Norwegian campaign.
(LUFTHANSA PHOTO-IMPERIAL WAR MUSEUM, LONDON)

coast of Norway, was in the hands of the Luftwaffe. Early in the morning a half-dozen Me-110s bombed the machine-gun emplacements at Sola (there were no antiaircraft guns). Paratroopers were then dropped to invest the field to be followed by transports (Ju-52s) carrying infantry battalions and a regimental staff. Meanwhile ships disembarked more troops and supplies in the harbor nearby. By the afternoon Sola was a German airfield.

To assure Luftwaffe prestige Göring sent Milch to command the newly formed Luftflotte 5, a temporary command which Milch held for three weeks when he returned to Germany to turn again to administrative details. Milch was succeeded by General Hans-Jürgen Stumpf. From bases established near Oslo, Christiansand, and Stavanger (Sola), the Luftwaffe operated most effectively against Norwegian and Allied troops as well as Allied shipping. The Focke-Wulf 200, the Condor, once the pride of Lufthansa's fleet, was pressed into active service

Junkers 88, the Luftwaffe's all-purpose aircraft. Its functions ranged from that of its original conception as a fast medium bomber through reconnaissance and *fighter plane. Designed in 1936 by a German, W. H. Evers, and an American, Alfred Gassner, the Ju-88 served in the Luftwaffe through the entire war.*

(U. S. AIR FORCE)

as an armed long-range reconnaissance aircraft. The first important use of the Junkers 88, flown by Kampfgeschwader 30, occurred during the Scandinavian campaign. The He-111 also was employed as was the now infamous Stuka.

The Allies sent small, ill-equipped reinforcements to engage in courageous but doomed ventures. Landings were made at Namsos, in central Norway, under command of Major General Carton de Wiart. The British forces soon came under heavy Luftwaffe attack and within days after the landings Namsos was bombed into an "unforgettable spectacle" of flame. General de Wiart informed London that he "could see little chance of carrying out decisive, or indeed, any operations unless enemy air activity is considerably restricted." The Luftwaffe continued to command the skies, just as their propaganda vaunted.

The aircraft carriers *Glorious* and *Ark Royal* were called in from the Mediterranean to assist in the delivery of aircraft, particularly fighters whose range would not permit their being flown directly from Britain. Since most of the best airfields were in German hands, the Allies were forced to construct their own airdromes under less than ideal conditions. The snow in one Norwegian airfield was packed down by a herd of several thousand reindeer. Bribed by the

The crew of an He-111 about to set off on a bombing mission. The Heinkel 111, a descendant of the single-engined He-70, was designed by Walter and Siegfried Gunther and first saw service in Spain and continued to be operational beyond its time. (NATIONAL ARCHIVES)

medical officer's pure alcohol, the keeper of the herd, a Laplander, drove the herd over the snow a few times to produce a perfect landing ground.

The British field was located on Lake Lesjaskog, near Aandalsnes in central Norway, where two hundred Norwegian civilians appeared to assist in scraping a runway under two feet of snow. Once prepared, the field was ready for the RAF: No. 263 Squadron dispatched eighteen Gloster Gladiators, the last of the biplane fighters, which took off from the deck of the *Glorious*. Led by a Blackburn Skua, an early Fleet dive bomber, the Gladiators flew through a snow flurry for nearly two hundred miles over unknown terrain and actually found the little icy strip on Lake Lesjaskog. Not long after, the ubiquitous Luftwaffe—Ju-88s and He-111s—appeared. Before the day ended ten of the eighteen Gladiators were out of operation. The planes had landed on April 24; by April 27 their effort was over, the Gladiators burned, and the pilots evacuated. The wreckage of some of the Gladiators may be found in the vicinity of Lake Lesjaskog even today.

In the north, at critical Narvik, the Allies were able to hold out longer because they were, temporarily at least, out of the Luftwaffe's effective range. A few airdromes were hacked out of the ice and forests, the most impressive of which was located at Bardufoss, about fifty miles northeast of Narvik. Once again the runways were created by civilians under the direction of British and Norwegian engineers and Royal Air Force technicians. Under the snow lay a six-inch coating of ice—and under that frozen soil, some of which turned to mud under the direct rays of the feeble sun. Work began on May 4 and by May 21 a great hand-carved network of landing strips, taxiways, and shelters was ready for occupancy. Once again No. 263 Squadron with its new Gladiators alighted in Norway. They were later joined by No. 46 Squadron, equipped with the modern Hawker Hurricane, based at another field near Skaanland, which lay closer to Narvik.

The Allied forces were, by this time, under double stress. Not only had the Germans enlarged their holdings in Norway, which included bases closer to Narvik, but Hitler had brought the "twilight war" on the Western Front to an end. Was holding Norway at great cost worth the risk of losing France?

Two Gladiators of No. 263 Squadron, RAF, camouflaged against German air attack at Aandalsnes, Norway, in the spring of 1940.

(IMPERIAL WAR MUSEUM, LONDON)

Flight Lieutenant Caesar B. Hull of the ill-fated No. 263 Squadron, which lost all of its Gladiators in and around Norway—although only two in combat; the rest were destroyed in operational mishaps, to German attack while on the ground, or, finally, when the aircraft carrier Glorious, *evacuating them from Norway, was sunk by the German Navy. Hull, wounded in the fighting in Norway, had not been aboard the* Glorious. *He returned to England and was killed while serving with No. 43 Squadron during the Battle of Britain.* (IMPERIAL WAR MUSEUM, LONDON)

Besides which, the tide of battle had turned severely against the Allies—British, French, and Polish troops. The air war was characterized by a quality of epic tragedy with overtones of the romance of air fighting in the First World War. In objective fact it was a clash of the past and the present with the outcome preordained.

On May 26 three Gladiators of No. 263 Squadron took off from the airfield at Bardufoss and flew south to a temporary field at Bodø. The three biplanes, led by Flight Lieutenant Caesar Hull, came upon a couple of He-111s which fired shots at the English planes but without inflicting damage. The Gladiators put down in the muddy strip at Bodø. While refueling was going on another He-111 appeared over the field. Lieutenant Anthony Lydekker immediately took off and engaged the Heinkel while Hull and the other pilot, Pilot Officer Jack Falkson, were briefed on their mission.

The Allies were retreating northward up a valley to the east of Bodø in an attempt to get to the sea and back to England. As Hull explained, the troops "were being strafed by the Huns all day." The three Gladiators were to interfere with the strafing.

The Heinkel having been chased off, Lydekker landed to refuel and the three British planes prepared to take off. This in itself was a major chore, for mud gripped at the wheels of the planes the instant they touched down. The stickier spots were covered with flat boards. In his report later Hull did not say that they took off; instead they "came unstuck about fifty yards from the end and just staggered over the trees." Falkson was not so fortunate and his plane crashed in the takeoff. Feeling certain theirs was a doomed mission, Hull ordered Lydekker to land and continued on alone.

"Saw some smoke rising," he reported, "so investigated, and found a Heinkel 111 at about 600 feet. Attacked it three times, and it turned south with smoke pouring from fuselage and engines. Broke off attack to engage a Junkers 52, which crashed in flames. Saw Heinkel 111 flying south, tried to intercept, and failed. Returned and attacked two Junkers 52s in formation. Number one went into clouds, number two crashed in flames after six people had baled out."

After attacking another Heinkel which raced south (toward the German lines) with smoke in its wake, Hull returned to Bodø to rearm. "The troops

Norway 1940: Norwegian skiers watch a Luftwaffe crew bomb-up a Stuka. The pilot waits upon one of the wheel pants. (NATIONAL ARCHIVES)

were cheered by the report," Hull wrote, "and I thought another patrol might produce more fun." It took a good deal of persuasion to convince the officer in charge of the strip to permit another takeoff from the viscous field. But Hull was most convincing, more planks were laid down, and he took off again. "This time the valley was deserted, and the only thing I could do was amuse the troops by doing some aerobatics. They all cheered and waved madly every time I went down low—I think they imagined that at last we had air control and their worries were over. Vain hope!"

That night, alternating in the remaining two Gladiators, the three pilots furnished air cover for the ships carrying the troops out of Norway. Fortunately there were no enemy aircraft aloft at midnight so Hull once again amused the troops by "beating up" the vessels as they left. By morning, however, it was agreed that the Bodø runway could no longer be safely used even with planks covering practically all of it. Also, at eight in the morning a jetty near the airdrome came under attack by Messerschmitt 110s and the Stukas. Only Lydekker succeeded in taking off immediately to save the Gladiator, but by the time he arrived at Bardufoss he was wounded and the plane a write-off.

Hull meanwhile had taken shelter in a barn and

Messerschmitt 109E-3 of Jagdgeschwader 77, based at Nordholz, near Cuxhaven, in northern Germany. JG 77

played an active role in the Scandinavian campaign, during which it was moved northward to Westerland at Sylt on the North Sea. (H. J. NOWARRA)

watched the dive-bombing for a while before noting that the field itself was not being attacked. He climbed into his plane and took off, climbed and attacked a Stuka at the bottom of its dive. He may have hit it, for the Ju-87 made off slowly over the sea. At that instant Hull was attacked by another Stuka, the shots shattering his windscreen. The force of impact had stunned Hull and he was "thanking my lucky stars" as he came to—only to hear the sound of guns from behind and the thudding of hits in his aircraft. The Gladiator turned into a right-hand dive, which Hull felt he would not be able to get out of, when at about two hundred feet the plane pulled itself out. Hull quickly gunned the engine to clear an outcropping of rocks in his path. This achieved, he was discouraged to hear the sound of machine guns from the rear again" . . . so gave up hope and decided to get her down."

The glutinous mud of Bodø would have been welcome as the screaming, strained engine pulled the Gladiator into the ground. The landing legs snapped and with a crashing roar and a ripping of fabric Hull's plane bounced along the frozen rocky ground in a spray of snow, crunching of trees, and a trail of oily smoke. With an injured head and knee, Hull crawled away from the wreck. The Tom-

mies, whom he had served so well in the hours before, sent him to the nearest British aid station, from which he was later evacuated by air to England. Within hours nothing remained of Bodø: jetty, airstrip, town, and forest blazed after a concentrated Luftwaffe attack.

As Hull had observed, it had all been a vain hope. By June 3 evacuation from Narvik was under way. A merciful stratum of mist and low cloud screened the frantic movement to the seaport from the Luftwaffe, whose planes thronged over the entire area at will, dive-bombing and strafing the troops, destroying communications and generally creating havoc.

The few surviving Gladiators of No. 263 Squadron were flown back to the *Glorious*. The ten remaining Hurricanes of No. 46 Squadron would have to be burned because the planes were not supposed to be capable of landing on a carrier deck. Unable to bring himself to destroy the Hurricanes, Squadron Leader K. B. Cross literally pleaded for permission to attempt the impossible. At this crucial moment every aircraft was priceless and the risk, it was finally decided, was worth it. At midnight, June 7, Cross led a formation of ten Hurricanes out of beleaguered Bardufoss and, after an hour's flight, all ten landed safely on the *Glorious*. Tragically this, too, was a vain hope.

The German Imperial Navy, which had inspired Hitler's Scandinavian adventure, had a final blow to deliver. The two battle cruisers *Scharnhorst* and *Gneisenau,* in Norwegian waters and cruising northward, learned from air reconnaissance and intercepted radio messages of much shipping activity between northern Norway and Scotland. The plane had also spotted a British carrier. On the afternoon of June 8 the German warships sighted the *Glorious* and its two escort destroyers, the *Acasta* and the *Ardent.* Outgunned by the German cruisers, all three British ships were sent to the bottom within two hours. Over fifteen hundred British seamen and airmen were lost in the icy sea—as were the twenty planes, ten Gladiators and ten Hurricanes, so splendidly evacuated from Bardufoss. There were only forty-three survivors, among them Squadron Leader Cross and one other member of his Hurricane squadron. For hours, as they waited for rescue, they saw twenty-five of their countrymen, even

some of their squadron mates, die in the Arctic cold.

It was a triumph for the German surface fleet—but with portentous qualifications not apparent at the time. In the battle with the *Glorious,* the *Scharnhorst* took a torpedo from one of the British destroyers. Within two weeks the *Gneisenau* was hit by a torpedo from the British submarine *Clyde.* Both German ships were under repair, and therefore out of action, for close to six months, a critical half year. In addition the cruisers *Königsberg* and *Karlsruhe* were destroyed in Norwegian waters, the former by Fleet Air Arm bombers and the latter by a British submarine. And during the battles of April 10 and 13 Royal Navy ships accounted for no less than ten of the destroyers which had brought German troops to Narvik. One half of the German Imperial Navy's destroyer strength, therefore, was eliminated within four days, and about a third of its cruisers. As a force at sea the German surface fleet counted for little after the Scandinavian campaign.

It was true, in the short view, Hitler had once

The British carrier Glorious, *which served in the Norwegian campaign, delivering aircraft and evacuating the* *wounded. It was sunk on June 8, 1940, during the withdrawal from Narvik with heavy loss of life.*

(NAVY DEPT., NATIONAL ARCHIVES)

again proved himself the supreme war lord, the blitzkrieg concept had proved insuperable, the Luftwaffe incomparable, but at what a price. In order to invade Britain Hitler would need all those ships which lay in dry dock or rusting in the fiords and coastal waters of Norway.

Many missed the full significance of the Scandinavian adventure: that the Luftwaffe had succeeded in disrupting the movement and operations of the most powerful Navy on earth. It was a lesson that would have to be painfully relearned before its implications were fully understood. Even so confirmed a ground soldier as Jodl had glimpsed this truth. His final report to the Führer on the Scandinavian campaign must have been the ultimate shock to Raeder, happy in his moment of hollow victory. "The Luftwaffe," Jodl submitted, "proved to be the decisive factor in the success of the operation."

Foreign Minister Joachim von Ribbentrop, however, spoke the ultimate in cant when he said, "Germany by its action has saved the countries and the peoples of Scandinavia from annihilation, and will now guarantee true neutrality in the north until the war's end."

4

WAS NUN?

"LIVE and let live was still the policy in the Saar," Bernard Fergusson reported from the Western Front, "and anybody who loosed off a rifle was thought to be thoroughly anti-social." In the positions where the British and French faced the Germans in the Siegfried Line the Germans twice in April "went through the motions of an attack, and the second time overran some French posts on our flank; this was considered to be extremely bad form, and not to be imitated."

This idyllic warfare abruptly ended on May 10, 1940, when the Nazi legions struck the Netherlands, Belgium, and Luxembourg. *Fall Gelb* ("Case Yellow"), the assault along the Western Front, erupted at dawn in Holland as the Wehrmacht smashed across the borders, parachutists dropped from the skies on airfields and other vital defense points, and the cry of the Stuka again shattered the peace of the countryside.

This had been preceded by a curious series of tentative and inconclusive actions during the "twilight war." As word of the attack on Poland flashed around the world, President Franklin D. Roosevelt appealed to all belligerents to refrain from unrestricted aerial warfare; in short, the bombing of cities. The British accepted on the same day, September 1, 1939; the French followed on the next day, and the Germans, having already devastated Polish towns and villages and with plans for the

bombardment of Warsaw in the offing, accepted Roosevelt's request on September 18. So it was that both sides confined bombing attacks only to absolute military targets: no bombs were to fall upon land lest civilians be placed in danger. Only ships at sea, therefore, were legitimate targets.

The RAF was devoted also to dropping propaganda leaflets, beginning with the first night of the war, when ten Armstrong Whitworth Whitley twin-engined bombers of Nos. 51 and 58 Squadrons delivered "Nickles," as the leaflets were called in code, to Hamburg, Bremen, and the industrial Ruhr. Although there was no interception by German fighter planes, the Whitleys did encounter bad weather, severe electrical storms, and icing. One plane crashed in France.

Nickle raids were not popular with crews, a view shared with them by Arthur Harris, commanding No. 5 Group of Bomber Command when the war began (by war's end he would command the bomber forces of Britain), who felt "that the only thing achieved was largely to supply the Continent's requirements of toilet paper for the five long years of war." By virtue of the irrational sapience rampant in the early weeks of the war, and of which there was little dearth throughout the war, the leaflets were marked "Secret" and carefully watched lest any of the British pilots read them. They were for the eyes of the enemy only, it seems. Harris, who

The Armstrong Whitworth "Whitley"—the "Flying Barn Door" to its crews—was one of Bomber Command's first modern bombers. Employed during the "phony war" in dropping propaganda leaflets, the Whitley accumulated impressive "firsts" during its tenure: it was the first British aircraft to drop bombs on German and Italian soil and the first to fly over Berlin to drop leaflets in what the crews called "bumphlet" raids on October 1, 1939. Earlier "marks" were powered by radial engines; beginning with the Mark IV the Whitley's performance was improved with the installation of in-line Merlin engines. By the spring of 1942 the Whitley was retired from Bomber Command; its day was over.

(IMPERIAL WAR MUSEUM, LONDON)

resented the additional complexity of handling the leaflets as secret documents, regarded them with typical acuity. "Many of the pamphlets," he said, "were patently so idiotic and childish that it was perhaps just as well to keep them from the knowledge of the British public, even if we did risk and waste crews and aircraft dropping them on the enemy."

While hazardous, the propaganda raids were useful in that they provided the air crews with training and reconnaissance flights over enemy territory—all of which would serve a more destructive purpose once the gloves came off. Also it became obvious that, against the "gloves off" day, new operational techniques were required particularly as applied to navigation; the conditions under which the crews were expected to operate required attention.

A typical raid of this type and period took place late in October 1939, when four Whitleys (originally five but one turned back) of No. 51 Squadron took off around dusk from a forward base at Villeneuve, France. The weather forecast was deadly: "rain, hail, and sleet showers, risk of thunder; cloud 7 to 9/10, low base 1000 feet, but 500 feet in showers; freezing level 1500 feet; heavy icing anticipated in shower clouds up to 12,000 feet." Except for the single turnback because of the weather, all planes proceeded to their assigned target areas in the Düsseldorf-Frankfurt region and dropped their Nickles under truly impossible conditions.

The Whitley, at best, could reach about seventeen thousand feet—and through most of the route snow clouds jutted up to eighteen thousand feet. While dropping the leaflets from the "dustbin," (a flare chute in the underside of the fuselage), it was not possible to use oxygen. The "droppers" were forced to walk around, cut the strings binding the bundles, and force them through the dustbin, all without oxygen and with little protection against the freezing temperatures. In one of the Whitleys the droppers—otherwise the navigator and radio operator—collapsed from anoxia. They revived on the way home, however, when the plane began icing up heavily and lost altitude. Controls became all but useless and great lumps of ice were flung back from the propellers and thudded alarmingly against the sides of the plane. Despite these problems and others, the pilot brought the plane safely back to Villeneuve.

Another Whitley had similar troubles, even before reaching Düsseldorf-Frankfurt. On the way to the drop zone the front gun turret and the trim tabs on the controls froze. And as the dustbin was being lowered, that too froze. The leaflets had to be transferred from one side of the plane to the other because of the jammed turret. During this painful operation, the crew discovered that it had taken along only a single charged oxygen bottle—all others were empty. As the Whitley lumbered toward the target, the front gunner passed out from the cold and lack of oxygen. The navigator and copilot relieved the pain of the cold by voluntarily butting their heads against convenient hard surfaces. When they descended to a lower altitude their aircraft came under antiaircraft fire. But they pressed on, despite the pilot's sickness from the cold, anoxia and bucking of the plane. More freezing afflicted the rear gun turret as well as the air-speed indicator. But the radio operator tripling also as navigator somehow managed to find his way back to base.

As with the other two aircraft, the third Whitley experienced trouble with frozen dustbins, but with variations and augmentation. The leaflets were scattered but only the combined efforts of the crew raised the dustbin out of the slipstream. The navigator passed out from the exertion. The pilot, after five and a half hours of exhausting flight, turned the controls over to the copilot and then joined the navigator in a loss of consciousness. When the pilot recovered it was to the sight of flames shooting out of his starboard engine. A six-inch coating of ice had formed on the wing. In a cloud, the distressed Whitley staggered into a dive. With the tail controls frozen solid, it took the strength of both pilot and copilot to pull the plane out of the plunge. Though leveled out, the Whitley continued dropping; the port engine, the one which wasn't burning, simply stopped under a thick coating of ice.

"The order was given to abandon ship by parachute," one of the crew later related; "as no reply was forthcoming from the front and rear gunners, the order was immediately cancelled. It was afterwards ascertained that the front gunner was unconscious due to a blow on the head from an ammunition magazine, and the rear gunner was unconscious from a blow on the head from the turret due to the dive and subsequent recovery.

"The aircraft then assumed a shallow high-speed dive. We opened the top hatch [all windows were solidly frozen over] to see where we were going, and the second pilot, who was at the controls, opened the side window. The aircraft emerged from the clouds in heavy rain at about 200 feet above the ground. All we could see was a black forest with a grey patch in the middle, for which we were heading; the second pilot pulled the aircraft over the trees brushing through their tops, and the aircraft dropped flat into a field, travelled through a wire fence, skidded broadside on and came to rest with the port wing against the trees on the further side of the clearing."

All climbed safely out of the Whitley and attempted, with little success, to extinguish the burning engine. The pilot climbed into the cabin to get an extinguisher, only to find that the crash had caused it to discharge. Finally the radio operator found another extinguisher and mounting the wing put out the flames. All were safe and unhurt and even managed a laugh when, the next morning, one of the local farmers asked, in French, "What time are you taking off?"

The fourth Whitley had little trouble on the way to the drop area, which was Munich, despite the blanket of hoary ice on the windows and snow underfoot in the front gunner's compartment. It was a cheerful crew, singing on the way to Germany —"Roll Out the Barrel" was an especial favorite —with particular and brilliant solo efforts praised over the intercom system. It was a noisy if frigid Whitley. Over Munich the Nickling was properly accomplished (with the usual freezing of the dustbin, the raising of which eventually exhausted most of the crew). As the plane neared the French border a cylinder head in the starboard engine blew off. With the loss of power the Whitley descended lower and lower into the thick clouds, after which the other engine began to sputter.

"Abandon aircraft," the pilot announced as the plane, flying at two thousand feet, bore down on some hills in the near distance.

First to jump was the front gunner, who entangled himself in the intercom wiring and dangled outside the aircraft, unable to get free, until the navigator gave him a push. The opening of his parachute knocked him out and when he next awakened he was startled at being ringed in by enormous brown eyes. He had dropped into a pasture and became the center of curiosity of a herd of cows.

The radio operator, who had been forced to jump with an oxygen bottle in his hand because his fingers had frozen to the metal, apparently landed in an adjoining field. He also proved that it was possible to cover a hundred yards in record time while encumbered by full flying regalia, complete to boots, and to hurtle a four-foot hedge while being pursued by a bull.

The navigator jumped, with a resultant sprained ankle; the pilot, after setting the plane in a flat trajectory, also jumped and landed gently in a meadow. The Whitley, ostensibly crewless, remained in flight for a few more minutes, plowed into the ground, and burst into flames. In the rear turret Sergeant A. Griffin, whose intercom had gone defective and who had not heard the order to jump, snatched a fire extinguisher and dashed into the front of the plane to save his fellow crew members. Extremely puzzled to find the crew gone, Sergeant Griffin limped to the nearest village, where he found the rest of the crew and learned that he had actually walked away from the crash of the Whitley. They were taken from the cafe in which they met, after being presented with bouquets, to a French hospital for treatment. By the evening all had returned to No. 51 Squadron.

Bomber Command was, however, engaged in more hostile operations during the period of the war's first days and through the twilight war. These incipient efforts were confined primarily to the North Sea approaches to Germany where the German fleet was concentrated. As with the Germans, the British began with good intentions: "The greatest care is to be taken not to injure the civilian population [the original order stated explicitly]. The intention is to destroy the German fleet. There is no alternative target."

Forty-eight minutes after the official declaration of war a Blenheim, with Flying Officer A. McPherson piloting and carrying a naval observer, took off on the first British aerial mission of the war. According to the Operations Record Book of No. 139 Squadron, the duty was "Photo. Reco." and the Time Up 1200 and Time Down 1650. The Remarks read tersely: "Duty successful. 75 photos taken of German fleet. The first Royal Air Force aircraft to cross the German frontier." The last sentence was a small concession to merited pride. It hardly suggested any of the hardships of the four-and-a-half-hour mission.

The Blenheim (a Mark IV, serial number 6215) came in from the North Sea over Wilhelmshaven at twenty-four thousand feet. The men aboard saw several German ships coming out of Wilhelmshaven and entering the Schillig Roads, among them the *Admiral Scheer* and the *Emden*. But they were unable to wire back the information, for, as with the leaflet-dropping aircraft, they were afflicted with the cold. Their radio frozen, McPherson and the naval observer (a Commander Thompson) could relay the intelligence only after they had returned to England. Thus was the first RAF target of the Second World War decided upon.

The major enemy was the weather, with minor contributions from High Command uncertainty. "The war was only 24 hours old," deplored Flight Lieutenant K. C. Doran, "but already the bombload had been changed four times. Lunch-time on 4th September found us standing by at an hour's readiness, the Blenheims bombed up with 500-pound S.A.P." McPherson's flight having located some German shipping in the region of the Heligoland Bight, it now devolved upon Doran to lead the bombers carrying Semi Armor Piercing bombs. But these too were changed for five-hundred-pound General Purpose (GP) with eleven-second delay fuses. This was a concession to the weather, which, as Doran noted, was reported as "bloody, and the only attack possible would be a low-level one."

With Doran in the lead aircraft, ten Blenheims (five from No. 107 Squadron and five of 110 Squadron) took off for Wilhelmshaven. Another five from No. 139 Squadron were also dispatched but because of the weather never located their target and returned to base without bombing.

Bristol Blenheims of No. 139 Squadron over France, 1940. Although hailed in the summer of 1936 as the last word in modern fast bomber design, the Blenheim proved vulnerable to the Messerschmitt 109 in France; it was also lacking in armament and protective armor for its crew. "XD" was the code for No. 139 Squadron, whose Flying Officer A. McPherson, in a Blenheim, was the first Briton to cross the German frontier when he photographed the German fleet at Wilhelmshaven on September 3, 1939. The following day, Blenheims of No. 110 Squadron made the first bombing raid of the war on Wilhelmshaven.

(IMPERIAL WAR MUSEUM, LONDON)

"Soon after crossing out over the North Sea," Doran of No. 110 Squadron noted, "we ran into bad weather . . . a solid wall of cloud seemed to extend from sea-level to about 17,000 feet." The formation thereupon dropped down to nearly sea level and flew through the clouds. They flew on instruments and dead reckoning. When they estimated they were over Heligoland, they turned and headed for what should have been Wilhelmshaven. They were barely fifty feet over the water when suddenly "a couple of barges appeared out of the murk and vanished." A dim suggestion of a coastline also emerged from the fog. "After a bit of feverish map-reading, we decided we were in the approach to the Schillig Roads. By an incredible combination and judgement we were bang on our track."

The Germans were not expecting any action in such dismal weather, and if anyone heard approaching aircraft no alarms were given. As Doran led the flights of No. 110 Squadron into the attack, now divided into two sections of two and three planes each, the cloud base lifted to around five hundred feet. Doran saw a large merchant ship—and just beyond it, the *Admiral Scheer*. The *Scheer* lay in

anchor, away from the shore, protected from the landward side by barrage balloons. Gaining as much altitude as possible—about five hundred feet —without losing sight of the target, Doran led the attack against the *Scheer*. Once the bombs went it would be necessary to make a sharp turn to the left to avoid hitting the cables of the barrage balloons.

Doran recalled seeing the laundry of the German seamen fluttering on the stern as he approached. The sailors seemed to be idling about, watching with little concern the approach of the Blenheims. Not until the first British bomber flashed over the *Scheer,* dropping its bomb, did the Germans realize what was happening. From then on the Blenheims were under heavy antiaircraft fire from both the ships and shore-based batteries. The bombs dropped by the first Blenheim struck the *Scheer* and —thanks to the delayed fusing—bounced off the deck and fell harmlessly into the water. The second plane, its crew under heavy fire, dropped short and the bombs exploded in the water. One Blenheim, its pilot misjudging his height or hit by flak, crashed into the forecastle of the *Emden*. It was the only serious damage done to any German ship in the attack and also killed some Germans and injured several more. No. 107 Squadron lost four aircraft in the attack and No. 110 Squadron one; it was a costly raid for small results. One half of the attacking force was lost in this first bombing attack by the Royal Air Force in the Second World War.

Later in the same day, September 4, 1939, fourteen Vickers Wellingtons, six from No. 9 Squadron and eight from No. 149 Squadron, made an attempt upon the *Scharnhorst* and the *Gneisenau*. Their presence at Brunsbüttel had been noted by the enterprising McPherson on his historic reconnaissance flight the day before. Bad weather and antiaircraft fire again took their toll and two of No. 9 Squadron's planes did not return. One of the bombers lost was attacked by Sergeant Alfred Held in a Messerschmitt 109 of Jagdgeschwader 77. It was the first British bomber of the Second World War credited to a German fighter pilot. Unlike the attack at Wilhelmshaven by Doran and the Blenheims, the Brunsbüttel attack, which was at a greater distance from the United Kingdom, afforded more time for an alarm to be given and a few aircraft to be dispatched to intercept.

In all, seven bombers were lost on the first day of offensive aerial warfare. It had not been a "wizard" day for the RAF—although it did mean much in terms of civilian morale and it did show what British aircrews could do under extremely difficult conditions. The "restricted bombing" policy naturally kept them from attacking the more likely target: the factories in the Ruhr. The Air Staff, however, waited, feeling that "this delicate and difficult problem may well be solved for us by the Germans, who are perhaps unlikely to refrain for more than a limited period at most, from actions that would force the Allies from all legal restrictions." The expression in vogue in the Air Ministry was that all were waiting for the hated "Hun to take off the gloves." When this occurred Bomber Command, too, would remove the gloves and unleash its force against more important targets than the ships of the German Imperial Fleet. But, in truth, the Bomber Command's bared fist consisted of less than five hundred aircraft, many of which were the out-of-date Battles and the hardly better Wellingtons, Whitleys, and Hampdens. The most effective bomber was the Blenheim, and its early

operations, as already described, were hardly comforting. Against the five hundred British bombers, the Germans, when ready to discard the gauntlet, could muster three times the number.

Nor were the Germans, certainly not the Luftwaffe at least, anxious to violate the restricted-bombing agreement. The Germans, like the British, were most active mining their respective coastal waters or bombing enemy warships.

This policy was in force when the first German bombers, Heinkel 111s and Junkers 88s of Kampfgeschwader 30, appeared over Britain. The bombers had been dispatched to attack the *Hood*, supposedly in the neighborhood of Rosyth in the Firth of Forth. On the morning of October 16, 1939, German reconnaissance aircraft had passed over Rosyth and the possibility of a raid on the port was noted. No. 607 Squadron was sent north from its home base closer to Rosyth. But the early-warning system broke down and No. 607 Squadron was not alerted to the approach of the German bombers until late. On the other hand, the Germans suffered some surprise, for they had been informed by intelligence that there were no fighters in the vicinity of Rosyth. There were two additional units, No. 602 (City of Glasgow) and No. 603 (City of Edinburgh), within striking range of the Firth of Forth.

Kampfgeschwader 30 found the *Hood* docked at Rosyth, therefore too close to land, and consequently civilians, to serve as a target. The small force of nine bombers was forced to select other targets as they approached Rosyth at twelve thousand feet. Captain Helmut Pohle, piloting a Ju-88, picked the *Southampton* for his attack. There was some tardiness in the reactions from antiaircraft gunners in the area, so that the bomb run was reasonably unmolested. One British gun battery was engaged in a practice drill when they saw German planes coming over. The gun crew hurriedly changed dummy ammunition for live, and began firing at the bombers.

By this time bombs had begun raining down on the ships. One bomb cut through three decks of the *Southampton* and careened out the side before exploding against an admiral's barge, sinking it. Damage was done to the *Edinburgh* and the *Mohawk*. Pohle, leading the attack on the *Southampton*, found himself in a good deal of trouble. His Ju-88 was struck by flak and the top housing of the pilot's compartment blew away in the dive. Worse, as he headed out to sea in a race for home he came under attack by a trio of Spitfires—the first he had ever seen. The German aircraft, crippled and yawing, staggered under the heavy gunning of the British fighters, which swarmed in three times. Pouring smoke and carrying two dead crewmen, the Junkers splashed into the sea near Dalkeith, Scotland—the first German aircraft brought down over Britain since the First World War. Captain Pohle survived and was taken prisoner. Another German plane, reported as a Heinkel, also fell into the sea. The credit for bringing down the first German plane was given to No. 603 Squadron, led by Squadron Leader E. E. Stevens.

Like the British raids on German naval ports, the German attacks on Rosyth and other havens for the Home Fleet were tentative, meager, almost haphazard skirmishes. They did not lead to great aerial battles, as had been visualized in the pulp magazines the young fliers had read in school. But they took their toll and the losses were bitter if not spectacular. The missing element of drama was finally provided on December 18, 1939, when two dozen British Wellingtons, of Nos. 9, 37, and 149 Squadrons, set out on an "armed reconnaissance" of the Heligoland Bight, specifically the vicinity of the Schillig Roads and Wilhelmshaven. (Armed reconnaissance eliminated the process of sending out one plane to spot targets and then sending out the bombers to strike them. The Wellingtons were bombed up and ready in the event that worthwhile targets were found.)

It was a perfect day, cloudless and sunny, with superb visibility. Two of the Wellingtons turned back because of mechanical trouble and the remaining twenty-two approached from the north, having kept away from the flak guns stationed on ships along the way. The four formations, at twelve thousand feet, then came in over Heligoland. It was about at this moment that the Messerschmitt 109s of Jagdgeschwader 77 intercepted the British bombers. Doggedly pressing on, the Wellingtons continued their reconnaissance, unable to drop their bombs upon the warships below because they were docked or in harbors and thus not to be attacked. The gunners in the Wellingtons did the best they could to fight off the darting Me-109s, which seemed to be coming in from all directions. The tail guns

of the Wellingtons gave the Germans the most trouble, but the bomb-laden Wellingtons, slow compared to the Me-109s, were terribly mauled. For about eighty miles from Heligoland until they were well out to sea the Wellingtons suffered the attacks of the Me-109s, as well as those of Me-110s which had also joined the battle. Taking advantage of the blind spots in the Wellington's defense, that is, where the guns were unable to traverse, the Messerschmitts accounted for no less than twelve of the British bombers (the claim was, however, for thirty-four) at a cost of two Me-109s (British gunners claimed twelve). Worst hit of the British units was No. 37 Squadron, which lost five of its six aircraft dispatched.

The surviving crews reported that many of the Wellingtons had crashed, burning and with fuel streaming from their tanks; it was a memorable argument in favor of self-sealing tanks. In time these would become standard equipment on all aircraft, but the lessons were always tragic and costly. It was learned also that bombers were susceptible to aggressive fighter attacks. If "the bomber always got through," so did the modern fighter get through the bomber's defenses. It was after this battle over the Heligoland Bight that the British High Command gave serious consideration to switching to night operations, when fighter attacks could be expected to be almost negligible.

Bomber Command's crews endured the worst of the Luftwaffe's effectiveness; but the fighter pilots, too, were subjected to the lessons to be learned in a new kind of warfare.

II

Contemporaneously with the attack on Poland, the northern invasions, the halfhearted bombings and Nickling raids, RAF units were sent to France to fight the Germans.

As in 1914, British aircraft crossed the English Channel shortly after the official declaration of hostilities. Ten squadrons of Fairey Battles of what was termed the Advanced Air Striking Force left for France in the afternoon of September 2. One of the Battles fell into the Channel because of engine trouble; it was the only incident of the crossing. The crew was saved and so the transfer was unremarkable and uncontested. The bomber squadrons were reinforced by four Hurricane squadrons of the Air Component attached to the British Expeditionary Force.

The Air Component, as its name implied, was to work with the BEF, as had, in a sense, the Royal Flying Corps a quarter of a century before, as cover for the troops and protective element for the reconnaissance and photo squadrons (Blenheims and Lysanders), also a part of the Air Component.

The Advanced Air Striking Force was to be employed in the more or less strategic bombardment of targets inside Germany with its Battles and Blenheims; the French, it had been agreed, would supply the fighter protection. The facts of war in its new form hindered the mission of the AASF. The

the French Air Force. Before the war regarded as one of the greatest air forces in the world, the Armée de l'Air was in reality antiquated, afflicted with an effete, defeatist command—in short, ineffectual. The young pilots were able and eager, but they had been betrayed. Neither their aircraft nor the policy under which they were expected to operate was anywhere equal to the task before them.

Burdensome also were the kid-glove bombing rules, observed equally by the Germans and the Allies. Neither side wished to unleash a bomber war on the cities. The French were particularly sensitive to the possibilities of an aroused Luftwaffe and did little to encourage strategic bombardment. It was a policy of kill and let kill just so long as

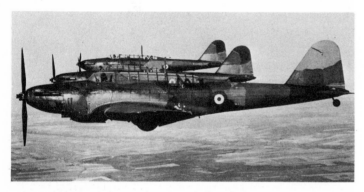

Fairey "Battles" of No. 218 Squadron, Advanced Air Striking Force in France, 1939–40. The Battle, although obsolete by 1939, was used in front-line service as a reconnaissance bomber during the "phony war" (when this photograph was taken), and as a bomber when the war in the west erupted in May 1940. It was shortly after used as a trainer.

(IMPERIAL WAR MUSEUM, LONDON)

Westland "Lysander," five squadrons of which operated as tactical reconnaissance and photo-survey aircraft for the British Expeditionary Forces in France. Slow, with a top speed of barely two hundred miles an hour (the Me-109 could do well over three hundred), the Lysander was maneuverable but vulnerable and not suited to modern air combat.

(IMPERIAL WAR MUSEUM, LONDON)

impact of the blitzkrieg, especially after the twilight war expired, necessitated the diverting of the bombers to attack the advancing German troops and armored vehicles rather than "strategic" targets behind the lines. The Battles proved less than suitable for modern war.

Late in September 1939, for example, five Battles of No. 150 Squadron were dispatched to reconnoiter ten miles inside the German frontier. They encountered a flight of Messerschmitts and in the battle that followed four of the Battles were destroyed and the surviving aircraft was a write-off on returning to base.

Another handicap was France's Armée de l'Air,

the war remained remotely "civilized." It was also a war of boredom. While the Germans reduced and decimated Poland and then instituted a new order, the French and the British dug in, hoping for the best.

These were tragic, equivocal days which stretched into the months of the twilight war.

The first British fighter squadrons to land in France, and which endured both the boredom of the "phony war" and the frantic humiliation of being pushed out of France, were Nos. 85 and 87 Squadrons of the Air Component and Nos. 1 and 73 Squadrons of the AASF. These Hurricane squadrons were among the first to engage the Luftwaffe, the first British airmen to face the German fliers since 1918. Thanks in part to the press, the opening of the Second World War, at least in the air, was but a sequel to the earlier war. Some of the traditions of that more romantic epic were revived as newsmen sought out aces, colorful characters, human interest stories. The lone fighter pilot engaged in aerial combat high in the heavens furnished good copy—this despite the official negative British attitude toward the glorification of the individual.

Among the first celebrities of the war was a husky, tall, young New Zealander, Flying Officer Edgar J. Kain, of No. 73 Squadron. The friendly, sportive twenty-one-year-old was best known by his

into the equally "impassable" Ardennes Forest. A mere four- or five-minute flight carried the British pilots over Germany. Despite the proximity of "Jerry" (a term which served the British for either the Germans or a chamber pot), the eager fighter pilots found little action in their sector. This was true also of No. 1 Squadron, nesting some thirty miles to the south of Verdun at Vassincourt airdrome near Bar-le-Duc.

At both bases, primitive by RAF standards, the Hurricanes proved their sturdiness, thanks to their rugged construction. Also the wide-track landing gear of the plane was capable of coping with the hazardous, often muddy condition of the landing strips. As for action, apparently the Luftwaffe de-

Among the first to arrive in France were the Hurricane pilots of No. 1 Squadron (right) and No. 73 Squadron. Although they endured the boredom of the

"phony war" they fought furiously after May 1940. Among the No. 73 Squadron members grouped around the antique vehicle is Cobber Kain (on right without hat). (IMPERIAL WAR MUSEUM, LONDON)

nickname "Cobber," an Australian-New Zealand term for "pal" or "chum." With his ready grin, his tousled hair, his crumpled uniform, and his fearless, almost madcap flair for fighting and flying, Cobber Kain seemed a reincarnation of the spirit of Albert Ball or Billy Bishop of the Great War and was the squadron's star performer.

By October No. 73 Squadron was stationed at Etain-Rouvres airdrome near Verdun. The base lay just behind the famed "impregnable" complex of fortresses, the Maginot Line, facing Germany's West Wall. The Maginot Line at this point petered out

voted itself chiefly to reconnaissance and dived into cloud cover and ran for home before the British could intercept.

Not until October 30—the war was nearly two months old—did an RAF fighter bring down its first German plane. Almost directly over No. 1 Squadron's field three German aircraft, Dornier 17s, were seen at high altitude. The airdrome defense section took off immediately in pursuit and Pilot Officer P. W. O. Mould (in Hurricane L1842) overtook the Dornier. The twenty-year-old pilot, the squadron's youngest—a distinction which

King George VI on a visit to an Air Component base in France. The three Hurricanes in foreground belong to No. 85 Squadron (VY), the others to No. 87 *Squadron (LK), which like Nos. 1 and 73 Squadrons were the first of the fighter units to serve in France. In the right background are a Blenheim and two Gladiators.* (IMPERIAL WAR MUSEUM, LONDON)

Destroyed German bomber in France. At left is the tail section (possibly of an He-111). French soldiers have begun to gather souvenirs from the scattered wreckage. (FRENCH EMBASSY)

A Hurricane I landing at Vassincourt, France. The aircraft, belonging to No. 1 Squadron, was then equipped with a wooden propeller. Pilot Officer Mould of this squadron, flying one of these early Hurricanes, scored the first RAF victory when he destroyed a Dornier on October 30, 1939.

(IMPERIAL WAR MUSEUM, LONDON)

earned him the nickname "Boy"—surprised the Germans and shot the Dornier down without a fight.

Two days later, November 2, 1939, Cobber Kain scored the first victory for No. 73 Squadron. The young giant had been lying sprawled on the ground scanning the skies through field glasses when he suddenly leaped up shouting, "I've spotted a Jerry!"

He ran for his Hurricane, which was in readiness, leaped in, and gunned the fighter down the field. Within nine minutes he had climbed to about twenty-seven thousand feet, above a lone Dornier 17, the "Flying Pencil," on a reconnaissance mission. As Kain closed in upon the German plane the rear gunner began firing at him. A few tracers flashed past the Hurricane's cockpit before Kain "squeezed the teat." One sudden flash of fear came into his mind: he hoped that his armorer had not forgotten to arm the eight machine guns in the Hurricane's wings.

The entire plane jolted as the eight guns burst into action—and it was over. Kain dipped onto one wing to watch the Dornier plunge to earth and strike near a small village not far from Rouvres. The German plane had, as described by Charles Gardner of the BBC, "dug a trench four feet deep across a village street, and all that was left of it was a flaming heap of rubble. Gruesome bits of the crew dangled from nearby trees, and the French children were running round with bits of fingers and hands which they had found lying around."

Kain, meanwhile, dived for home and jumped into a vehicle as soon as he had landed to cheers and back-pattings. On arriving at the crash site Kain had to be reassured that no one in the village had been injured by the Dornier. Kain walked over to the twisted, smoking tangle of metal. Three fellow humans had been horribly mangled in the wreckage. It was difficult for Kain to determine which was worse: the sight of the French children playing with bits of Boche or the head of one of the crew, lying at his feet, intact in the helmet and eyes wide open. Kain stood at the edge of the smoldering trench, his face drawn and grimy. Turning away he was heard to say softly, "Well, it was either them or me."

It was not to be a cinematic, pulp-fiction war after all. And it would become grimmer. This was apparent in the build-up of the German fighter squadrons along the Western Front in preparation for Hitler's frequently postponed and permutated *Fall Gelb*. The Messerschmitt 109 squadrons, free of the Polish campaign, and soon outnumbering the French and British squadrons, proved to be more aggressive than they had once been. By the first of the new year 1940, despite the fact that the invasion of France for which the Allies thought they were ready had not yet come off, there was clearly something in the wind. Up to the end of 1939 the RAF had succeeded in destroying about twenty German aircraft—not an impressive number.

The tenor of the air war was, however imperceptibly, changing. Among the first to experience this was the doughty Cobber Kain. While leading a three-Hurricane flight on patrol, Kain spotted a dozen Messerschmitts. With characteristic dash, he announced to the other two pilots, "Get going, chaps," and dived into the middle of the German formation.

In the first minute or so of the attack, Kain blasted one of the Messerschmitts out of the melee. But he also watched one of the by then crippled Hurricanes racing for the ground and a forced landing. The other Hurricane, Kain noted, was the center of attention of five Messerschmitts. He pulled back on the control stick and came up under one of the German planes, squeezing the gun button. Another Messerschmitt fell out of the battle, streaming black smoke.

It was now Cobber Kain's turn: rushing toward him was a Messerschmitt with guns twinkling. In his rear-view mirror, Kain saw another German plane pouring shells into the Hurricane. Ignoring the rear plane for an instant, Kain activated the eight guns against the oncoming fighter. Nothing happened—Kain had used up his ammunition supply. Luckily his companion knocked the Messerschmitt off Kain's tail—but not before a shell rammed into the engine of Kain's aircraft. There was a burst of flame and thick black smoke filled the cockpit—the air filled with colorful New Zealand profanities. In desperation Kain attempted to ram a German fighter which loomed ahead of him in the thick smoke. But his engine was rapidly dying and the Messerschmitt whisked away.

Cobber Kain was at twenty thousand feet, his plane aflame and he himself choking in the oily smoke. He jerked the stick forward and pushed the nose down. The flames spread and Kain rammed

Squadron scramble by No. 87 Squadron, France 1940. Second plane in the foreground is a Hurricane fitted *with the de Havilland three-bladed propeller, an improvement over the old wooden prop.*

(IMPERIAL WAR MUSEUM, LONDON)

the cockpit hood open and was about to bail out. Then he remembered, when he had taken off he hadn't bothered to fasten his chute properly. He sank back into the smoky cockpit hoping to correct the oversight. He then noted that the dive had smothered the flames, although the cockpit leaked oil and effused smoke. And then the engine came back to life. Hoping to save the precious Hurricane, Kain sought out a place to land and quickly found a spot just at the edge of an airdrome near Metz. He brought the plane down and then hopped out of the tattered Hurricane and, as he himself said, "I fell flat on my bloody face. Passed right out, like a sissy boy."

Kain's cavalier attitude toward regulations (he should have properly adjusted his parachute before ever leaving the ground) had nearly cost him his life. He might easily have been court-martialed for his breach of discipline. As it was, Squadron Leader

Brian Knox would from time to time vent his Dublin Irish on the young New Zealander—this was known as "tearing off a strip" (presumably, and metaphorically, of flesh).

The strip tearing might be earned for some slighting of military courtesy or bearing—the RAF pilots had already begun to fashion curious variations in dress. Kain affected uncreased trousers stuffed into flying boots. Around his neck he generally wore a scarf; a small chain dangled outside his jacket—this carried his identification disks and a small green tiki, the image of a Maori god, as a good luck charm. Like other pilots, Kain liked to wear turtleneck sweaters. Another shared characteristic was the dashingly wind-blown mop of hair. Members of the Senior Service, the Royal Navy, frowned upon this unkempt noncomformity with some disdain, referring to the bulk of pilots as "the Brylcreem boys." The raffish, tradition-free fighter pilots further dis-

A trio of Hurricanes in attack formation—German-eye view. These aircraft are in a neater formation, however, than was possible in combat. But several German fighter and bomber pilots undoubtedly had a glimpse *of Cobber Kain leading a couple of his chaps into a fight in a formation that for an instant may have looked as it does here.*

(IMPERIAL WAR MUSEUM, LONDON)

turbed the "naval types" when aboard ship by referring to the bow as "the pointy end of the boat."

Drinking became an off-duty pastime, as it had during the First World War, for the young fighter pilots. Every squadron had its favorite "boozer" in nearby French villages. It was quite unlike their local pubs, back home, with the traditional dart board and the pints of bitters. Champagne was easily obtained in the boozers and it was a reasonable substitute for the delectable English beers. It was, of course, dubbed "giggle water."

Victories were celebrated either in the local boozer or in the squadron mess. And, since victories were few in the early weeks, the officer pilots were frequently invited to the sergeant's mess for a blow. Or else a group of men from one squadron visited another squadron. After much imbibing of giggle

water such blows became rather destructive and lacking in decorum. Visiting dignitaries were requested to stand on their heads, as a kind of squadron initiation. Or a playful wrestling match resulted in a battle royal and the eradication of the supply of chinaware, chairs, and even tables.

It was following one of these parties that four members of No. 1 Squadron poured themselves into their car to return to their squadron. Two, in the rear seat, were completely out. The other two, the squadron leader—whose car it was—and a pilot, Paul Richey, manned the forward seat.

Soon they were racing through the darkened French countryside. The following (authentic) conversation took place:

"Not so fast, Paul," cautioned the squadron leader.

Edgar J. "Cobber" Kain of Christchurch, New Zealand, and No. 73 Squadron, RAF. The first official British ace of the Second World War with seventeen victories, Kain was killed while "beating up" his airdome in France just before he was to have returned to England to become a flying instructor.

(IMPERIAL WAR MUSEUM, LONDON)

"OK."

A few minutes later the squadron leader spoke again, "Ease off a bit, old boy."

"OK," Richey hazily agreed.

Three minutes later Richey addressed the squadron leader.

"Hey, I'm not driving, you bloody fool, you are!"

"Am I?" said the squadron leader. "Oh, so I am."

The Brylcreem boys were forming their own traditions and Cobber Kain represented them in the first months of the war. The subject of discipline was not taken too seriously. He smiled (if only inwardly) when Squadron Leader Knox tore off a strip, but rebelled when Knox went a step beyond and grounded him. A really drastic punishment was to put Kain in charge of the operations tent, where

he heard the sounds of the battle over the radio to his discomfiture and frustration.

On March 26, 1940, after completing a full day in the operations tent, Kain had reached the limit. On hearing of much enemy activity over the frontier, he sprinted out of the tent and pulled away in his Hurricane in company with two other No. 73 Squadron men.

"In the Luxembourg corner," Kain later reported, "I saw a number of enemy aircraft and proceeded to investigate at 2:30 p.m. I gave a message on R/T [radio telephone] to Flying Officer Perry and Sgt. Pilot Pyne, who were with me—'Enemy aircraft ahead'—and proceeded to attack. I turned into the enemy which had started to climb and gave a burst at the leader who pulled up, turned on his back and spun away in flames. I then noticed 5 more M.E. 109's working round behind me, so I turned hard right and took a sight on the near machine. I fired a burst at him, he dived away and I took three deflection shots at another M.E. 109 which was slowly turning ahead of me. I got behind this aircraft and gave it a burst. He turned on his starboard side and dived right down towards earth."

Suddenly the sky was clear of aircraft, except for Kain's, so he searched for the other Hurricanes. Seeing nothing, he turned south just as his Hurricane was struck by two shells, one hitting the cockpit and the other the fuel tank.

"The explosion of the hood of my cockpit rendered me unconscious," Kain reported, "but I came to diving steeply. After a while I managed to pull out of the dive and tried to bend down and turn off the petrol, but the flames burnt my face. I headed towards France to gain as much ground as possible and when the flames got too intense I decided to abandon my aircraft."

Heaving himself out of the burning plane, Kain pulled the ripcord at twelve thousand feet. At ten thousand feet he emerged from the clouds where he found that it "was all very still and I thought I was in heaven." Afraid that he would land in Germany, Kain yanked at the strings of the parachute, slipping the air and hastening the descent. He painfully struck the ground near Ritzing in the vicinity of a woods. He gathered up his chute, ran for the woods, hid the chute, and set out in a southerly direction hoping he would find himself in France. He was soon challenged by a French captain and after being properly identified, Kain was sent to Evendorff for first aid. He had been burned and was limping badly. The captain informed Kain that he had dropped into No Man's Land, between the French and German positions.

A French staff car returned Kain to Rouves where the squadron medic, Flight Lieutenant R. M. Outfin, spent two hours cleaning up the burns. Kain's uniform was in tatters and had to be abandoned. As he stood up to leave, Kain winced.

"What's wrong with your leg, Cobber?" Outfin asked.

"I don't know, doc," Kain replied. "Some things went in and I don't think they came out." Whereupon Cobber Kain collapsed. The doctor proceeded to remove over twenty pieces of shrapnel from his leg.

Two hours later, when the officers prepared to go to the sergeant's mess as guests for an evening of "fun and games," Cobber Kain's shouts echoed through the village. He would not be muzzled until he was taken in a stretcher by the doctor and a medical orderly to the sergeant's mess. Kain drank to his comrades' good health. They returned the compliment and the happy Kain was carried back to his billet through the village.

Upon recovery Kain was given a ten days' leave in London, where he was awarded the Distinguished Flying Cross, the first bestowed upon a British airman in France. On rejoining his squadron on April 11, Kain seemed to have changed slightly. He was as good-humored and as eager to fly as ever, but he was more businesslike, even neater. Cobber Kain had become engaged while in London and was to be married in June. Soon he was back in action and had scored about twelve official victories. Even so, the days were short on combat despite the improvement in the weather. What was Jerry up to?

III

At dawn, May 10, 1940, they found out. Massive Nazi columns surged over Dutch, Belgian, and Luxembourg's frontiers as Luftwaffe assaults smashed and scorched the airfields behind the lines. It was the third, and to date the most effective, demonstration of blitzkrieg. The twilight war erupted into a nightmare of panzer and Stuka: *Fall Gelb* had finally come.

The extent of this nightmare was soon obvious in air battles such as were not experienced during the first eight months of the war. Typical was the tragic epic of the Maastricht bridges, which furnished the Germans crossing over the Albert Canal in Belgium. Once secured these would serve as bridgeheads for pouring German troops into northern France.

The desperate Belgians had failed to blow the bridges and appealed to the Allies for aid. Counterattacks by ground troops did not drive the Germans away from the bridges, which by May 11 carried streams of armored vehicles, troops, supplies, and ammunition across the Albert Canal. On this same day the Germans carried out one of the brilliant coups of the war: the capture of Fort Eben Emael, reputed to be the most modern, strongest fort in Europe. It was situated a few miles south of Maastricht overlooking the juncture of the Meuse River and the canal. This formidable position was taken from above, by air-borne troops flown in silently by glider. These were towed by Ju-52s from Cologne and released over Aachen, about twenty miles from the fortress. Nine gliders gracefully landed atop the fort and specially trained troops proceeded to put the fort out of action with explosives, grenades, and flame throwers. Reinforcements arrived by parachute and by the afternoon of May 11, with additional help from the Stukas and ground troops, the Germans had taken Fort Eben Emael. Simultaneously with this, air-borne troops also dropped upon the bridge sites to the north of the fort. One, at Canne, was destroyed by the Belgians, but two, at Veldwezelt and Vroenhoven, fell into German hands.

The task of denying the use of these two bridges to the Germans fell to No. 12 Squadron, known as the "Dirty Dozen." Air Vice-Marshal P. H. L. Playfair, commanding the Advanced Air Striking Force, although realizing the mission was undoubtedly foredoomed, asked for volunteers. Characteristically, the entire squadron stepped forward, but only six Fairey Battles were scheduled for the attack, three for each bridge. Leading one section, Flying Officer Norman M. Thomas was to strike at the concrete bridge at Vroenhoven while Flying Officer Donald E. Garland led the other section against the metal bridge at Veldwezelt. That their four 250-pound bombs could do much damage, especially to the concrete bridge, was questionable. So was their breaking through a Luftwaffe-infested sky, let alone the flak. But they would try.

"You British are mad," a German officer later told one of the Battle pilots, I. A. McIntosh. "We capture the bridge [in this instance the one at Veldwezelt] early Friday morning. You give us all Friday and Saturday to get our flak guns up in circles all around the bridge and then on Sunday, when all is ready, you come along with three aircraft and try and blow the thing up."

But they did try, although "at all costs," as the orders had read.

Early on Sunday morning six Battles warmed up on the tarmac at Amifontaine. Then it was discovered that one of the planes in Thomas's section had a defective radio; the crew switched to another Battle, which, it developed, had a malfunction in the hydraulic system. Only five aircraft took off for the bridges. Thomas led his section, consisting only of one other Battle, piloted by Flying Officer T. D. H. Davy. Garland led his full section, the other two planes of which were flown by Pilot Officer I. A. McIntosh and Sergeant F. Marland.

Thomas and Garland had disagreed upon the tactics of the mission. Thomas believed that the approach should be from a high level while "Garland was determined," as Thomas explained, "to carry out a low-level attack, thinking it not only the best form, but the safest.

"My parting words to him were 'it will be interesting to see the result, and may we both be lucky enough to return.' "

An escort of six Hurricanes from No. 1 Squadron had been supplied to clear the air of German fighters. Thomas and Davy flew at six thousand feet— at a thousand feet seven-tenths cloud cover obscured the ground and afforded some protection from flak batteries. While the Hurricanes tackled the Messerschmitts Thomas led the attack on the Vroenhoven bridge. Enemy fighters bore in upon Davy's plane, however, and a brief exchange of fire ensued in which the gunner of the Battle shot down one Messerschmitt. Other German planes went down in the battle, but five of the six Hurricanes were lost.

Over Vroenhoven the two Battles ran into a wall of flak and machine-gun fire. Diving through this murderous barrage, through the clouds, the two Battles raced for the concrete bridge. Fragments of both planes whipped back into the slipstream as the flak hammered at them. The determined British dropped their bombs on the bridge, some of them from so low that the Battles were endangered by their own bomb blasts. Almost negligible damage resulted to the bridge.

When Thomas pulled his Battle out of the dive he realized the plane was too battered to remain in the air. The engine quickly sputtered out and he had to land. Thomas found an open field and brought the Battle in for a wheels-up landing. Within minutes Thomas and his crew were taken prisoner.

Davy too had engine trouble and a badly sieved aircraft. But he hoped to return to base. When it appeared that the Battle might drop out of the air at any moment, he ordered the other two men to jump. This was in the vicinity of Liége, where one of the crew was captured (mistakenly as a German) and manhandled by Belgian civilians until the police arrived. Davy, even with the lighter load, could not keep the Battle air-borne all the way to Amifontaine. He crash-landed inside Belgium.

Garland's section, meanwhile, had proceeded to the Veldwezelt bridge. Determined to carry out a surprise attack from low level, Garland ordered the fuses on the bombs to be set at eleven-second delay. Thus Garland planned to swoop down, drop the bombs, and just have time to get away. As the three Battles approached the bridge the screen of flak fire roared into a frightful crescendo. McIntosh's plane was the first to be hit and the Battle burst into flame. The pilot kept it on its bomb run as long as possible until the observer released the bombs (although with scant if any accuracy). The burning plane crashed shortly after and the crew pulled the near-unconscious McIntosh from the wreck. The three men found refuge, momentarily, in a ditch.

The air over the bridge was an inferno. The twenty-one-year-old Garland, just newly commissioned a flying officer, was resolute. He led his section, now consisting only of his plane and Sergeant Marland's, into the fury over Veldwezelt. He carefully lined up the Battle on a suicide run and accelerated the slender bomber into the barrage. Just as coolly, his observer, Sergeant Thomas Gray, took meticulous aim before releasing the small bomb load. Whether or not these men saw that their bombs scored direct hits upon their target is not known. The terrific flak onslaught ripped the Battle to pieces. Marland also may have scored hits on the bridge but possibly neither he nor anyone else ever knew.

From the ditch in which he was sheltered, McIntosh saw one Battle still in the air, the focus of the relentless flak guns. "We saw this Battle trying to get away," he said. "Then it suddenly stood on its tail, climbed vertically for about a hundred feet, stalled, and nose-dived to earth." They did not know whose plane it was. It hardly mattered, for all three Battles had been knocked out of the sky and only

McIntosh and his crew survived. For their efforts in the attack Garland and Gray received the Victoria Cross, posthumously, Britain's supreme award and the first given to RAF personnel. But the third crew member, Leading Aircraftman L. R. Reynolds, radio-gunner, inexplicably received no award at all. Davy, who tried to bring his plane back to base, was given a Distinguished Flying Cross.

All five aircraft had been lost, two crews of three men each had been killed, two crews had been captured, and one had made it back to Allied lines. This expensive, almost quixotic, show of valor had achieved only slight damage to the bridge and cratering of the approaches at Vroenhoven. The Veld-

A camouflaged Battle of No. 218 Squadron, Advanced Air Striking Force, in France, 1940. The ground crew prepares the aircraft for combat which, during the "Phony War" never materialized but which, following the unleashing of Fall Gelb (*Plan Yellow*) *on May 10, 1940, became devastatingly sufficient. Ten out of the eleven Battles of No. 218 Squadron which had been*

sent to help hold up the German advance at Sedan were destroyed on May 14 in a futile attempt. Despite losses of more than half the RAF bombers which participated in the attack at Sedan and despite the concerted effort by both French and British Air Forces, the Germans rolled on into France.

(IMPERIAL WAR MUSEUM, LONDON)

wezelt Bridge suffered serious damage to its western truss and was out of use—temporarily.

The Maastricht carnage was but a prelude. As the seemingly invincible German armored forces overran the Netherlands and Belgium, the French—to the south—were shocked by the unexpected materialization of a German vanguard in the form of Ewald von Kleist's Panzer group thrusting through the "impassable" Ardennes Forest. Soon German armored cars and tanks had crossed the Meuse at Sedan. Even earlier, on May 13, General Erwin

Now, on the morning of May 14, 1940, an attempt was made to stop the flood of Hitler's troops passing over pontoon bridges at Sedan. Ten Battles were dispatched from Nos. 103 and 150 Squadrons of the Advanced Air Striking Force. They attacked their targets and, encountering no fighters or flak, all planes returned safely. Air Marshal A. S. Barratt, in command of all British air forces in France, then planned to send bomber forces to deal with Rommel's panzers at Dinant. He was requested by the French to lend all-out effort to a counterattack at Sedan. Because of the command situation in

A Battle of No. 150 Squadron shot down during the Battle of Sedan, during which forty (mostly obsolete) aircraft vainly attempted to stop the Wehrmacht from crossing the Meuse. (H. J. NOWARRA)

A Ju-52 drops men of Fallschirmjäger-Regiment 1— paratroopers—upon Waalhaven, near Rotterdam, as Hitler began the blitzkrieg into the Low Countries. (H. J. NOWARRA)

Rommel, leading his 7th Panzer Division (attached to Günther Hans von Kluge's Fourth Army), had breached the Meuse at Dinant. The stunned French called for aerial interference of the establishment of German bridgeheads at Monthermé and Sedan.

The latter town had particularly tragic overtones in French history. It had been at Sedan, in 1870, where the Germans defeated Marshal Patrice Mac-Mahon's army, captured Napoleon III, and brought an end to the Second Empire. During the First World War, Sedan, a town of about thirteen thousand people, situated on the north bank of the Meuse on the edge of the Ardennes Forest about five miles from the Belgian frontier, had been occupied by the Germans.

France, Barratt was forced to comply. Instead of Dinant, they would attack at Sedan.

His bomber force had dwindled in just the few days since the blitzkrieg had reignited. On May 10 there had been 135 operational AASF bombers on hand; by the evening of May 12 only 72 remained.

But the early morning bombing of Sedan boded well. Around noon the second wave of Allied bombers was sent in; this consisted of a few French aircraft, which were so badly mauled that the French air effort for the day was ended. Then, beginning at three in the afternoon, all available RAF medium bombers—Battles and Blenheims— were hurled at Sedan.

By this time of the day, which the Germans at

the time called "the day of the fighters," the air over Sedan was alive with German fighters (Messerschmitt Bf-109Es), which were superior in speed to the Hurricane. The Battles and Blenheims were so many sitting ducks. Among the elite units the ill-fated British planes encountered were Jagdgeschwader 2, the "Richthofen" unit named for the First

of the eight planes sent on the mission). More than half the Battles did not return to their bases: No. 12 Squadron lost four out of five planes; No. 88 one out of ten; No. 103 three out of eight; No. 105 six out of eleven; No. 142 four out of eight; No. 150 all four of its planes; No. 218 Squadron ten out of eleven; and No. 226 three out of six. A total of

Flood tide: Ernst Udet, Adolf Galland, and Werner Mölders. During the Battle of France Udet was head of the Luftwaffe's Technical Office, Galland the op-erations officer of Jagdgeschwader 27, and Mölders the top-scoring ace of Jagdgeschwader 53 ("Richthofen"). (NATIONAL ARCHIVES)

World War ace, and Jagdgeschwader 53, in whose third *Gruppe* (i.e., III/JG 53) was the famed Hauptmann Werner Mölders. On May 14 Mölders added another victory mark to the tail of his Me-109: it was his tenth.

As relentlessly as the British came in to attack Sedan, just so relentlessly did the Luftwaffe take its toll. In all, eight Battle squadrons were dispatched along with two Blenheim squadrons (which lost five

thirty-five Battles were destroyed of the sixty-three sent. Counting the Blenheims, the British lost forty aircraft out of the seventy-one they had been able to muster for the attack on Sedan.

There was but a momentary pause in the German thrust across the Meuse; by nightfall Heinz Guderian's panzers crossed the bridgehead and seized the bridges over the Ardennes Canal. The way was open for a drive toward the north and the English Channel; it would outflank the British Expeditionary Forces and the French armies backing up the Dutch and the Belgians. The beaten, demoralized French Ninth Army fell back from an ever widening German front.

By this same morning of May 14 the fate of the Netherlands had already been decided and reached a grim climax in the bombing of Rotterdam. Within four days after the German attack it was clear that the Dutch were beaten. Queen Wilhelmina and the government had fled to England. Some pockets of resistance held, and they were troublesome, but obviously the small, "neutral" country was no military match for the Germans. Still their stubborn fight interfered with the rapid German advance toward France through Belgium, also neutral.

Orders had come from General Georg von Küchler, commanding the small but potent Eighteenth Army, that resistance in and around Rotterdam must be broken "by every means." By eight o'clock in the morning of May 14 surrender negotiations had begun although not without hairsplitting demands on the part of the Dutch commander in Rotterdam, Colonel P. Scharroo. He refused to deal with Dutch civilians sent by Oberstleutnant Dietrich von Choltitz, whose forces were attempting to cross the bridges into Rotterdam. A stickler for form, Scharroo rejected another, this time more official, capitulation proposal from General Rudolf Schmidt (commanding the XXXIX Corps) because it did not carry the proper "rank, name, and signature."

This same ultimatum, however, carried the threat of an aerial attack upon Rotterdam unless Scharroo surrendered. The plans for this attack had already been formulated: one hundred Heinkel 111s of Kampfgeschwader 54 would bomb the center of Rotterdam. The first bombs fell at around three o'clock in the afternoon even while surrender negotiations were under way.

Immediately before the German bombers took off they had been informed of the possibility of a Dutch surrender. If this came about before they reached the target in Rotterdam red Very pistols were to be fired from the ground and the bombers were to return without dropping their high-explosive bombs. While this may seem a humane precaution on the part of the Germans, it is difficult to understand how it was expected that the bomber crews might discern from bombing altitude the red lights in the haze and flame of the battle below. At best, it was a halfhearted precaution.

The crucial question of time reveals the split-second development of the calamity. It had been around noon that General Kurt Student, leading the air-borne troops in Holland, radioed Schmidt's XXXIX Corps headquarters that "bombing attack Rotterdam postponed owing to surrender negotiations." The attack was set for 3 P.M. Just five minutes before, at 2:55 P.M., General Schmidt sent yet another communiqué to Scharroo outlining surrender terms, giving the Dutch commander three hours in which to come to a decision—that is, until six o'clock.

Obviously communications between the German ground and air forces had become inefficient. The Dutch courier hastened across the Willems Bridge. He had barely reached the other side when a hundred Heinkels appeared over the city.

Recall orders had obviously been sent from Luftflotte 2, but as the planes were on their bombing run, and their receiving antennas having been retracted, the messages were not heard by the bomber radio operators. According to German accounts, desperate attempts were made to divert the bombers by discharging Very pistols into the air, but either the crews did not see them or mistook the signals for Dutch antiaircraft fire. Bombs began falling into the heart of Rotterdam.

Just as his plane's bomb load was dropped, Oberstleutnant Otto Hohne, commander of III/KG 54, spotted two red flares ascending through the smoke below. He shouted the recall order code word to his radio operator, who wired to the rest of the formation and prevented the dropping of all but a few bomb loads. It did not matter a great deal to the Dutch by this time, however.

Just over half of the hundred Heinkels had dropped hundred-pound and five-hundred pound bombs into the center of the old city: a total of ninety-seven tons. Within hours Rotterdam was in

---

Rotterdam after the May 14, 1940, "error" bombing by the Luftwaffe. Although the bombing mission had been called off because surrender negotiations were in progress, more than fifty aircraft dropped ninety-seven tons of explosives into the city, which burned uncontrollably.

(PRESS & INFORMATION SERVICES, ROTTERDAM)

flames: the small fire department was all but help-less because a bomb had hit a margarine factory. Burning oil spread to the timbered buildings and the heart of Rotterdam disintegrated in smoke. A twelve-year-old boy wrote that "There is a funny smell in the air like burned meat and a funny yellow light all over the country from the incendiary bombs. [This is an error. No incendiaries were used.] . . . I went out for a while and they were taking dead people out of the bombed houses. . . . It is awful to watch the people standing by their bombed houses. They don't do much. They just walk around and look at them and look sad and tired."

Rotterdam on that May 14, 1940, became a sym-bol of German *Kultur* like Guernica and Warsaw. The casualties, turned to propaganda uses by the Allies, were exaggerated. The official Dutch figure at the time—and it may have been an honest er-ror—reached thirty thousand dead.

The actual figure would be closer to a thousand men, women, and children—killed in the seven and a half minutes the Heinkels remained over Rotter-dam. In all, twenty thousand buildings were de-stroyed by bombs and the ensuing fires; seventy-eight thousand people were rendered homeless. A square mile of the city smoldered for days. By six o'clock in the evening the Dutch had capitulated. The blitzkrieg had crushed the Netherlands in five days.

Belgium was next on the Nazi timetable. The Belgians, led by King Leopold and reinforced by French and British troops, fought bitterly. The pat-tern was repeated and within eighteen days—on May 27, 1940—Leopold asked for a German peace. This action, however inevitable, was taken without proper consultation with his allies, and placed the French and British forces in serious jeopardy and possible annihilation. Already under pressure by the German forces which had broken through at Sedan, the beleaguered Allies, falling back into France, were left with their left flank exposed. The exhausted armies were rapidly encircled in steel, the panzers, the Stukas, and the Wehrmacht, drawing them closer to the sea at their backs, until the entire British Expeditionary Force, the French First Army as well as units of the Seventh and Ninth Armies, along with Belgian and Polish troops converged upon the French port of Dunkirk.

IV

There were two miracles at Dunkirk, one British, the other German.

The German "miracle" came to pass in the eve-ning of May 24 when from the headquarters of Von Rundstedt's Army Group A an order was issued halting the armored thrust from the south and the west. Panzer Group Kleist and Guderian's 19th Corps pulled up roughly on the line of canals run-ning from Gravelines on the Channel coast and southeasterly through Saint-Omer to Bethune. Rund-stedt had convinced the Führer that the tanks, after the surprising swing through France from the breakthrough at Sedan, should be rested for the major battle of France to come. With the Führer's backing there was no questioning the stop order, despite the objections of Commander in Chief Wal-ther von Brauchitsch. Hitler, who waxed manic-depressive, was one moment decisive and the next cautious. The success of the Lowlands campaign and the breach in the Ardennes was difficult to as-similate. And then Göring promised to destroy the fleeing allies on the Channel with his Luftwaffe. Why exhaust and deplete the Panzer forces if the Air Force could do the job? It was this con-sideration, not the fatuous one that Hitler had elected to spare the British, which resulted in the stop order.

Göring's vanity prompted him to offer more than the Luftwaffe could deliver. Many of the bomber *Geschwader* were still based far from the Dunkirk area, which fact would require long-distance flying and little time over the target. But the Wehrmacht and the panzers had been snatching most of the glory in the Lowlands, while the Luftwaffe con-tinued in a subservient role. Göring longed for a Luftwaffe coup, pure and simple, with no portion of the credit to the Army or Navy.

That the British had already begun to plan Opera-tion Dynamo, the evacuation, was not known to the Germans. That the British would attempt to evacu-ate from such ports as Calais, La Panne, and Dun-kirk seemed likely, but to the land-loving Ger-mans and to Hitler especially, for he had no sea sense at all, any large-scale withdrawal was un-thinkable.

The beach at Dunkirk: troops of the British Expedition-ary Forces awaiting deliverance by "the little boats" and the Royal Navy after being driven into a pocket *by the Wehrmacht. During the nine days of Dunkirk more than 300,000 men were rescued from the beaches of Dunkirk despite the efforts of the Luft-waffe.* (NATIONAL ARCHIVES)

*An RAF Coastal Command Lockheed Hudson flies
over the beaches of Dunkirk. Oil storage tanks have
been set aflame by Luftwaffe bombers.*

(LOCKHEED PHOTO)

The British miracle (without qualifying quotation
marks) was a stunning accomplishment of flexible
planning, courage, civilian participation, imaginative
improvisation, and sheer British doggedness. History's most heterogeneous armada gathered along
the southeast coast of England. At Dover Vice-Ad-
miral Sir Bertram Ramsay took charge of Operation Dynamo. Besides the craft of the Royal Navy,
the Admiralty had pressed civilian motorboats into
service. "At the same time," Winston Churchill has
written, "lifeboats from liners in the London docks,
tugs from the Thames, yachts, fishing-craft, lighters,
barges, and pleasure-boats—anything that could be
of use along the beaches—were called into service.
By the night of the 27th a great tide of small vessels began to flow towards the sea, first to our
Channel ports, and thence to the beaches of Dun-

kirk and the beloved Army." A total of 860 vessels
of every description took part in the "Dunkirk deliverance," as Churchill called it. Seven hundred
were British ships, the rest were French, Polish,
Belgian, and Dutch. Nearly 250 ships of the armada
were sunk, most of them by the Luftwaffe.

As the men of the British Expeditionary Force
limped or were carried ashore, their eyes revealed
the harrowing experience they had undergone. Their
hollow-cheeked faces were begrimed by the smoke
of oil fire, burning vehicles, and shells. These
wearied men, returned with only what they wore—
for their weapons were abandoned on the beaches
at Dunkirk—grateful for their deliverance, brought
a bitter question with them.

"Where was the bloody RAF?"

The infantryman, whose concern is generally confined to the few feet of ground he occupies, has little
conception of the airman's war. On the Dunkirk
beaches the infantryman was only aware of the
bombing and strafing of the Luftwaffe. Rarely did
he see or recognize a British aircraft overhead. He

did not see the Blenheims of No. 107 Squadron bombing the advancing German columns on May 27—the day the evacuation officially began. Coincidentally, it was also the day on which the Rundstedt-Hitler stop order was withdrawn, after a two-and-a-half-day pause.

At dawn on Monday, May 27, the Heinkels began the bombardment of the defense perimeter around Dunkirk; then came Richthofen's Stukas to pin-point the targets. The Dorniers followed. These last were surprised on being attacked by Spitfires of No. 74 Squadron—the first major encounter with this new fighter. Hurricanes of No. 145 Squadron also joined the battle, but the British were always outnumbered by the Messerschmitt 109s and 110s. However, it was soon obvious that the Spitfire was a match for the Me-109 and superior to the Hurricane as a high-altitude fighter.

Even so, great numbers of German bombers broke through the Spitfire and Hurricane formations and bombed the beaches and the ships in the Channel. Oil storage tanks on the western outskirts of Dunkirk were set afire and the black smoke rose as a thick, curling beacon to friend and foe alike. But when the weather turned damp and the ceiling descended this same oily smoke combined with the smoke from the fires in the town and mist to afford cover for the evacuation.

A pilot of No. 43 Squadron described the scene as he saw it from above: "All the harbour at Dunkirk seemed to be on fire with the black smoke from the oil dumps," he said. "The destroyers moved out of the pall of smoke in a most uncanny way, deep in the water and heavily laden with troops. I was flying at about 1000 feet above the beach and the sea. And there I could see the *Brighton Belle,* and the paddle steamers, and the sort of cheerful little boats you see calling at coastal towns on Sunday. Hundreds of boats! Fishing boats and motor boats, and Thames river craft and strings of dinghies, being towed by bigger boats. All packed with troops, and people standing in the water and awful bomb craters in the beach, and lines of men and groups of people sitting down. Waiting, I suppose. And I could see rifles—stacked in threes. And destroyers going back into the black smoke. And wrecked ships on the beach: wrecked ships of all sizes, sticking out of the water. And a destroyer cut in halves by a bomb. I saw it!"

On the beach itself all was a horror. A British gunnery officer sensed "a deadly evil atmosphere . . . a lurid study in red and black. . . . A horrible stench of blood and mutilated flesh pervaded the place. There was no escape from it. Not a breath of air was blowing to dissipate the appalling odour that arose from the dead bodies that had been lying on the sand, in some cases for several days. We might have been walking through a slaughter-house on a hot day. The darkness, which hid some of the sights of horror from our eyes, seemed to thicken this dreadful stench. It created the impression that death was hovering around, very near at hand. . . ."

The aerial battles generally occurred out of sight of the besieged ground troops. Although German planes did attack mercilessly, the Luftwaffe did not gain mastery of the air over Dunkirk because of the defense afforded by the Hurricane and Spitfire squadrons of No. 11 Group under the command of Air Vice-Marshal Keith R. Park. To contend with the massive formations of German fighters and bombers Park had only sixteen squadrons available —that is, about two hundred fighters. From their bases in southern England the fighters would have to be flown at least fifty miles to the battle area— without the advantage of radar to pin-point the

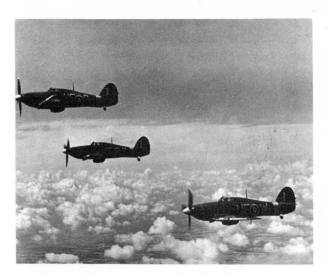

"Where was the bloody RAF?" The Hurricanes (and the Spitfires) operated above the clouds in fighting the Luftwaffe and so were rarely seen by the beleaguered ground troops at Dunkirk. Although RAF fighters intercepted German bombers, some broke through to bomb the beaches. (U. S. AIR FORCE)

German attacks. This meant that fuel limitations enforced about a forty-minute stay over Dunkirk for the Hurricanes and Spitfires.

To send all sixteen squadrons to cover the entire evacuation area was impossible (it was attempted on the first day, May 27, but the wasteful fuel consumption rendered such tactics infeasible; it also left England open to air attack, and the defense of the home islands was the major function of Fighter Command). Beginning on May 29, Park devised a patrol system over Dunkirk, using four squadrons at a time. Consequently there were stretches of time when no RAF fighters patrolled directly over Dunkirk. Also, while attempting to attack the bombers, they were in turn attacked by the Messerschmitts. Two very large formations of German bombers, including the vulnerable Stuka and the vaunted Junkers 88, assaulted the beaches while no British fighters were present. Three other formations, however, had been mauled by the British fighters.

In the turmoil as much, possibly more, shipping was lost through collision as to German bombs. Also owing to the confusion of battle—and faulty aircraft recognition, especially on the part of the Royal Navy—the men in the Dunkirk perimeter fired indiscriminately at friend and foe alike. All aircraft were taken to be hostile by the harassed troops crowding into the sea. Rear Admiral William Wake-Walker recalled several such incidents on June 1, the sixth day of the evacuation. Spitfires flying low over the beaches received the same attention from the British guns as did a Messerschmitt—even after Wake-Walker hoisted the cease fire flag. Later he witnessed a similar piece of action as he stood talking with Captain W. G. Tennant, the senior naval officer in charge of shore operations, when "a Lysander Army Co-op plane came over very low and flew over the pier. It was fired at by several Bofors guns and Tennant said, 'I'm sure that damn fellow is a Hun—he has been flying over here all day.' I then realized," Wake-Walker reported, "it was the plane flying over at my request to see if the pier was being shelled, and I felt sorry for the poor chap; though he seemed none the worse."

Not all the errors were made on the ground, for Spitfires and Hurricanes attacked each other above the clouds also.

The Luftwaffe attacks on June 1 had been so vicious—Stukas by the dozen not only attacked the ships but also came in low to strafe the struggling figures in the water—that Ramsay realized that the evacuation could be continued only at night. The German ground forces had also begun to press in on the perimeter and the sands of Dunkirk erupted with the shelling from German artillery.

The fighting in the air too had become desperate; the initiative belonged to the Luftwaffe, which could muster great numbers of bombers with escorts. As the battle progressed, and as the German infantry closed in, the Luftwaffe gained airdromes closer to battle site. Only the weather and the RAF interfered. But from time to time, such as on May 29 and June 1, the sun broke through and cleared the mist, and the Germans concentrated with fury on Dunkirk. And so it went, intermittently for the nine days.

"Well, another day is gone," wrote Flight Lieutenant R. D. G. Wight of No. 213 Squadron to his mother, "and with it a lot of grand blokes. Got another brace of 109's today, but the whole Luftwaffe seems to leap on us—we were hopelessly outnumbered. I was caught napping by a 109 in the middle of a dog fight and got a couple of holes in the aircraft, one of them filled the office with smoke, but the Jerry overshot and *he's* dead. If anyone says anything to you in the future about the inefficiency of the R.A.F.—I believe the B.E.F. troops were booing the R.A.F. in Dover the other day—tell them from me we only wish we could do more. But without aircraft we can do no more than we have done—that is, our best, and that's fifty times better than the German best, though they are fighting under the most advantageous conditions."

On the morning of June 4, with the Germans within two miles of the beaches, Operation Dynamo was officially closed. About forty thousand French troops remained behind to hold off the Germans —just as they had during the nine days at Calais and Cassel. Theirs had been an enormous contribution to the miracle of Dunkirk—a contribution frequently slighted in view of the performance of the "little boats" and their own political and military leaders subsequently.

Dunkirk was no military victory. The Germans had permitted practically the entire British Army to escape. True, they were weaponless and most of their equipment lay abandoned along the beaches

German troops haul in a trophy from the English Channel, the tail section of an RAF Hurricane shot down during the desperate fighting of the last weeks of the Battle of France. (NATIONAL ARCHIVES)

at Dunkirk, but it was a tough, experienced army. The Luftwaffe had not been able to achieve—if, indeed, they were achievements—a Warsaw or a Rotterdam. This despite the ease with which the smoking, water-outlined target could be found even in bad weather.

The cost of Dunkirk in shipping was high: 6 destroyers were sunk, 8 personnel ships, 5 minesweepers, 17 trawlers, a hospital ship, a sloop, 3 tugboats, 3 yachts, and 182 other assorted craft. The RAF lost over 100 aircraft and 80 pilots in the Dunkirk battles. The Luftwaffe lost about 150 planes, although claims were made for twice that number.

Churchill reminded the British that "Wars are not won by evacuations. But there was a victory inside this deliverance, which should be noted. It was gained by the Air Force. . . ."

If it was not a spectacular victory, even an almost negligible one, it was, on a small scale, a prologue to the coming battle over Britain. It might have served as portent to the Luftwaffe of things to come.

Dunkirk had not been a victory for the British, although 338,000 men had been snatched out of the jaws of the devouring blitzkrieg. But it was a triumph of the British spirit, best expressed by Churchill during the nine days when he said, "Of course, whatever happens at Dunkirk, we shall fight on."

Churchill had been handed the reins of government, taking over from the ailing and tottering Chamberlain, in the early evening of May 10, 1940 —that morning the Germans had struck in the Low Countries. Reveling in crisis, defying adversity, and spoiling for a fight, the once discredited Churchill, whose warnings of a burgeoning military Nazi Germany had not contributed to his popularity, was the embodiment of the British spirit. He watched the fighting in France with concern, but never with the loss of hope so evident in the French government and High Command.

When the Germans attacked there were eight Hurricane squadrons in France, the Air Component's Nos. 3, 85, 87, 607, and 615 Squadrons and the AASF's Nos. 1, 73, and 501 Squadrons. By May 12 these were joined by Nos. 79 and 504 Squadrons sent to the dwindling Air Component taxed with the support of the BEF. Under the onslaught of the blitzkrieg in the north of France the seven squadrons of the Air Component had been reduced to about three on May 17; four days later the remnants were ordered back to England.

The fighter pilots who had complained about the "phony war" and the scanty air activity had little cause for gripes after May 10. Their fields were bombed and strafed and they were air-borne from dawn till dusk. The bombers of AASF were spent in bombing the advancing Nazi columns while the Hurricanes furnished fighter cover. There was plenty of action for eager fighter pilots, German as well as British and French.

On May 12 Adolf Galland, one of Germany's outstanding airmen, scored his first "kill," a Belgian Hurricane. Flying with a wingman in an Me-109E, Galland had stolen some time away from his desk job. The two Germans spotted a formation of eight Hurricanes flying at nine thousand feet near Liége. Diving from above, Galland opened on an unsuspecting Belgian. The first burst from Galland's guns startled the Hurricane pilots and the formation scattered. The German concentrated on his victim, now clumsily trying to evade the guns of the Messerschmitt. The poorly trained pilot in the antiquated Hurricane had no chance. Galland's second burst shot away the Hurricane's rudder and the plane spun away. Before striking the ground the aircraft shed parts of its wings. Galland then turned to the remaining Belgian planes. Finding one Hurricane attempting to dive away from the battle, Galland in his superior Me-109 pulled up to within a hundred yards of it. The plane whipped away in a half roll and through an opening in the clouds. But the experienced Galland remained locked to the Hurricane's tail. A burst of gunfire and the Belgian plane pulled up for a moment, stalled, and dived straight into the ground. In the afternoon of the same day, while on a routine patrol flight, Galland accounted for another Hurricane—his third victory of the day.

On the day after the Dunkirk evacuation, June 5, Werner Mölders, the leading German ace with twenty-five "kills" to his credit, joined a battle in the vicinity of Amiens. The contenders were French Dewoitine 520s, the best—and rarest, because of the inefficiency of the Production Office—fighter the Armée de l'Air could muster. Only one group had been supplied with the D-520s before the Germans opened their attack on France. It was the group's planes which Mölders came upon fighting off the Messerschmitts. He fired at one of the French planes and lost it in the general melee: there were nine French aircraft standing off more than two dozen Messerschmitts. Mölders turned back to the center of battle. Suddenly his cockpit burst into flame and smoke, his throttle was shot out of his hand, and the Me-109 flipped into a vertical dive. Struggling inside the smoky cockpit, Mölders found the release catch and sent the cockpit hood off into the slipstream. Unexpectedly the Messerschmitt leveled for a second from its dive, which had pressed Mölders into the cockpit, and he jumped. Mölders, floating down into France, watched his plane crash into the ground. Thus it was that Germany's hero-ace was taken prisoner of war. When the French surrendered subsequently, however, Mölders and all the other German pilots taken prisoner in France were released.

On June 5 also the Germans opened their new offensive, *Fall Rot* ("Case Red"), across the Somme and the Seine. Before long their armor had crossed the Marne—the familiar names of an earlier war echoed the sound of disaster. Refugees filled the roads, fleeing from northern France to the south: these too were familiar scenes. The Luftwaffe contributed innovations by strafing and dive-bombing the clogged highways. By this time there were too few targets to keep them occupied.

The British pilots remaining in France, the rem-

Werner Mölders, who was shot down over France after the Dunkirk evacuation and taken prisoner; with the fall of France he was released and served later in the war as commander of Jagdgeschwader 51 on the Eastern Front. Mölder's official victory score for the Second World War was sixty-eight (and fourteen in Spain); he was killed in an air crash later in the war. (H. J. NOWARRA)

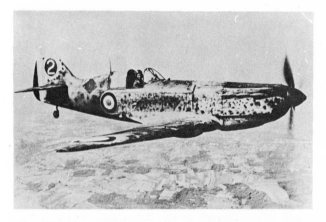

The French Dewoitine 520, the best of the few French fighters operational during the Battle of France. The German ace Mölders was shot down by a French pilot in a D-520. (MUSÉE DE L'AIR)

nants of Nos. 1, 73, and 501 Squadrons, later joined by Nos. 17 and 242 Squadrons, fell back to emergency landing strips southwest of Paris. The constant nervous strain, exhaustion, and high-altitude flying took its toll along with the German fighters. Individual pilots flew patrol after patrol until fatigue caused them to fall asleep in their cockpits while they were refueling and being rearmed. When their Hurricanes were ready, the ground crew had to punch the pilots awake. One pilot reported that he had fallen asleep three times while flying over German-occupied territory. Another pilot landed and fell asleep in the cockpit. He was lifted from the plane and when all attempts to awaken him failed, he was shipped to England. He awakened forty-eight hours later wondering how he had ever got back home.

Meanwhile, France lay broken and without hope in the path of the overwhelming German armies, now being lent close support by the Luftwaffe. Even small pockets of resistance were crushed under the Stukas working with the panzers. The French demanded more British fighter squadrons to deal with the Stukas. But the outcome of the battle was obvious and Churchill, after sending additional Hurricanes, relented and sent no more. Of the necessity of this decision he had been forcefully convinced by Fighter Command leader Air Marshal Hugh Dowding. The latter had estimated that fifty-two fighter squadrons would be required to defend Britain from the attack that must come once France was defeated. On hand were a mere twenty-five; if an additional ten squadrons were sent to France, only to be destroyed in the French holocaust, Britain too must fall. As early as May 15, 1940, Dowding had warned the Air Ministry that "if the Home Defense Force is drained away in desperate attempts to remedy the situation in France, defeat in France will involve the final, complete and irremediable defeat of this country."

Churchill, who was romantically inclined and could not leave a friend or an ally in trouble, was seriously tempted to send an additional ten Hurricane squadrons to France. The French were calling for no less than twenty. The dispatch of ten squadrons was being seriously considered when Chief of the Air Staff Air Chief Marshal Cyril Newall learned from Air Marshal A. S. Barratt, commanding the two British air forces in France,

that even if ten squadrons were sent there would be bases for no more than three.

Instead, at Newall's suggestion, six squadrons based in the south of England rotated to France: three each morning and three to relieve them in the afternoon. Soon after, upon witnessing the chaos and hopeless desperation in France himself, Churchill concurred and no further fighter squadrons were sent to France.

The extent of the disorder and near paralysis of the French High Command was revealed when Benito Mussolini, concerned that his German colleague had so brilliantly outdistanced him in the race for conquest, declared war upon France and Great Britain. With the German Army within thirty miles of Paris it was safe no doubt for the Duce's legions to attack the Riviera. On May 10, 1940, Hitler had himself a partner in war: it would, in time, cost them both dearly.

It had been agreed in the French and British Supreme War Council that in the event of a declaration of war by Italy British aircraft were to be bombed-up to attack industrial targets in northern Italy.

So it was that in the early afternoon of May 11 No. 99 Squadron (Wellingtons) landed in France, near Salon, to refuel on the way to bomb Genoa. The longer-ranged Armstrong Whitworth Whitleys of Nos. 10, 51, 58, and 102 Squadrons accompanying the Wellingtons were to refuel in advance bases in the Channel Islands (instead of France) and proceed to targets in Genoa and Turin.

The Wellingtons had barely landed when Group Captain R. M. Field, in charge of the bomber force at Salon, was informed by the French that the planes were not to take off for Italy. Still wondering what this was about, Field received an order from the Air Ministry to send the bombers to Italy. The phone rang; it was the French commander again reiterating that bombing operations against Italian targets were forbidden.

From three-thirty in the afternoon till almost midnight Field was involved in a whirl of order and counterorder; it seemed his phone never stopped ringing. The French High Command had even gone to Barratt, at British Air Forces in France headquarters. Barratt called London attempting to get Churchill. He learned that the Prime Minister was in France. Churchill was, in fact, just sitting down

to dinner with French Premier Paul Reynaud, Supreme Allied Commander General Maxime Weygand, General Charles de Gaulle, and members of Churchill's party including Anthony Eden and Chief of the Imperial Staff Sir John Dill.

Churchill was reached through General Hastings Ismay, at Weygand's headquarters, and the Churchillian view was constant: "All our [that is, English] minds ran much more on bombing Milan and Turin the moment Mussolini declared war, and seeing how he liked that."

Insofar as he was able to judge, after sifting the various orders, views, and opinions, Captain Field must dispatch the Wellingtons to bomb Italy. The Whitleys in the meantime had already taken off from the Channel Islands.

As the Wellingtons taxied for the takeoff at Salon, the distracted French added the final touch. French trucks, lorries, and carts were driven onto the airfield and stalled strategically in the path of the British bombers. Thus effectively blocked, and not wanting to fight it out with his allies, Field canceled the mission to Italy. The Whitleys, however, continued on and of the thirty-six sent only thirteen bombed their targets. Bad icing conditions and storms over the Alps greatly curtailed the mission.

It required four additional days of discussion before the field at Salon was cleared of the French obstructions. Eight Wellingtons took off to bomb Genoa but again storms interfered and only one plane found the target.

The situation in France had deteriorated so thoroughly by this time that such missions seemed without point. On June 14 the triumphant Germans marched into Paris. On June 17, 1940, Marshal Henri Pétain, succeeding Reynaud as Premier, asked for an armistice. On the afternoon of June 21 Hitler appeared for less than a half hour in the Forest of Compiègne, some forty-five miles north of Paris, the site of the hated German surrender of 1918. Hitler literally danced at Compiègne and then left the technicalities of the signing of the new treaty to others. France was finished and the British were driven off the Continent again. Cobber Kain's No. 73 Squadron, after covering the final evacuations from Nantes and Saint-Nazaire, was the last to leave. On June 18, as the surviving six Hurricanes thundered down the runway, all non-operational

Where do we go from here? Göring (sixth from right) and his staff gazing from the coast of France across the English Channel at Dover, England. Hav- *ing won a quick victory the Luftwaffe—and the Wehrmacht—had made no real plans to cross that Channel.* (NATIONAL ARCHIVES)

aircraft, supplies, and equipment were set ablaze. France had become a vast funeral pyre.

Looking down upon his stricken country from six miles up, author-pilot Antoine de Saint-Exupéry saw the devastation and the futile burning. "But how many villages have we seen burnt down," he speculated, "only that war may be made to look like war? Burnt down exactly as trees are cut down, crews flung into the holocaust, infantry sent against tanks, merely to make war look like war. Small wonder that an unutterable disquiet hangs over the land. For nothing does any good."

Hitler was jubilant; Versailles was truly avenged. In an outburst of largess he created a flowering of field marshals: Brauchitsch, Bock, Kluge, Leeb, Rundstedt, Reichenau, Witzleben, and Keitel. The Luftwaffe too was honored as Kesselring, Sperrle, and Milch were given their batons.

But there was an unutterable disquiet in the German camp too. The forces of National Socialism, the great German Reich, the Wehrmacht, the immortal Führer himself had achieved incredible heights.

Was nun? "What now?" was the question all the conquerers asked as they stood peering through their glasses across the English Channel. *Was nun?* they wondered as they studied the stark chalk cliffs of Dover.

Was nun? Victory had come so quickly. Poland: twenty-six days; Norway: twenty-eight days; Denmark: twenty-four hours; the Netherlands: five days; Belgium: eighteen days; and France, with its Maginot Line, its great Army and Air Force: thirty-five days.

As they stood arrogantly, assured but questioning the next move, the invincible victors had no idea that, in truth, not even the Führer knew. The tottering British must be added to the victory timetable. All agreed to that.

But how?

BOOK II
The Battle of Britain

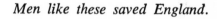

Men like these saved England.

AN AIR MINISTRY ACCOUNT OF THE
GREAT DAYS FROM AUGUST 8–OCTOBER 31, 1940

5

ADLERANGRIFF

"THINKING now of those days," an English flight lieutenant said in recollection of July–October 1940, "I find that what remains most clearly in my memory is not the sweating strain of the actual fighting, not the hurried meals, the creeping from bed at dawn, not even the loss of one's friends; but rather those odd stolen moments of peace in the middle of all the pandemonium—the heat haze lying lazily over the airfield while we sat munching a piece of grass, waiting to take off; that curiously lovely moment of twilight after the last Spitfire had landed, after the last engine had been switched off, and before the first night fighter took the air, the first search-light split the darkness and the first wail of the siren was heard again—that moment when the evening lay spread out against the sky, giving for an instant a mocking glimpse of stillness and peace before night fell suddenly like a curtain and the whole hideous cacophony of war broke out afresh.

"But, above all, the thing that remains most clearly imprinted on my memory is the spirit which then existed—the same spirit which inspired everybody from the Station Commander to the lowest air-craft-hand. . . . For that was the first trial, the first flush of battle, and it was a great hour."

Another pilot remembers: "We always had a devil-may-care sort of happiness. Lying in the sun waiting at readiness, there were moments of great beauty; the colours in the fields seemed brightest and the sky the deepest blue just before taking off for a big blitz. At dusk everything became peaceful. We were all happy at the thought of another day accomplished, our Hurricanes standing silhouetted against the sky, looking strong and confident, the darkness hiding their patched-up paintwork. In the morning whilst it was still dark, the roar of engines being tested woke us for another day's work."

"They were wonderful, weird, exciting days," a squadron leader recalled. "Days when aircraft left beautiful curving vapour trails high in the sky, days when some of our friends took off and never came back, when others came back maimed and burnt, never to fight again."

It was, despite the pervading ubiquity of death, an exhilarating time. The warriors were young—the average age was twenty—they were vigorous, and they felt they would never die, at least, perhaps, not today. They were a small band of men, Winston Churchill's "few," who must hold back Hitler's conquerers. They were the despised "soft English," the comic "weekend pilots," the unprofessionals, and surely they must soon be overwhelmed by the unbeatable Luftwaffe. In their Hurricanes and Spitfires they took off from airfields in Kent and Sussex. And here lay some of the root of the spirit: the gentle, trim English countryside—home for so many —was the last thing they saw before climbing five miles up to do battle.

The people of Britain too exhibited a spirit of mordant defiance, a quality of tough fatalism, of

Fighter types: typical RAF men of the Battle of Britain. Standing (right), wearing a "Mae West," is Peter Townsend, who on February 3, 1940, shot down the first German aircraft that fell on England—long before the Battle began. Later Townsend went to France to command No. 85 Squadron and returned to fly in the Battle of Britain, during which he became an ace. (IMPERIAL WAR MUSEUM, LONDON)

recognizing that they would soon be fighting for their very survival—and finding a fearful elation in the thought. In their small island—*their* small island and they intended to keep it—arose a mood of Shakespearean poetry-drama. Winston Churchill gave voice to this mood and was the living paragon of the Briton whom Hitler must defeat before he could win the war in the west.

With the defeat of France came an easy temper of complete victory in the German Army; plans were made for a victory parade in Paris and lists were drawn up of divisions to be dispersed home.

But the final days of June slipped away and there was no indication that London was seriously considering the peace feelers Hitler had sent through neutrals. This was puzzling, for surely, Hitler thought, the British were beaten. The ex-corporal, now the greatest living field marshal, looked with a wistful corporal's heart at the cold, treacherous English Channel. Certainly the British must come to terms.

Instead the contentious Prime Minister dictated reams of warlike minutes, pithy bits of advice, questions, assurances, demands, criticisms, and suggestive comments to his War Cabinet, the High Command, Members of Parliament. The subjects ranged from wicked—often impractical—devices of war to the defense of London. The common refrain was one of challenging preparation. To Mr. Josiah Wedgwood, M.P., Churchill wrote that "You must rest assured that we should fight every street of London and its suburbs. It would *devour* an invading army, assuming one ever got that far. We hope, however, to drown the bulk of them in the salt sea."

Finally in the German camp on July 2, 1940—eleven days after the signing of the armistice with

Waiting: pilots of No. 611 Squadron, with a ready Spitfire (note parachute on wingtip), enduring one of war's characteristic experiences, tedium. During the Battle No. 611 Squadron, then based at Digby, suffered numerous casualties.

(IMPERIAL WAR MUSEUM, LONDON)

The Ditch, the English Channel from thirty-five thousand feet. Calais is at lower left and Dover's white cliffs above. Only the Ditch—and the RAF—stood between Hitler and, in the phrase of Wehrmacht Chief of Staff Jodl, "The final German victory over England . . ." which he believed to be "only a question of time." (ROBERT C. CHAPIN)

France—Keitel issued instructions to all three services to prepare for an invasion of Britain. Hitler did not make his own directive No. 16 for the Conduct of the War, official with his signature until two weeks later. Directive No. 16 opened with these words: "As England, in spite of the hopelessness of her military position, has so far not shown herself willing to come to any compromise, I have decided to begin to prepare for, and if necessary to carry out, an invasion of England.

"This operation is dictated by the necessity of eliminating Great Britain as a base from which the war against Germany can be fought, and if necessary the island will be occupied." This was to be

Operation *Seelöwe* ("Sealion"), and Hitler's own equivocal posture is revealed in the conditional phrases closing each paragraph.

Colonel General Alfred Jodl, Chief of Staff of the Wehrmacht, was more definite when he wrote that "The final German victory over England is now only a question of time. Enemy offensive operations on a large scale are no longer possible." He was correct in the last sentence, but in the first he raised "the question of time." And it was time which the Germans were all but deliberately bestowing upon the British. Jodl too could wax happy, for he knew his army would be spared the initial phases of dealing with the British. The major burden must fall upon the Imperial Navy and the Luftwaffe. Admiral Raeder, as early as November 15, 1939, had instructed the Naval War Staff to look into the chances of invading England. At that time he had not expected to pay so heavily for the conquest of Norway. The loss of half his cruisers and destroyers placed Raeder in no position to deal with the British in the Channel—the German Navy had not even been able to interfere very effectively with the Dunkirk evacuation. Operation Sealion would be spread over a sea front of more than two hundred miles, from Lyme Bay to Ramsgate. How the German Navy could clear, protect, and convoy over so large an area was a serious and, Raeder knew inwardly, an impossible question.

On July 19, 1940—a full month after the last Hurricane took off from France and three days after he had signed the *Seelöwe* directive—Hitler appeared before the Reichstag. The German press was to hail the speech made that day as a "peace offer," Britain's last chance before the blow fell.

"In this hour," Hitler said, "I feel it to be my duty before my own conscience to appeal once more to reason and common sense in Great Britain as much as elsewhere. I consider myself in a position to make this appeal since I am not the vanquished begging favors, but the victor speaking in the name of reason. I can see no reason why this war must go on.

"It almost causes me pain to think that I should have been selected by Fate to deal the final blow to the structure which these men have already set tottering. . . . Mr. Churchill ought perhaps, for once, to believe me when I prophesy that a great Empire will be destroyed—an Empire which it was

never my intention to destroy or even to harm. . . .

"Possibly Mr. Churchill will brush aside this statement of mine by saying it is merely born of fear and doubt of final victory. In that case I shall have relieved my conscience in regard to the things to come."

Göring, who had drawn up an ambitious plan for dealing with the British "by attacking the enemy air force, its ground organizations, and its own industry" on June 30, hoped too that the stubborn British would realize the precariousness of their position. He took little interest in the invasion studies being made by the Army staffs. He found little comfort, as the days passed and no word of surrender came from Britain, in watching the emphasis of "the things to come" devolving upon the Luftwaffe. But then his bravado prevailed and he was certain, after the successes of the Luftwaffe since the beginning of the war, that England could very well be blasted out of the war by air power alone.

From the Führer's headquarters on August 1, 1940, was issued the "Top Secret" Directive No. 17 for the Conduct of Air and Naval Warfare Against England:

In order to establish the conditions necessary for the final conquest of England I intend to continue the air and sea war against the English homeland more intensively than before.

Therefore, I order the following:

1. The German Air Force is to overcome the English air forces with all means at its disposal and as soon as possible. The attacks must at first be directed at flying formations, their ground organizations, and their supply organizations; secondly, against the aircraft production industry and the industries engaged in production of antiaircraft equipment.

2. After we gain local temporary air superiority the air war is to be directed against harbors, especially those important to the food supplies, and also against inland food storage facilities. Attacks carried out against the south coast harbors must bear in mind future operations we may wish to carry out and must therefore be restricted to the minimum.

3. The war against enemy warships and merchant ships must, however, take secondary position in the air war unless such ships present attractive opportunity targets, or is an additional bonus to attacks carried out under paragraph 2 above, or where it may be used for training of crews for specialized tasks.

4. The increased air war is to be carried out so that the Air Force can support naval operations on satisfactory opportunity targets with sufficient forces

as and when necessary. In addition, the Air Force must remain battleworthy for Operation Sealion.

5. Terror raids as reprisal I reserve the right to order myself.

6. The intensified air war may begin on August 5. The opening date may be selected by the Air Force itself upon completion of preparations and taking weather conditions into account. The Navy is authorized to begin intensified operations on the same date.

—*Adolf Hitler*

On the following day an order alerting Luftflotten 2, 3, and 5 was issued. They were to begin preparations for *Adlerangriff*—"Eagle Attack." No date

land would surely bring out the RAF and then, perhaps, the legend would fade.

Finally, with the help of Milch, also present at Karinhall, it was decided that *Adler Tag* would take place on August 10, weather permitting. But the weather turned for the worse and *Adler Tag* was postponed until August 13.

The main burden of the attack fell upon Luftflotte 2, with headquarters in Brussels and whose units were deployed in northern Germany, Holland, Belgium, and France north of the Seine, and Luftflotte 3, with headquarters in Paris and units based in western France. Luftflotte 5 would make its

The armourers . . . Give dreadful note of preparation: *while Hitler offered Britain his truculent "peace offer" and Göring wished that Britain might sink into the sea,*

the Luftwaffe got ready for its next objective. Lehrgeschwader 1 (left) *ground crews check their Ju-88s and armorers of Jagdgeschwader 51 load the guns of the Me-109.* (H. J. NOWARRA)

was set for the first day of the intensified attack. High-level, and argumentative, meetings were held at Göring's Karinhall to determine general policy and set an *Adler Tag* ("Eagle Day"). There was disagreement between Sperrle (Luftflotte 3) and Kesselring (Luftflotte 2), the former advocating the operations against the RAF, the ports, and supply centers, as Hitler had outlined. Kesselring leaned toward a concentration on a few targets (he had earlier suggested attacking Gibraltar rather than take on the RAF over England). He was soon shown the light and reluctantly agreed, though he had wanted to maintain the legend of the Luftwaffe's invincibility. A direct attack upon the British home-

thrusts from bases in Norway and Denmark. Two *Fliegerkorps* (air corps), 2 and 8, were assigned to establish air superiority over the English Channel and to disrupt, if possible to stop, all shipping into Britain. Fliegerkorps 2 (more correctly designated with Roman numeral), based on the Pas de Calais within Stuka strike of the Straits of Dover, was under command of General Bruno Loerzer, Göring's old First World War best friend. Loerzer's units would operate within the boundaries assigned to Luftflotte 2—an imaginary line, not always observed, which ran across the Channel northerly from Le Havre, cut the English coast near Portsmouth, and continued upward passing slightly to the west of Oxford and, farther north, to the west of Birmingham up through Manchester. All targets to the left of this line, theoretically, were the responsibility of Luftflotte 2; those to the right belonged to Luftflotte 3.

The other *Fliegerkorps,* number 8, based just south of the *Luftflotten* boundary at Deauville, was commanded by Generalmajor Wolfram von Richthofen. Once the chief critic of the Stuka, Richthofen was celebrated as the master of close support and a Stuka virtuoso. His *Fliegerkorps* consisted mainly of Ju-87s.

Ringing the British Isles and poised for *Adler Tag,* therefore, were three massive German air fleets —bombers, dive bombers, single-engined and twin-engined fighters, reconnaissance craft—about 3500 aircraft. Normally about two thirds of the total strength might be serviceable for any given day, however. As of August 10, 1940, for example, Luftflotten 2 and 3, the major units participating in *Adlerangriff,* had at their disposal 1232 long-range bombers (875 serviceable), 406 dive bombers (316 serviceable), 813 single-engined fighters (702 serviceable), 282 twin-engined fighters and fighter-bombers (227 serviceable), as well as about 50 long-range reconnaissance planes.

Across the Channel Air Marshal Sir Hugh Dowding prepared his Fighter Command for the onslaught he knew was coming. The presence of Dowding, like that of Churchill, at this time and at this place, was providential. A brilliant administrator, a sound strategist, and a shrewd tactician, Dowding was, in personality as well as a leader, the opposite of his opponent Göring. For that matter, the aloof Air Officer Commander in Chief, Fighter Command (to use his correct title), shared little in common with his own fighter pilots, who called him "Stuffy," a term of rakish affection rather than scorn.

The words of Churchill must have spurred Dowding, as he took full advantage of the seven weeks between the end of the Battle of France and the opening of the Battle of Britain. "The whole fury and might of the enemy must very soon be turned on us," Churchill had said. "Hitler knows that he will have to break us in this island or lose the war. If we can stand up to him, all Europe may be free and the life of the world may move forward into broad, sunlit uplands. But if we fail, then the

Air Chief Marshal Sir Hugh C. T. Dowding—"Stuffy" to his irreverent but affectionate pilots. For all his diffidence Dowding was a brilliant strategist and proved it as leader of Fighter Command during the Battle.
(IMPERIAL WAR MUSEUM, LONDON)

whole world, including the United States, including all that we have known and cared for, will sink into the abyss of a new Dark Age, made more sinister, and perhaps more protracted, by the lights of perverted science.

"Let us therefore brace ourselves to our duties," Churchill concluded, "and so bear ourselves that, if the British Empire and its Commonwealth last for a thousand years, men will say, 'This was their finest hour.'"

Dowding had sixty squadrons on hand in time for *Adler Tag* with 704 operational aircraft at their disposal (and 289 in reserve). Of these aircraft 620 were Hurricanes and Spitfires (about 400 of the former and 200 of the latter). The rest were Bristol Blenheims, two-engined light bombers em-

The backbone of Fighter Command during the Battle of Britain: the Hurricane. The Hurricane's performance was limited and was no match for the Me-109 at high altitudes. (HAWKER SIDDELEY AVIATION, LTD.)

ployed as fighters, and the Boulton Paul Defiant, a two-seat fighter which resembled the Hurricane. Over Dunkirk, where the Defiant went into action for the first time, it had proved most successful. German pilots, mistaking it for the Hurricane and not realizing a second crew member manned the rear-firing machine guns, attacked from the rear and were shot down. This advantage lasted briefly, for soon the Germans realized the Defiant was a different plane and dealt with it harshly, for it was no match for the Me-109. Nor was the Blenheim; even less the Gladiator, of which a single flight (six planes) remained operational in one squadron.

The Hurricane was obsolescent by August 1940, though a sturdy fighter and a good aircraft. It was Dowding's plan to have the Hurricanes attack the German bombers, which were slower and less maneuverable than the fighters, and leave the Messerschmitts, the 109s and the twin-engined 110s, to the faster, more nimble Spitfires. The Spitfire was a better high-altitude performer than the Hurricane— and the German fighters too fought well above twenty thousand feet.

Dowding's major concern at the Battle's inception was not aircraft, but pilots. Churchill had appointed newspaper publisher Lord Beaverbrook (William Maxwell Aitken) to head the Ministry of Aircraft Production in May 1940. Beaverbrook's disdain for red tape, his dynamism and highly charged personality contributed to the rise in aircraft production. In this he was, of course, helped by the urgency of the time, the robust defiance that vitalized all Britons after Dunkirk. Beaverbrook's son, John William Aitken, had served in France with No. 601 Squadron and was flying a Hurricane with the same unit based in Tangmere near the coast of southern England.

The air fighting in France had taken a heavy toll —320 RAF pilots killed or missing and 115 taken prisoners of war. Of the 959 planes lost in France, 229 had been fighters. British workers could replace the planes. The young men, "the effete, pleasure-mad youth of Britain," as Hitler called them, had to be trained, and this took time.

A fraction of the deficiency was alleviated by the "loan" of fifty-eight pilots from the Fleet Air Arm. In time No. 1 Squadron Royal Canadian Air Force joined in the battle and refugee pilots from Poland and Czechoslovakia were formed into squadrons. The latter two proved especially savage fighters.

II

When *Adler Tag* finally dawned Dowding could call upon 1253 pilots—almost 200 short of his authorized establishment. These pilots were deployed throughout the main island of the British Isles, in England, Wales, and Scotland. The greater concentration of squadrons were based in south England —in the counties of Sussex, Surrey, and Kent. To reach London from the bases in northern France the Luftwaffe fighters and bombers would have to cross this area, most of which lay in the province of No. 11 Group, Air Vice-Marshal Keith Park, Air

Lord Beaverbrook, William M. Aitken, who as head of the Ministry of Aircraft Production during the Battle of Britain slashed through red tape and made certain that Fighter Command did not lack Hurricanes or

Spitfires. With him is his son, John ("Max") Aitken, a fighter pilot with No. 601 Squadron. At war's end Aitken's victory score stood at sixteen.

(*Daily Express,* LONDON)

Officer Commanding. To the west of this area lay No. 10 Group's domain, Air Vice-Marshal Sir Christopher Brand, AOC. To the north, into Essex and Suffolk counties, Air Vice-Marshal Trafford Leigh-Mallory commanded No. 12 Group. Scotland and the northern tip of England were the responsibility of No. 13 Group under Air Vice-Marshal Richard Saul.

The bulk of the heavy air fighting was to take place over the domains of Nos. 11 and 12 Groups. No. 11 Group consisted of twenty-two squadrons (fifteen Hurricane, six Spitfire, and one Blenheim) and No. 12 Group of fifteen squadrons (seven Hurricane, five Spitfire, two Blenheim, and one Defiant).

To contend with the attack the Air Ministry also established antiaircraft divisions, a Balloon Command with its barrage balloons (a throwback to the First World War), an Observer Corps, and, of the greatest import to Fighter Command, a network of so-called Chain Home Stations operating Radio Direction Finding equipment. In time this RDF came to be called *"ra*dio *d*etecting *a*nd *r*anging," which by mid-war the Americans had abbreviated to "radar." The brain child of Robert Watson-Watt, radar was a decisive factor in the outcome of the Battle of Britain.

In the summer of 1940 a system of radar stations stood along the northern, eastern, and southern coasts of the main island. The spindly masts of the

Radar towers on the English coast, an early detection system that contributed greatly to the outcome of the Battle of Britain.

(IMPERIAL WAR MUSEUM, LONDON)

With radar detecting the Luftwaffe forming up while it was still over France, the RAF was able to send its fighters to meet the German formations. Radar would locate the German formations and enabled the British to ignore diversionary sweeps and concentrate on the main point of attack. It also saved the RAF from wasteful patrols. Pilots were scrambled only when necessary—at least in the ideal situation. Pilots could also keep informed of the rapidly shifting air situation by radio from the ground radar stations tracking and plotting the oncoming Germans. Furthermore, pilots could talk with each other in the air. The German communications system was not as well developed. There was no ground control with radar and while pilots could talk with each other within their own units there was no intercommunication in formations except by signal: the fighters had no radio connection with the bombers. In general this meant operations were dependent upon the orders issued before they had taken off; there was little leeway for the unexpected.

Thus the situation stood when the Germans impatiently girded for *Adler Tag.* Göring, warming up to what was to be the world's first great air battle, expected that the defenses of southern England would be shattered in four days and that the Luftwaffe would take four weeks to eliminate the Royal Air Force. After this, Operation Sealion could be launched and a triumphant Third Reich would be free for more important conquests (especially that of the Soviet Union, which Hitler now seriously considered).

Although the all-out assault was set for the August "Eagle Day," the Luftwaffe ventured over the English Channel before this. On the night of June 5/6 about thirty German bombers flew over the east coast dropping bombs on airfields and upon the vicinity of airfields. Nighttime accuracy, even with the help of a radio beam (code-named *Knickebein,* and quickly jammed by the British), left much to be desired. Such harassment raids were of little military value except to provide the crews with night-flying practice. Also, the raids kept the British on their toes, although they interfered somewhat with production as the workers sought shelter upon the sounding of air raid sirens.

The scattered raids of June were of no great consequence, although some damage was done, and there were a number of casualties, as well as small

transmitting and receiving towers were concentrated in the southeastern counties opposite France. Additional stations were erected inland. At the time of the Battle's opening there were twenty-one operational CH stations and thirty CHL (Chain Home Low) stations. The former were capable of picking up objects at a distance of 120 miles but missed low-flying aircraft; the CHL stations supplemented the CH stations on low-flying aircraft up to fifty miles distant. By no means absolutely perfect or foolproof, the English radar system was superior to anything the Germans had developed. And because they had not been able to devise a good system the Germans characteristically assumed the British had also been as unsuccessful.

Before the curtain rose on the Battle of Britain the Luftwaffe began scattered raids against various port cities on the southeast coast of England and upon vital British shipping in the English Channel. On the left

German bombs fall on Portland, which was attacked for the first time on July 11, 1940. On the right, a view from the nose of an He-111 of English ships under attack in the Channel. (NATIONAL ARCHIVES)

German losses. July saw the beginning of more intensified daylight attacks, particularly upon the port cities—Portland, Falmouth, Plymouth, Dover—and upon shipping in the Channel. By the end of July daylight passage through the English Channel, even for convoys, became hazardous under the attacks of the Stukas, the Messerschmitt 110s, the Dornier 17s, and escorting Me-109s.

Loerzer had selected Johannes Fink as Kanalkampfführer (Channel Battle Leader) to lead a small battle group, Kampfgeschwader 2, to attend to shipping through the Straits of Dover; Richthofen's Stukas did the same to the west. In addition to his own *Geschwader*'s Dorniers, Fink could call upon two *Gruppen* of Stukas (Ju-87s) and two fighter *Geschwader*, JG 26, led by Adolf Galland, and JG 51, led by Werner Mölders. The two

Jagdgeschwader, commanded by the stars of the Luftwaffe, were equipped with the latest Messerschmitt 109Es. Mölders, a great tactician and teacher, was then the high-scoring Luftwaffe ace. He was, interestingly, an ardent anti-Nazi, an aberration for which he was tolerated because of his achievements as a fighter pilot.

If the early July Channel encounters were not conclusive, they were no less deadly for the participants. Flight Lieutenant Alan Deere, leading B Flight of No. 54 Squadron on a convoy patrol—the fourth scramble of the day—crossed the English coast at Deal. At this point the English Channel, that is, at the Straits of Dover, is barely twenty miles wide. Deere, a New Zealander, had been flying since he was nineteen and was a confirmed ace with five official victories to his credit. Shot down over Dunkirk, Deere had joined the "brown jobs" (Army men) and was evacuated by ship back to England.

Leading his flight of six Spitfires, Deere had spotted a silvery plane flying low, escorted by a dozen Me-109s at about a thousand feet and another five serving as top cover. The silver seaplane was a Heinkel 59 decorated not only with the traditional black crosses of the Luftwaffe, but also with a red cross identifying it as an Air-Sea rescue plane. Obviously it was searching for German pilots who had crash-landed in the Channel in the day's early fighting. The RAF had orders to attack the He-59s, red cross or not, for while they rescued the pilots they also reported the British convoys in the Channel.

Ordering half of his flight to attack the seaplane, Deere led two Spitfires to deal with the top-cover Messerschmitts. The German fighters immediately formed into a defensive circle. Diving through the circle Deere shot down one of the German planes and then, as he tells it himself, "straightening out from my favorite defensive maneuver of a tight turn, I found my self head-on to another [Me-109].

"As we sped towards each other at a combined speed of over 500 mph there was little time to think. For my part, the thought of a collision did not enter my head—had it done so I have no doubt I would have tried to avoid it—and when I realized it was to be the inevitable outcome it was too late for evasion action. At one moment the Me-109 was a blurred outline filling my reflector sight and the next it was on top of me blotting out the sky ahead as it passed marginally above, avoiding a direct collision perhaps by a last-minute alteration of course by the German pilot.

"But collide we did; propeller hit propeller, the shock of the impact throwing me forward in my seat, saved only from being crushed on the dashboard by the restraining cockpit harness which bit cruelly into my shoulders.

"The next few moments I recall as a panic-stricken blur as I fought to regain some control over my now vibrating, pitching Spitfire already gushing ominous black smoke into the cockpit. Gain control I did, but sufficient only to keep the aircraft in a too-fast-for-comfort dive towards the English coast, with throttle jammed open but a happily unresponsive engine seized solid by a propeller which under the impact had bent double and dug itself progressively into the engine housing before finally ceasing to turn."

But now fire had begun licking out of the smoke in Deere's cockpit and he knew he had to jump.

The Heinkel 59, which, despite the red crosses painted on its sides (not on this one, however) because of its function as an Air-Sea Rescue plane, was consistently shot down by the RAF. Churchill believed they were used also to make reconnaissance observations during rescue operations. (H. J. NOWARRA)

The Messerschmitt 109, the standard single-seater Luftwaffe fighter during the Battle of Britain. Superior to the Hurricane, it was an even match for the Spitfire. Air battles between the Me-109 and the Spitfire were decided either by pilot skill or luck.

(U. S. AIR FORCE)

Heaving at the cockpit hood he was dismayed to learn that the collision had jammed it shut. Nor could he jettison it mechanically. There was no choice; Deere had to stay with the burning Spitfire, bring it down, and hope to get out somehow on the ground.

"Half-choked by the smoke, licked at by flames I somehow kept the Spitfire heading inland and under a measure of control. I could see nothing directly ahead and only a little to the side as my now burning fighter plunged towards a resting place in the Kentish fields, barely discernible through the smoke and flame. . . .

"I must have prayed, but I don't remember. What I do remember is the crunching sensation as the aircraft hit the ground, fortunately in open country, launched itself in the air again, returned to earth and ploughed a skidding and erratic passage through a field studded with wooden posts, put there as a deterrent to an enemy airborne glider force, shedding bits of fuselage en route."

When the shuddering, bouncing Spitfire finally came to a stop Deere desperately hammered at the perspex of the canopy, broke it open, dived over the side, and ran from the burning wreckage. The Spitfire had come to rest in a cornfield now resounding to the firing of the plane's guns, which had become heated by the flames.

By some miracle, except for slightly burned hands, singed eyebrows, bruised knees, and the cuts from the shoulder harness, Deere was not seriously injured and was back in the battle the next day. His plane, named *Kiwi*, was a total loss, however.

The Me-109 with which he collided had not shared Deere's luck. The tail of the German fighter had been sheared off and, trailing bits of fuselage, the plane fell into the Channel.

August brought a quickening of the tempo of Luftwaffe attacks; by the end of the first week the bombing became heavier and more fierce. Göring waited for an improvement in the weather, however, to launch the all-out attack, set for August 10. Dowding, meanwhile, held his fighters in check, not wishing to waste pilots and aircraft in the preliminary phases of the big battle that must inevitably come. Fighting over the Channel was a risky business; wait for the Luftwaffe to come farther inland to the limit of their range, Dowding wisely cau-

The Messerschmitt 110, the ill-fated Zerstörer *(destroyer), which was supposed to operate in the dual role of fighter and bomber and proved to be neither.*
(H. J. NOWARRA)

tioned. Avoid combat as much as possible with fighters—get the bombers; they carried the lethal burden.

But the English weather proved to be characteristically unreasonable. On the evening of August 9, with the Channel socked in with cloud and with Britain under cloud and rain, Göring canceled the large-scale attack of the following day. *Adler Tag,* weather permitting, then was set for August 13.

On the twelfth the prelude to *Adler Tag* took place. While continuing to harass shipping in the Channel and the ports, the Luftwaffe attacked airfields and radar installations. The expanding battle was moving inland.

Spearheading the assault was an *Erprobungsgruppe* (Experimental Group) 210, a mixed unit of fighters, Messerschmitt 109s and 110s, converted to fighter-bombers. The formation, led by Hauptmann Walter Rubensdörffer, consisted of eight Me-109s, some carrying five-hundred- or thousand-pound bombs under their bellies, and a dozen Me-110s, similarly armed. Their targets were the radar antennas along the Kent and Sussex coast. The steel structures, 350 feet tall, rose up out of the marshes and apple orchards of Kent like strange devices from another world.

These spindly antennas were Fighter Command's ace in the hole. Their existence eliminated the Luftwaffe's element of surprise.

On this day the Messerschmitts split up and sped

Me-110s in flight. According to the original conception, these planes were supposed to be able to fight off attackers while on bombing missions, or to serve as escort for heavier bombers. They proved to be sitting ducks for the guns of the RAF. (MUSÉE DE L'AIR)

toward their individual targets upon reaching the English coast. Except for patches of mist the weather was good and the Messerschmitts dropped down out of the sun and raced toward the masts at Pevensey, Rye, Dover, and Dunkirk (the latter on the south bank of the Thames near Canterbury). Although the radar stations had picked up the approaching bombers, the formations appeared small enough to require little more than watching. Almost at the same moment all of the radar stations came under attack and all bombers loosed their bombs on target. The earth shook, buildings collapsed, smoke rose into the air—but, as the Messerschmitts wheeled around for home, the men saw that the masts remained standing.

At Dunkirk two huts had been destroyed but the station continued operating. At Rye all the huts had gone up in the explosions, but by noon the station was back in action. Bombs cut the main electric cable at Pevensey, putting it out for two hours. At Dover the aerials took slight damage and the working quarters were smashed to bits—but Dover continued to operate. These stations were "manned," so to speak, by young women of the Women's Auxiliary Air Force who endured the bombings with exemplary calm.

Though triumphant on returning to their base at Denain, the pilots and crews of Experimental Group 210 found their jubilance premature. Luftwaffe

Communications Chief General Wolfgang Martini learned through detection devices that the radar stations continued to operate despite the on-target attacks by the fighter-bombers.

There was an exception. Just before noon, while more than sixty Ju-88s attacked Portsmouth Harbor, fifteen aircraft veered off and dived toward the radar installation at Ventnor on the Isle of Wight. The heavy bomb concentration destroyed most of the buildings, caused fires which could not be put out because of a lack of water, and seriously damaged the site. Ventnor was out of action for eleven days.

While the radar stations were recovering from the morning attacks the afternoon opened with assaults upon British airfields. Even as the pilots of No. 65 Squadron ran for their Spitfires, the bombs from the Dorniers fell upon Manston, an advance base near the coast. Another airfield, Hawkinge, was also bombed. The fleeing Ju-88s left two hangars destroyed, the workshops afire, and the landing strips cratered. Five people had been killed and four aircraft damaged. For the second time in the day, the airfield at Lympne (actually an unimportant emergency landing field) was bombed. Manston was hardest hit, although like the other stations it was back in operation by the following day. *Adler Tag* eve had cost the RAF 22 fighters and the Luftwaffe 31 aircraft. The toll from July 10 through this August 12 was 150 RAF fighters and 286 German aircraft, including fighters and bombers. And the Battle proper had not yet begun.

Kanalkampfführer Johannes Fink—whose friends lightly called him *Kanalarbeiter* ("Sewer worker")—did not take his position lightly. By seven in the morning of August 13—*Adler Tag,* at last—his Dornier 17s of Kampfgeschwader 2 were air-borne. Fifty-five aircraft roared toward the airdrome at Eastchurch on the south bank of the Thames estuary. All along the coasts of France, Belgium, Holland, and Norway aircraft of the three great *Luftflotten* would converge upon the stubborn British for the Attack of the Eagles.

As was its wont, the weather had turned bad overnight—there were clouds over the Channel and mist and drizzling over the target. Eastchurch, Fink did not know, was a Coastal Command station—not a fighter field. The target of the Luftwaffe was RAF Fighter Command. This was not the only slip of the morning.

When he arrived at the rendezvous point with the fighter escort, the Messerschmitt 110s of Oberstleutnant Joachim Huth's Zerstörergeschwader 26, Fink was annoyed with the behavior of the fighters. Huth's Messerschmitt bore down upon Fink's Dornier, dived, turned, and came back at him. Fink good-naturedly attributed it to the typical fighter pilot's high spirits in celebration of *Adler Tag*. The performance of the Destroyers was ridiculous but understandable. Fink proceeded toward Eastchurch. After cutting through a cloud bank, Fink was further piqued to note that no Messerschmitts were visible anywhere. They had lost one another in the clouds. There was nothing before him except the forbidding coast of England and scattered clouds.

In their stations the radar operators had begun tracking Fink as soon as his planes formed up over Calais. The still inexperienced operators could not predict the Dorniers' destination.

The cloud had thickened so Fink ordered the planes to loosen the formation in order to lessen the chance of collision. When the Dorniers broke through the mist Fink was delighted to see Eastchurch about three miles ahead—and ten thousand feet below. Anxiously peering out of the cockpit, Fink ascertained an unfortunate truth: no fighter escort. The cautious, fifty-year-old leader found some consolation in the sight of the aircraft on the field below neatly lined up, wingtip to wingtip, waiting for them.

Fink led the Dorniers to the attack. At about the same moment some Spitfires of No. 74 Squadron, the only unit dispatched to deal with "a few aircraft," pounced upon the rear of the formation. Oberleutnant Heinz Schlegel's Dornier bucked under the scattered fire from the Spitfire's eight guns. The right engine ground to a stop and began smoking, and Schlegel had trouble keeping the plane from pulling to the left. Another burst from a diving Spitfire solved that problem: the other engine was damaged and, because two of his crew were wounded, Schlegel crash-landed the Dornier in an English meadow. Schlegel and his crew were taken prisoner.

Fink, unaware of the attack going on behind him, dropped his bombs upon Eastchurch. The men on the base below reacted with astonishment as explosions erupted in the early morning. Five Blenheims of No. 35 Squadron went up in smoke. Twelve

men died in the rubble and fire and forty were injured. A direct hit destroyed the operations building. When Fink ducked his plane into the clouds and raced for France, great black clouds of smoke rose up from Eastchurch.

But some of the smoke may have been that of his own planes, for during the fighting Fink lost four aircraft.

Furious because he had had no fighter protection, Fink called Kesselring at Luftflotte 2 headquarters as soon as he had landed. The tone and language of the usually mild Fink prompted a visit from Kesselring, who brought a personal explanation.

A Spitfire harries a Dornier-17, the "Flying Pencil," over England. (NATIONAL ARCHIVES)

Adler Tag had been postponed because of the poor weather. Fink's mission had been canceled although word had come only after he had taken off. The fighters had been informed, which explained not only their absence, but also the odd behavior of Huth's Messerschmitt 110. Fink learned that as he was attacking Eastchurch other uninformed aircraft, the Ju-88s of Kampfgeschwader 54, with Me-110 escort, attempted to bomb the Royal Aircraft Establishment at Farnborough. Fighter interception from No. 11 Group prevented the attack and at least five of the Me-110s, Göring's pet Destroyer, went down under the Spitfire guns. The rest fled for home. The same occurred with a formation of more than eighty Stukas—only they fled before attacking and thus were spared, temporarily, a full-scale encounter with the British fighters. Only Fink's resolute, and vulnerable, formation had succeeded in the morning of Eagle Day.

An attempt to save the glory of the day was made in the afternoon despite the worsening weather. A fighter formation (Me-110s) was sent to the vicinity of Portland to draw off the English fighters. While these engaged the Hurricanes and Spitfires it was expected that the Ju-88s might break through the defenses and bomb the docks and warehouses at Southampton. Most of the bombers got through, causing serious damage while the Me-110s, possibly

Channel near Cherbourg, hoped to find airfields in the Portland area. But cloud cover again interfered —and so did No. 609 Squadron. Diving through the Me-109 escort formation, scattering them, the Spitfires pounded at the "dreaded" Stuka. The slow, clumsy craft was no match for the Spitfire and within minutes five of them lay smashed on the countryside below.

In the same encounter Pilot Officer D. M. Crook of No. 609 Squadron fired at an Me-109, which burst into flame and joined the hapless Stukas in a fiery dive to the ground. The fleeing Stukas spread their bombs over three counties.

The Ju-87 Stuka, once the scourge of the air, reached the end of the road over England in the summer of 1940. (U. S. AIR FORCE)

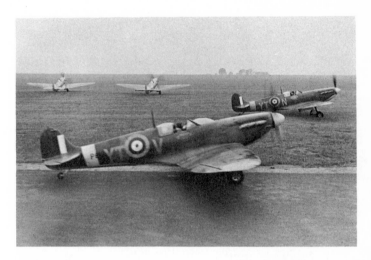

Aroused Spitfires of No. 65 Squadron take off to confront the Luftwaffe. On "Eagle Day" this squadron drove off an attack by the Stukas.

(IMPERIAL WAR MUSEUM, LONDON)

mistaken for bombers, engaged the fighters. The more sprightly Spitfires dived and twisted through the defensive circle which the Messerschmitts had formed under attack. In the savage fighting, five Me-110s fell. Clearly, the escort required an escort.

During the afternoon attacks also Richthofen's Ju-87s had succeeded in bombing the airfield at Detling, while its fighter escort dueled with the British fighters. Another formation of Ju-87s, aimed at a fighter base at Rochford, could not find it because of cloud cover. When attacked by the Spitfires of No. 65 Squadron, the Germans jettisoned their bombs across Canterbury and fled.

Farther west and south, more Stukas, crossing the

As evening fell the Attack of the Eagles subsided into the scattered detonations of wasted bombs and the desperate scream of the Stuka, the onetime Scourge of the Blitzkrieg, running for home. Small night attacks by bombers did not add to the accomplishment of the day. The eagle's wings had been clipped. The German pilots had not lacked courage, only that required efficiency in the High Command which makes sense of complex, large-scale operations.

When *Adler Tag* officially closed, the Luftwaffe had lost forty-five aircraft—thirty-nine to the British fighters—and the RAF Fighter Command had lost thirteen planes, but only seven pilots in combat.

It was not an auspicious beginning.

6

TARGET: RAF

THE FAT ONE was in a sour mood. His Eagle Day had not gone off as planned, what with the breakdown in command which set it off piecemeal. It was that damned English weather, unpredictable, obstinate, capricious—now bright and sunny, then moody and threatening: like the English themselves. Göring was not at all pleased with the course of the battle. The weather on the day following Eagle Day, August 14, had proved too poor for large-scale operations, although the Luftwaffe flew 489 sorties with the concentration upon the airdromes in southeastern England.

On that morning Göring called a conference at Karinhall with his staff and the *Luftflotten* commanders for the next day, August 15. He was obviously not in a joyous temper. He was concerned with the vulnerability of the Stuka and ordered increased fighter escorts for the dive bombers: as many as three *Gruppen* of fighters per *Gruppe* of Stukas.

As for the heavy bombers, he sarcastically invoked one of his pet comments of the period. Göring suggested that they attend to the British aircraft industries and "not the lightship off Dover."

He waxed serious: "We must concentrate our efforts on the destruction of the enemy air forces . . . including the targets of the enemy aircraft industry allocated to the different *Luftflotten*. . . .

"For the moment other targets should be ignored. . . .

"Our night attacks are essentially dislocation raids, made so that enemy defenses and population shall be allowed no respite; even these, however, should wherever possible be directed against air force targets. . . ." That was the heart of Göring's master plan: the great German Air Force would erase the British Air Force.

Having committed his air force to the extinction of the RAF, Göring then proceeded to do the same to the Luftwaffe with a series of blunders in High Command. "It is doubtful," he concluded, "whether there is any point in continuing the attacks on radar sites, in view of the fact that not one of those attacked has so far been put out of action." Even as he said this repairmen were working against time to put the Ventnor station back into operation and not succeeding very rapidly. Göring, however, had no comprehension of radar's significance. It was yet another one of his decisions which would cost others their lives.

At almost the same moment Göring spoke and decreed, once again the order to postpone the day's missions because of weather had gone astray. In the absence of Loerzer, who was with Göring and the others at Karinhall, his chief of staff, Oberst Paul Deichmann, upon personally viewing the weather conditions—bright, sunny, with some cloud over the Channel—initiated the day's operations. Picking up the field phone, he dispatched the Stukas for England.

For the first time all three *Luftflotten,* based from Norway in the north to Brittany in the south, engaged in co-ordinated daylight attacks. In terms of

Göring with two aides who unconsciously let him down. On the left is the Chief of Air Intelligence, Josef "Beppo" Schmid, whose appraisal of the enemy's air power was frequently inaccurate; in the center, Chief of the Technical Branch of the Luftwaffe, Ernst Udet, who preferred flying airplanes to theorizing about them. Göring, however, betrayed both of them and the Luftwaffe as well by virtue of simple incompetence.

(H. J. NOWARRA)

numbers it was a more impressive German showing than Eagle Day itself.

The day began serenely enough with a few reconnaissance patrols by the RAF. Air Vice-Marshal Park dispatched a squadron from No. 11 Group to keep an eye upon two convoys just off the Thames estuary, but without incident.

That something big was to be expected was noted on the radar screens when just before eleven o'clock large formations were detected. These were the Stukas, with Me-109 escort, meeting over Calais for the twenty-minute flight across the Straits of Dover to attack the RAF airfields in Kent. When the German formations reached the English coast at eleven-thirty, they were met by a squadron each of Hurricanes and Spitfires. Of the nearly fifty Stukas participating in the attack, only four fell to the British fighters. The rest pushed through the defenses to bomb the airfields at Lympne and Hawkinge. The latter, a fighter base, was not seriously damaged, but Lympne, actually a secondary field, was knocked out for two days. Clearly the Luftwaffe was out to get the Royal Air Force Fighter Command.

While this fighting continued, and radar screens blipped with German air activity in the Channel

Stukas en route to their targets—and, more often than not, their doom.

(EMBASSY OF THE POLISH PEOPLE'S REPUBLIC)

area, another development to the north was unfolding on the screens in the Operations Room of No. 13 Group. Shortly after noon "twenty or more aircraft" were reported approaching from the North Sea. This estimate was increased soon after to three distinct formations aimed at Northumberland: "thirty plus," was the new figure. In reality, the radar operators were plotting a *Gruppe* of seaplanes on a diversionary flight toward the Firth of Forth, to the north of the true path of the other aircraft groups.

Unfortunately for the attacking Luftwaffe, the second group, the bombers of Kampfgeschwader 26,

cort planes with adequate range for the flight from the Luftwaffe base, four-hundred miles distant, at Stavanger, Norway. In his high-flying Messerschmitt, Restemeyer planned to direct the battle against the British fighters.

The forewarned Spitfires of No. 72 Squadron had climbed above the approaching Germans. From out of the sun they pounced upon the German formations. Among the first planes to come under attack was Restemeyer's Messerschmitt. With its eight guns firing, the mottled, graceful Spitfire struck the German fighter. The Messerschmitt staggered momentarily in mid-flight, shedding bits of metal, and then

Spitfire takeoff with wheels beginning to tuck into the wing. Early Spitfires required the pilot to crank the *wheels up (and down) manually; later models were equipped with automatic wheel gear.*
(IMPERIAL WAR MUSEUM, LONDON)

sixty-three He-111s with an escort of twenty-one Me-110s of Zerstörergeschwader 76, were off course. Instead of approaching their targets, British Bomber Command bases at Dishforth and Linton-on-Ouse, the German bombers converged upon the English coast at almost the same point as the seaplane feint.

Having been stirred up by the seaplanes, No. 72 Squadron's Spitfires intercepted the formation of Heinkels and Messerschmitts about thirty miles off the English coast. The bombers droned along at about fifteen thousand feet. A thousand feet above them flew the Me-110s, led by Hauptmann Werner Restemeyer. The heavy fighters were the only es-

with an orange flash exploded. The mangled aircraft spun burning into the North Sea.

While some of the Spitfires engaged the Me-110s, which quickly formed into their customary defensive circle, the others flitted through the bomber formation. The suddenness of the attack, and perhaps the sight of Restemeyer's stricken plane descending, unnerved many of the crews in the Heinkels. Bombs were jettisoned harmlessly into the sea as the Heinkels lightened the loads for evasive action. Many ducked into cloud bank over which they had been safely flying just moments before.

After the first shock of the Spitfire attack had

worn off, the German planes pushed on toward their assigned targets. The fighters had to contend with yet another squadron (No. 79) of Spitfires which had been vectored to the heaving, lofty battleground. The Germans were outnumbered and fought with courage, although handicapped by their aircraft, none of which equaled the Spitfire in maneuverability. Once again the Zerstörer proved itself no match for the darting Spitfire. Although hits were scored by the German fighters and many claims made for "kills," British records do not reveal any losses of any of No. 13 Group's aircraft in the day's battle. Besides Restemeyer's plane, another eighteen

some homes in Portland, destroyed by the loosed bombs.

The surviving German planes turned and scuttled for home. Eight bombers did not return. The "surprise" flank attack by Luftflotte 5 cost twenty-seven aircraft and their crews. The expenditure was high for little return.

The other formation contributed by Luftflotte 5, unescorted Junkers 88s from Aalborg, Denmark, had been detected almost simultaneously with the Heinkels and Messerschmitts farther north. This flight made landfall at Flamborough Head, north of the Humber River. These were fifty aircraft of

He-111s over a German base. (NATIONAL ARCHIVES)

Me-110s were shot down and others returned to their bases in Norway badly shot up, with wounded aboard and crews demoralized.

Meanwhile, also under attack, the Heinkels pressed on for England. Spitfires now harassing the bombers were joined by Hurricanes of No. 605 Squadron. More bombs fell into the sea, joined by smoking Heinkels. Those that passed over the beaches and flew inland were then put upon by antiaircraft guns, further adding to the Heinkel's torment. Bombs scattered willy-nilly across the coastal villages—Seaham Harbour, Portland—but to no military point. The most serious damage was to

Kampfgeschwader 30—their target: the airfield at Driffield, home of No. 4 Group of Bomber Command.

This attack fell into the province of Leigh-Mallory's No. 12 Group. Around one o'clock—while the battle raged to the north—No. 12 Group's Spitfires, Defiants, and Hurricanes were ordered up. No. 13 Groups, though heavily engaged, dispatched a squadron of Blenheims to this battle also. It might be noted that the Defiants were specifically dispatched to patrol a convoy in the Humber River. Neither the Defiants nor the Blenheims could have been expected to fight on equal terms with German

Heinkel bombers heading out for targets in Britain.
(H. J. NOWARRA)

*An He-111 disintegrates under the eight-gun assault of
an RAF fighter attack.*
(IMPERIAL WAR MUSEUM, LONDON)

*Ju-88, the Luftwaffe's best bomber of the Battle of
Britain.* (U. S. AIR FORCE)

fighters; however, if, as it was hoped, the German formation contained only bombers the obsolescent aircraft might fare reasonably well. Even so, the Ju-88s were more capable of dealing with Blenheims.

The Spitfires of No. 616 Squadron intercepted the Ju-88s just offshore at Flamborough Head. Instead of breaking up for combat, the German formations dived into the clouds and eluded the British planes—at least temporarily. Then a flight of Hurricanes joined the battle as the Junkers crossed the coast line. The air over Flamborough Head was crisscrossed with machine-gun fire and from time to time the sky became smudged with oily smoke and flame as a Junkers fell under the eight-gun fighters.

Despite the heavy opposition about thirty German bombers broke through and found their targets. With amazing accuracy, considering the harassment, their bombs fell upon Driffield. Four hangars erupted under the onslaught, three blocks of buildings burst open and fell burning, and ten Whitley heavy bombers were destroyed under the heavy bomb concentration.

One of the Junkers was shot down by antiaircraft. But the formation had split up and while the larger one bombed Driffield another dropped its bombs on Bridlington, destroying some houses, and hitting also a nearby ammunition dump.

Then the Junkers turned and ran for Denmark, pursued by the Hurricanes and Spitfires a hundred miles out to sea. The Blenheims joined the pursuit but could not catch up to the swifter Junkers. Ten of the Ju-88s, however, remained smoking and tangled on the Yorkshire countryside or at the bottom of the sea.

Luftflotte 5 had lost, in its first—and last—full-scale daylight attack almost one eighth of its bomber force and one fifth of its heavy fighters. Nor had the feint succeeded in drawing the British fighters away from southeast England. Dowding had not permitted that and as the German bombers of Luftflotten 2 and 3 launched their attacks upon Kent, Essex, and Suffolk, the Spitfires and Hurricanes of No. 11 and No. 10 Groups rose up to meet them.

Even so, Me-110s of Erprobungsgruppe 210, accompanied by swarms of Me-109s and Stukas—about a hundred aircraft in all—slipped across the Channel northeast of London to strike the airfield at Martlesham Heath in Suffolk. While the Messerschmitt 109s held off those few British fighters which

Hurricanes of No. 85 Squadron on patrol awaiting the word to vector in on approaching Luftwaffe forma- *tions. Ideally, the Hurricanes took on the slower bombers while the Spitfires mixed with the Me-109s.*

(IMPERIAL WAR MUSEUM, LONDON)

had come upon them, the Stukas dive-bombed a radio installation and the Me-110s concentrated upon the airfield itself. No. 17 Squadron, part of which was based at Martlesham, had been sent off to intercept a formation of attackers and then suddenly vectored back to their station. The Hurricanes arrived only in time to see columns of smoke rising from Martlesham. It was too late; the German planes had already left for their bases in France.

The Operations Rooms in the sector stations were swamped with German activity in the vicinity of Calais and the Channel. Hundreds of Me-109s swept across the Straits of Dover, contributing to the confusion on the radar screens. And then, around the same time the Me-110s and Stukas freely dealt with Martlesham, the Dornier 17s of Kampfgeschwader 3, with Me-109 escort, had made landfall and were speeding westward over Kent. Almost a hundred bombers made up this formation, plus even

more fighters. Four British squadrons (forty-eight aircraft at best), then patrolling in the general area of penetration, were sent to deal with the Germans. They were easily held off by the high-flying Me-109s. Even the added strength of three more British squadrons did not improve the odds, and the Dorniers continued on to their selected targets. One was the Coastal Command station at Eastchurch; others were radar stations along the southeast coast.

A formation of more than thirty Dorniers pushed on to Rochester, where the most serious strike was successfully made. Bombs—fragmentation, incendiary, and delayed-action—literally rained down, cutting across hangars, workshops, and runways. Rochester, like Eastchurch, was not a Fighter Command station—but it was the home of aircraft factories, among them the important Short Brothers works. It was here that the first of the four-engined heavy bombers, the Stirling, was being built. The destruction to the facility delayed the heavy-bomber time-table several months. It was a crucial blow to the long-range plans of the British.

The British fighters attacked the Germans savagely, but outnumbered, nine Hurricanes and Spitfires were lost. The Germans lost only four planes in the fighting. Still, not all of the British pilots were lost. Flying Officer John Gibson, a New Zealander of No. 501 Squadron, contemplated his sad condition. He had made a pass at a German plane and found himself the victim of the enemy. Over Folkstone, at the edge of the sea, he gingerly sat in his blazing Hurricane planning his next action.

Gibson did not want the burning aircraft to crash on land with the possibility of striking a town, a village, or a farm cottage. He pointed the blistering nose of the Hurricane toward the Channel. Then he had another thought. Gibson wore, as was the wont of many an RAF pilot, new beautiful, hand-made boots. The thought of what the sea would do to such fine craftsmanship gave him pause. Gibson worked off the shoes and tossed them over the side, watched them drop for a second toward the earth below. Once over the water and down now to about a thousand feet, he flipped the Hurricane over and dropped out himself. His chute opened and, shoeless, Gibson wafted down into the waters of the English Channel. The blazing Hurricane dived smoldering into the sea.

For his action John Gibson was awarded the Distinguished Flying Cross. More: a Kentish native, upon finding the handsome boots, mailed them off to a nearby airfield and soon after Gibson was as dashingly booted as before his encounter with a Messerschmitt. It had been an action-packed hour.

Then, inexplicably, at the height of the battle there came a pause. Having, to a great extent, thrown Fighter Command off balance by its massive raids, feints, and fighter sweeps, the Luftwaffe permitted the English nearly two hours in which to refuel and rearm. The activity, up to this point, had fallen primarily upon Kesselring's Luftflotte 2. As soon as his forces had completed their missions, Sperrle's Luftflotte 3 should have taken over. Such timing is not always possible under actual operating conditions. Only in retrospect, in the warm security of their armchairs and with the even greater security of time (and the warranty of history), can those who were never there sit in judgment of What

German pilots recounting their experiences during the Battle of Britain. Hauptmann Georg-Peter Eder of Jagdgeschwader 26 (right) carries signal flare cartridges in his flight boots. (H. J. NOWARRA)

Pilots of Jagdgeschwader 27 prepare to take off on an escort mission to England. (H. J. NOWARRA)

Might Have Been. At any rate, the British were granted a breathing spell instead of having to contend with Sperrle's bombers and fighters immediately following Kesselring's quite effective attacks. It should also be remembered that even as these attacks were in progress both Kesselring and Sperrle were at Karinhall listening to their intrepid leader, no mean armchair strategist himself, on how to win the Battle of Britain in just a few days.

By five in the afternoon the radar screens again picked up large formations of German aircraft, perhaps two hundred or more, moving from Luftflotte 3 bases in northwestern France. As the fighter escorts, Me-109s, milled around waiting for the bombers and consuming fuel, No. 10 and No. 11 Groups prepared for the attack. The bombers, Ju-88s, were twenty minutes late: this not only gave the British time to prepare but also limited the time the Me-109s might afford protection for the bombers over England. Also in the German formations were Stukas and Me-110s. Even before the first group of German planes crossed the south coast (roughly in the area of the Isle of Wight) eight fighter squadrons—Hurricanes and Spitfires—were air-borne and waiting.

The evening sky erupted with battling aircraft. The Ju-88s of Hauptmann Jochen Helbig's 4th Staffel (of Lehrgeschwader 1) came under severe attack by swarms of Spitfires which had dropped down out of the setting sun. In seconds Helbig's bomber was punched full of holes by the swift British planes—the Spitfire was nearly a hundred miles an hour faster than the Ju-88. The eight guns of the Spitfire converged upon the German bomber with smashing force. Helbig's gunner managed to wing one of the attackers, which fell smoking out of the fight.

Helbig himself sought the safety of lower altitudes, where the Spitfires could not torment him in diving attacks. With his plane in poor condition he could only continue south for home—the Orléans field in France. But of his seven planes, only two returned. It had been a disaster for Helbig's *Staffel.*

The fighting at this point was a great confusion of tumbling aircraft, of hammering noise, of planes shedding fragments, of silent guns and dead gunners, of great burning veins across the sky—of screaming plunges and the abrupt, bursting crashes of a stricken aircraft. Their scorched, obscene resting places were marked by great scars in the earth. Small cottages burst open to admit precipitate, uninvited death. Orchards were left a burning waste —a village street a litter of scorching brick, glass, wood, and innocent, twisted dead. These were all reminders that the war in the air must finally come to earth.

In the melee of the attack which had decimated Helbig's *Staffel,* although many of the Ju-88s jettisoned their bombs, two formations fought through the British fighters. Three Junkers succeeded in bombing the naval air station at Worthy Down at Southampton. Another formation of a dozen Ju-88s pressed on farther to the north and struck the important sector station of Fighter Command at Middle Wallop. Even as the bombs shattered across the airfield, striking two hangars and runways, Spitfires of No. 609 Squadron were taking off. The German survivors of this attack reported they had hit Andover airfield (not a fighter base), not realizing the importance of Middle Wallop as a sector station which housed the radar equipment for operational control of the fighters in that sector.

A total of twenty-five German aircraft were lost in this phase of the day's fighting: eight Ju-88s, four Stukas, and thirteen Me-110s. This was at a cost of sixteen Hurricanes and Spitfires.

The scarred, crippled, smoking remnants of the once massive formations had hardly dashed for Cherbourg when another formation was plotted forming over Calais. This was an attack on the left flank after the attack on the south. Sixty or seventy aircraft were coming in over the Straits of Dover and many of No. 11 Group's planes were in need of fuel and landing. No. 501 Squadron's Hurricanes were still air-borne, although after two encounters they were low on fuel and ammunition. Air Vice-Marshal Park could do nothing else but dispatch the Hurricanes to Dover. He quickly added an additional four squadrons from Kent and, later, four and a half others.

At six-thirty Test Group 210, which had bombed the airfield at Martlesham Heath earlier in the day, was returning to bomb two sector stations, one at Kenley and the other at Biggin Hill. Hauptmann Walter Rübensdörffer's test group had enjoyed unusual success: it had also put out the Ventnor radar station on the Isle of Wight three days earlier— and its morning had been fruitful. Now it was returning in freshly bombed-up Messerschmitts (both 109s and 110s) as well as Dornier 17s. Jagdgeschwader 52 was to furnish the escort of Me-109s.

Leading his formation of twenty-three aircraft, Rübensdörffer wondered where the fighter escort was. His bomb-laden Messerschmitts, his fighter-bombers, would not be effective bombers until they had reached their targets and dropped the bombs. Another formation of his test group, twenty-seven Dornier 17s, made up the rest of the attacking force. But where were the fighters?

If he had lost the fighters in the darkening sky, now misting up in the early evening, Rübensdörffer had also lost his way. The Dorniers which were assigned Biggin Hill as their target bombed West Malling instead. Although no sector station, West Malling was put out of operation for several days.

Rübensdörffer made an even more serious error. On descending through the mist he spotted an airfield which he believed to be Kenley. He was only four miles off target, but the field he saw was Croydon, ten miles from London. Hitler's standing order was that Greater London, London itself, was not to be bombed. He still hoped for a negotiated peace and to keep the English reprisal bombers away from German cities.

It was almost seven o'clock in the evening when the Me-110s began dropping bombs on Croydon from an altitude of two thousand feet. The Hurricanes of No. 111 Squadron, patrolling at ten thousand feet, plunged down to the attack. The alarming sudden appearance of the Hurricanes resulted in an almost random spilling of bombs. Although the airfield was struck, causing much destruction to hangars, workshops, and runways, bombs fell haphazardly across the Croydon area. Small war production factories were hit, but so was the Bourjois perfume factory. Sixty-two people died as a result of the bombardment, more than a hundred were injured, many seriously. Once again Rübensdörffer's unit had proved effective, even if in error.

But he himself was in trouble. As he tried to get away from the scene of the attack, a Hurricane caught up with his Messerschmitt. Try as he might he could not shake the British fighter, flown by pilot J. M. Thompson of No. 111 Squadron, as he attempted to speed over Kent and return to France. The Me-110 burst into flame, and still the Hurricane harried them.

Alan Christopher Deere, the indestructible New Zealander who, though shot down more than a half-dozen times, survived the war with a victory score of twenty-two. (IMPERIAL WAR MUSEUM, LONDON)

They had to land. He sought for a likely place in the fields of Kent. He jerked the plane over a small cottage that suddenly came into view, then over a gentle hill and toward a valley beyond. The Messerschmitt trailed sheets of flame and molten metal dripped in its path. And then it was finished for the commander of Erprobungsgruppe 210 as his blazing aircraft struck the earth. Five other Me-110s had also not returned after No. 111 Squadron's Hurricanes attacked them over Croydon. An Me-109 also was lost. The other aircraft of Test Group 210 raced for Calais.

In the twilight moments of the day's battles the smaller skirmishes scattered across the skies of Kent. On his second patrol of the day Flight Lieutenant Alan Deere in a Spitfire (No. 54 Squadron) had in headlong frustration pursued an Me-109 all the way across the English Channel to the Calais-Marck nest of the German fighters. When he sud-

A Spitfire, victim of an Me-109, goes down burning.
(H. J. NOWARRA)

denly realized what he had done, he was himself being stalked by Messerschmitts. Faster than the Spitfire, the German fighters swept into range.

"Bullets seemed to be coming from everywhere and pieces were flying off my aircraft," Deere told the story later. "My instrument panel was shattered, my eye was bleeding from a splinter, my watch had been shot clean off my wrist by an incendiary bullet which left a nice diagonal burn across my wrist and it seemed only a matter of moments before the end."

With his Merlin engine full out Deere raced for England, feeling that never had thirty miles of water seemed so expansive, nor had his Spitfire seemed so slow. But still the hunted, he reached the coast near Folkestone. The German Me-109s, unwilling to repeat his mistake, turned off and returned to Calais-Marck.

Deere was now only eight hundred feet above the ground, and within a minute or so after the enemy planes turned back his straining Merlin engine burst into flame.

"Desperately I tore my straps off, pulled back the hood and prepared to bail out. I was still doing about 300 miles an hour, so I pulled my stick back to get a bit more height. At about 1,500 feet I turned on my back and pushed the stick hard forward. I shot out a few feet and somehow became caught up by the bottom of my parachute. I twisted and turned, but wasn't able to get either in or out. The nose had now dropped below the horizontal and was pointing at the ground which appeared to be rushing up at a terrific speed."

The twisting, plunging Spitfire, now burning fiercely, carried Deere for some minutes when his parachute unsnagged from the seat and the pilot was blown backward along the fuselage. The tail struck his wrist and then he was clear of the plane. He pulled the ripcord.

"None too soon. I hadn't time to breathe a sigh of relief before I landed with a mighty thud in a plantation of thick shrubs." Deere's luck truly held, for his parachute had opened dangerously close to the ground—the shrubs broke the impact of his fall. In a nearby field his Spitfire demolished itself in flame and dust.

After his injuries had been attended to in the hospital, the chief surgeon called Deere's station commander to inform him that the pilot was safe.

In his relief Wing Commander Cecil Bouchier could only say, "Keep him there, he's costing us too many Spitfires!" On that August 15, 1940, Alan Deere—who had shot down his thirteenth German aircraft earlier in the day—had "bent" his fourth Spitfire.

The great air battles of the day ended, a day of very heavy fighting, like a summer storm with the fury spent and small flashes and distant thunder. For the Germans it had been the true Eagle Day, with all three *Luftflotten* taking part in 1786 sorties (to RAF Fighter Command's 974). It was not until much later that the participants realized that August 15, 1940, had been the most active day of the Battle of Britain. It had also been a decisive day. It finished Luftflotte 5 as a daylight threat to England and underscored the vulnerability of the Stuka and the Messerschmitt 110.

The battle had raged over a five-hundred-mile

The remains of an Me-109 brought down on August 15, 1940. Winston Churchill observed the battle in which this fighter participated.

(IMPERIAL WAR MUSEUM, LONDON)

front, from near Tynemouth in the north to Southampton in the southeast. This battle front, however, was three-dimensional and moved inland as well as vertically in a continually shifting pattern. The radar screens, in most instances, were capable of tracing this pattern for the sector stations, from which the sector controller could direct the individual squadrons. It was on this day that Göring ordered the attacks upon the radar stations to stop.

The excited, exhausted pilots of Fighter Command claimed 182 aircraft in the day's fighting. The five massive assaults had come so swiftly that in the confusion of battle several pilots claimed the same plane. The true figure was 89—though not as spectacular it is nonetheless a formidable figure, for many of the aircraft carried multiple crews. The Luftwaffe claimed 82 Spitfires and Hurricanes, plus 5 Curtiss Hawks (which were non-existent in the

RAF) and 14 additional aircraft: a total of 101 British planes. The RAF in fact lost 42 fighters (not counting those destroyed on the ground); but 17 pilots, like the indestructible Alan Deere, walked away from their crashed planes.

The bombing of Croydon, so near to central London, infuriated Hitler, who wanted to court-martial the hapless Oberst Paul Deichmann, who had initiated the savage fighting of the day with the Stukas. But this rage was forgotten in the rush of other, bigger matters. Hitler had the Eastern Front on his mind, although he continued discussing Sealion, the invasion of England. Preparations for the invasion must be ready by the end of August; the landings must be made by September 15. At the conference on July 21, 1940, Hitler had pointed out that among the important prerequisites was "complete mastery of the air."

On August 15, only two days after Eagle Day, the Luftwaffe may not have lost the Battle of Britain; but neither could it win it.

7

HELL'S CORNER

For all their vaunted Teutonic efficiency, the Germans were not very well served by their intelligence services, Abteilung 5, under the command of Major Josef Schmid, a non-flying friend of Jeschonnek. Ambitious, hard-working, and convivial, Schmid, who liked being called "Beppo," brought some organization to his not very efficient department with the introduction of new members, most of them men he could trust and who would not menace his position. But he fell into the usual trap of underestimating the British air potential and supplied his superiors with the kind of information they liked to hear. In July 1940 Schmid composed an intelligence paper, "Comparative Survey of Royal Air Force and Luftwaffe Striking Power." The gist of the paper was revealed in the third section, "Conclusion," which opened with the very words Göring wished to see: "The Luftwaffe is clearly superior to the RAF as regards strength, equipment, training, command, and location of bases."

Following the great engagements of August 15, the Luftwaffe High Command estimated, basing this figure on Schmid's reports and upon the reports of fighter "kills," that the Royal Air Force had only three hundred fighters on hand. There were, in fact, more than double that number of operational Hurricanes and Spitfires. As the battle became progressively attritional the Luftwaffe pilots grimly joked about those "last fifty Spitfires." Their High Command had assured them that the RAF was all

but depleted, though frequently many more than the last fifty met the German formations near the Channel day after day.

Schmid did not so much as mention the radar system (a subject which wouldn't have interested Göring in any case) and he oversold the German aircraft as compared with the British planes. For example, he noted in his "Comparative Survey," referring to the Hurricane and Spitfire, that "In view of their combat performance and the fact that they are not yet equipped with cannon guns both types are inferior to the Me-109, and particularly the Me-109F, while the individual Me-110 is inferior to *skillfully* handled Spitfires." The emphasis is Schmid's. So is the ignorance of the fact that the Me-109F was not in use by the operational units engaged in the Battle of Britain. The tale of the Stuka came to a sad ending over Britain. This aircraft too was overvalued by the Germans. It was a good close-support plane and capable of precision bombing, but was a deathtrap in aerial combat.

On Sunday, August 18, following a relatively quiet day, the pressure upon Fighter Command was resumed in the morning with heavy attacks upon airfields and some strikes upon radar stations. Kenley and Biggin Hill were severely hit with considerable damage especially at the former. Its being knocked out of operations for two days crippled Fighter Command in the Kenley sector.

In the afternoon there was a concentration of

attacks upon Coastal Command and Fleet Air Arm Stations off the south coast at Gosport, Thorney Island, and Ford. The formations were from Luftflotte 3, consisting of Ju-88s, Ju-87s, and great swarms of Me-109s. The Stukas dive-bombed Thorney Island. At the same time, to the northwest nearby Poling, with its radar installations, was attacked by Stukas of Stuka Geschwader 77. The radar station was knocked out for the rest of the month—and the Stuka was knocked out of the Battle of Britain. Tangling with Spitfires of No. 152 Squadron and Hurricanes of No. 43 Squadron, the Stukas paid for their success. Twelve of the twenty-eight Ju-87s dispatched by *StG* 77's first *Staffel* were destroyed, some falling to earth and others

A Spitfire goes down under Luftwaffe guns; although the plane was replaceable, the pilot, if injured or killed, was not. The Battle of Britain reached a critical phase during the daylight raids because of pilot shortage.
(NATIONAL ARCHIVES)

into the sea. Of the sixteen that managed to return to France, six were so badly shot up that they were of little further use. Another thirty were either lost or so severely damaged that they had to be junked. Over a period of just a few days the losses in Stukas all but wiped out an entire *Gruppe*. Richthofen withdrew his *Fliegerkorps* VIII from Cherbourg to the Pas de Calais area, awaiting the day when Sealion would be launched and there would no longer be an RAF. The Stukas could then be employed against the Royal Navy in the forthcoming invasion. Except for an aborted flurry at the end of the month, the Stuka appeared for the last time over England on August 18, 1940. Its legend was dead.

Mercifully bad flying weather closed in on the next day and for nearly a week only sporadic activity was possible. Both camps had time to consider their positions. The most serious problem confronting Air Chief Marshal Dowding was the shortage of experienced pilots. He was reluctantly given some from Bomber Command by the Air Ministry and the training period for new pilots was continued at two weeks instead of the customary four. It had been hoped that the four weeks' course would be reinstated, but the cost of the battle canceled that. Pilots were posted to front-line squadrons with merely ten or at best twenty hours of solo flying.

The strain on experienced pilots took its toll also and replacements were hard to find. For example, in the period from August 8–18 Fighter Command lost 154 pilots, either killed or wounded seriously enough to be out of action. In the same ten-day period only 63 new fighter pilots were graduated from the training schools. And it was Fighter Command that Göring had selected as the primary target of the Luftwaffe.

On the day following the Stuka slaughter the German Air Force High Command again assembled at Karinhall on August 19. Göring's temper had not improved since the last conference. His four-day timetable for the destruction of the defenses of south England was definitely off. Obviously someone was at fault; losses were too high. He listened to the complaints of the bomber commanders—the fighters, they argued, did not fly close enough to the bombers to give proper protection. By the time they arrived upon the scene, the British had swooped in and shot up the bomber formations.

The fighter commanders argued for the "free hunt" technique, which placed the fighters high above and around the bombers. This made it possible for them to achieve flexibility, important to a fighter, and not be chained to the slower bombers. This close-support tactic, it was argued by the German fighter commanders, sacrificed both fuel and the fighter's ability to move about the sky to trouble points.

But the bombers had been suffering terribly under Spitfire and Hurricane attacks. The fighter protection must be doubled, tripled, Göring insisted.

"We have reached the decisive period of the air war against England," Göring told them. "Our first aim is the destruction of the enemy's fighters. If they no longer take the air, we shall force them into battle by directing bomber attacks against targets within range of our fighters." The lesson of Luftflotte 5's misadventure had not been lost on Göring and the ravaged Stuka *Gruppen* of the day before had impressed him also.

"At the same time," Göring decreed further, "and on a growing scale, we must continue our activities against the ground organization of the enemy bomber units. Surprise attacks on the enemy aircraft industry must be made by day and by night. Once the enemy air force has been annihilated, our attacks will be directed as ordered against other vital targets."

This was a passing reference to Sealion, in which Göring had scant interest—and, though they would not have cared to inform him, in which his Luftwaffe High Command had little hope. Time was running out for Sealion, for the autumn days were fast approaching and the Channel would be impossible to cross even without RAF interference. The Royal Navy, still intact, would chop the invaders to bits—those who survived the treacherous Channel waters.

Coincidentally, on that same August 19, 1940, from his No. 11 Group headquarters at Uxbridge, Kent, Air Vice-Marshal Keith Park also issued orders. Having noted that the German attacks had been moving closer inland and with greater concentration upon airfields, Park instructed his controllers in the sector stations upon several points. The main gist was the preservation of pilots.

"Despatch fighters to engage large enemy formations over land or within gliding distance of the coast," Park emphasized. "During the next two or

three weeks we cannot afford to lose pilots through forced landings in the sea." The enemy bombers were the major threat. Little was gained by clashing with the Me-109s. "Against mass attacks coming inland despatch a minimum number of squadrons to engage enemy fighters. Our main object is to engage enemy bombers, particularly those approaching under the lowest cloud layer." These, of course, were frequently missed by radar and bombed with devastating accuracy.

When the weather finally cleared enough for full-scale operations on August 24, and continuing through September 6 (when Göring or Hitler issued another fatal decision), the airfields of No. 11 Group came under concentrated attack. The full

Air Vice-Marshal Sir Keith Park, commanding officer of No. 11 Group, whose squadrons were stationed in Kent, in southeast England, and over which most of the fierce fighting of the Battle of Britain occurred.
(IMPERIAL WAR MUSEUM, LONDON)

impact and ferocity of it almost succeeded in realizing Göring's dream of destroying Dowding's shaken Fighter Command.

Kentish skies became an expansive battleground, the setting for desperate encounters between the RAF and the Luftwaffe. In accordance with Park's order to keep the British pilots inland, whenever possible, the fighting occurred over the hop fields and apple orchards of Kent, which to the Germans in this period became known as "Hell's Corner." If the contending pilots suffered in the vicious battles, so did the people below upon whom the de-

Kentish skies became an expansive battleground: *a formation of He-111s approach their bomb run.*

(H. J. NOWARRA)

tritus of battle fell—shell casings, spent bullets, burning pieces of aircraft: the aircraft themselves and jettisoned bombs.

The Luftwaffe's primary targets for the next two weeks were Park's airfields, with emphasis upon the inner fields ringing London. Under Park's command were seven sector stations—Tangmere, Debden, Kenley, Biggin Hill, Hornchurch, North Weald, and Northolt—in southeast England. Twenty-one fighter squadrons were based on these airfields and the Hurricanes, the Spitfires, and the few Blenheims were flown by about four hundred pilots. Although in a pinch Park could request help from the other groups, it would have to be a tight pinch. Dowding did not want to leave his other sectors open to attack while their fighters were engaged in "Hell's Corner." Although the main blow was struck at

No. 11 Group, the Germans at the same time confused the picture by diversionary feints, attacks upon ports, minelaying, as well as night raids upon various industrial targets. Nor were No. 11 Group's airfields the only ones attacked during the period August 24–September 6. They were, however, the worst hit. And its stations lay within range of the Messerschmitt 109s escorting the bombers.

That there was a new tactic was obvious to the British pilots when they met the German formations head on. The Me-109s outnumbered the German bombers about three to one—and the fighters all but clung to their charges. Breaking through such defenses was costly for the Hurricane and Spitfire pilots, if not impossible. Sheer courage was not enough and despite nearly superhuman effort and sacrifice, the bombers frequently managed to get through.

Of the sector stations, Biggin Hill, just to the south of London, sustained the worst attacks. The sector station had been hit heavily on Friday, August 30—which opened what became known as "the Bad Weekend" at Biggin Hill. The new German tactics of mass formations—few bombers and many fighters—of feints along a broad front, confused the tracking of the radar stations as well as the ground observers. It was difficult to determine, once the plots began coming in, just where the main effort would be.

It was around this time that Park instituted the now famed "Tally Ho!" procedure, which he hoped might clarify the situation. Formation leaders were to sing out this cry upon spotting German formations, along with the approximate number and type of aircraft, the altitude, course, and position of the formation when sighted. This actual visual information would help to prevent the dispatch of a single squadron of twelve Spitfires to intercept a hundred enemy aircraft, most of them fighters.

In the battles with such formations, the point of attrition became critical for Dowding. This was aggravated by the onslaught on the fighter bases and especially so in the case of the sector stations. Biggin Hill's Bad Weekend illustrates what might have been had the attacks continued systematically. Friday's raid was followed by an even heavier one on Saturday. Late in the afternoon low-flying Dorniers—only eight in number, but carrying thousand-pound bombs—slipped by the Observer Corps, radar, and the "Tally Ho!" Biggin Hill, which lay on the route to London, was attacked from the north, an approach which misled the defenses, which generally looked for the German planes to come from either the south or the east. The Dorniers flew up the Thames toward London, then turned sharply to approach Biggin Hill, still under repair from the previous day's attack as well as the morning's raid.

This afternoon raid was devastatingly effective. The bombs from the Dorniers cut across the main part of the installation, cutting power lines and gas and water mains, demolishing workshops, gutting hangars and storage facilities. The worst was a direct hit upon the crowded Operations Room; the projectile ripped through the hutment's roof, struck a steel safe, and deflected into the adjoining room before shattering with fulminating shock.

The building plunged into darkness and the air filled with debris, pulverized plaster and shards of eviscerating glass and steel. Instinctively, perhaps, Group Captain Richard Grice had ordered everyone in the Operations Room to get under tables as soon as he heard the approaching whistle of the bomb. Otherwise casualties would have been higher. As

An RAF Operations Room, from which fighters in the air could be controlled from the ground by radar and radio. WAAFs (Women's Auxiliary Air Force) keep track of oncoming German raiders on the mapboard.
(IMPERIAL WAR MUSEUM, LONDON)

it was, more than sixty died or were seriously wounded in the attack. The women of the WAAF inside the Operations Room acquitted themselves admirably, without panic and with a good deal of courage. They continued to carry on with their duties even though services were seriously curtailed. Sergeant Helen Turner and Corporal Elspeth Henderson remained at their phones despite the damage of the direct hit.

Other sector stations were hit on the same day—Duxford of No. 12 Group and two others of Park's No. 11 Group: Debden and Hornchurch. During the raid on the latter Alan Deere experienced another of his incredible adventures. Around the same time that Biggin Hill was being attacked, more Dorniers swung in over Hornchurch. All the aircraft had been hastily scrambled when it became clear that the sector station would be the target. Just as the Dorniers appeared over the field, No. 54 Squadron was taking off. Two sections raced into the air before the bombs began falling. The last section of three planes, led by Alan Deere, was not so fortunate.

The three Spitfires were under way when the first detonations ripped the runway. With the shouting of the controller in their ears and the sound of bomb bursts around them the Spitfires swung into the wind. Deere had the nose of his plane pointed in the right direction, only to find that one of the planes in his section blocked his way.

"Get the hell out of the way, Red Two," he shouted and gunned the engine. Red Two jinked aside and he too had his tail up and the engine roaring. Then all three Spitfires sprinted into the wind: they were air-borne. In seconds they were off the ground and their wheels began retracting into the aircraft. It was at this moment that the bomb hit.

"One moment they were about twenty feet up in close formation," wrote pilot Richard Hillary, who saw the incident, "the next catapulted apart as though on elastic." A bomb had erupted directly under the three planes. Deere's aircraft was thrown up and over on its back before crashing to earth upside down. For a hundred yards the Spitfire crunched and screeched along the runway before jolting to a stop, reeking of highly flammable fuel.

The number three man, Pilot Officer Eric Edsall, had fallen to earth right side up, but with such

force that leg injuries made it impossible for him to walk. He crawled toward Deere's Spitfire, which showed no sign of life. The number two man of Red Section, Sergeant J. Davies, was simply blown out of the airfield, across the boundary fence, where he landed without injury although the Spitfire's tail snapped off. He was missing for a long time that day, for in order to get back onto the airfield he had to walk for miles along the fence.

When Edsall reached Deere's overturned Spitfire he was amazed to find his flight leader still alive,

Prime Minister Winston Churchill on a visit to the Vauxhall Motors plant in Luton, Befordshire. Appropriately, the tank was known as the "Churchill."
(HOME COUNTIES NEWSPAPERS, LTD.)

although trapped inside the plane. Deere's most serious injury—which looked worse than it was—was a badly gouged head and the loss of some hair. With Deere pushing from inside and the crippled Edsall pulling from outside, they succeeded in forcing the cockpit door of the Spitfire. Fearing fire, they got away from the plane as quickly as they could hobble. Deere helped Edsall to Station Sick

Quarters. By the next day all three pilots were ready for action again.

The long day came to a close with a night bombing of Liverpool. The technique of night fighting (with the use of radar) was but a primitive idea and there was little that could be done at night, except with searchlight and antiaircraft guns. It was yet another pressure upon Fighter Command. August ended with the heaviest losses for Fighter Command on any single day of the Battle of Britain: thirty-nine fighter planes were destroyed by the Luft-

Luton after a visit from the Luftwaffe; although an aircraft factory had been the target, bombs fell on the city itself and upon the Vauxhall factory, setting some oil barrels aflame.

(HOME COUNTIES NEWSPAPERS, LTD.)

waffe. Fourteen pilots were killed, in addition to those injured or killed in the bombings themselves. The cost to the Luftwaffe, night and day, was forty-one aircraft. The loss ratios were less disproportionate, however than in July, a bad sign for Dowding's Fighter Command. Within days a serious crisis must develop, the tired Air Chief Marshal realized. The "few" were becoming too few.

II

There were no front lines in the sense that they had existed in France. And despite the aerial aspects of the Battle of Britain, the fighting and bombing took their toll on the ground also. On the day that the Bad Weekend at Biggin Hill began, Friday, August 30, 1940, the German raiders pushed through the interceptors and reached the city of Luton, some thirty miles northwest of London. Although some of the bombers jettisoned their bombs while under British fighter attack, the others found Luton at around four in the afternoon.

Luton was a manufacturing town, its main staple being the hat industry. It was also the site of Vauxhall Motors, Ltd., which turned out trucks and the so-called "Churchill" tank. Percival Aircraft, Ltd., manufactured training aircraft (the Oxford and the Proctor) as well as the de Havilland Mosquito. Also located in Luton were the Skefko Ball Bearing Company and Hayward-Tyler & Co., Ltd., which built engines for Admiralty barges.

War had come to Luton on the first day of the war when the city was designated a reception area (defined as "not immune to danger but an improbable target") for evacuees, mainly children, expectant mothers, and the blind from London. Besides the refugees from London (who eventually became homesick and returned) other signs of the war were seen in the narrow streets of Luton. These were smoke screen generators in which sawdust and tar blocks were burned to obscure Luton from possible German bombers. The generators succeeded primarily in coating the hills and homes of Luton with a black oily deposit. Later oil burners were installed for the purpose and were not as dirt-depositing.

But except for such inconveniences, and the alarums of the air raid alarms for raids that never materialized, Luton remained out of the front line until August 30.

Sometimes after, a German communiqué was issued which read: "A squadron of our bombers in daylight on August 23 [sic] raided a plane parts factory in Luton, northwest of London. The first aircraft initiated a great fire, and subsequent aircraft were thus guided to the target, which they completely destroyed."

This is not quite what happened. The bombs fell

A lone German bomber swooped down and dropped its bomb upon a factory in Luton—a factory devoted *to Luton's major industry, the manufacturing of women's hats.* (HOME COUNTIES NEWSPAPERS, LTD.)

first upon the airport, but did not focus there. The explosions ripped across Vauxhall, moving ever closer into the city itself; the bus depot was struck, killing one employee, and a double-decker bus was flung up into the roof of the garage, where it dangled over the rubble. The string of bombs "walked across" Luton, making shambles of the little brick dwellings (most of them belonging to the poor). Bombs even fell upon Vauxhall's cricket ground; the duds gave the bomb disposal crews much work to do.

It was a shocking new experience for everyone. A six-year-old boy ran into his grandmother's house to tell her of his adventure. The very earth had opened up and lifted him right into the air! When he took her to show her the place, another boy was found there dead. In all, 53 people were killed in Luton that day and 140 injured.

Vauxhall, not a plane parts factory, as the German communiqué claimed, was worst hit. As for the "great fire," while it served admirably as a guide, it was merely some oil barrels at Vauxhall. It did little damage, nor was it a great loss. The damage to the truck assembly factory was more serious, but within a short time even this was cleared away.

Throughout the rest of the war Luton was treated

A not unusual pastoral scene in Kent during the summer of 1940. A Spitfire has just destroyed a German plane, which has come to rest in a sheep meadow.
(SYNDICATION INTERNATIONAL)

to such harsh though not very decisive raids (including some with V-2 bombs toward the close of the war). On October 15, 1940, as the Battle of Britain itself was coming to an end (at least in its intensive phases), the Luton sirens sounded. Shortly after, a lone German bomber appeared high in the sky and dropped a bomb. What its target could have been must remain one of the mysteries of the Second World War. The bomb struck a factory, true, but it was the W. O. Scales and Co., Ltd., a hat factory.

The sportive face of war is no less tragic than its grimmer visage. The explosion of the bomb blasted sewing machines in every direction: some sharp fragments even went into the factory adjoining and killed a young bride who had just come to work that morning. Ribbons, hats, brick, wood, and mortar intermingled in a colorful outburst of swirling death. New Bedford Road brightened when its trees were

suddenly festooned with gaily colored ribbons. But out of this ludicrous gaiety came thirteen dead, most of these dead being women or young girls employed by Scales. There were in addition thirty-five wounded. It took two and a half hours to dig young Tommy Walker out of the debris. The fourteen-year-old boy kept up the spirits of his rescuers by singing all the while.

But Luton was not in Hell's Corner and the people of Kent, who were subjected to much more of such accidental bombings, crashes, and shootings, remained generally in good spirits also. The continual air raid warnings took their toll in loss of sleep as well as loss of production. Watching dogfights even became an interesting pastime, once the initial fears were overcome. This came to be known as "goofing," that is, instead of taking shelter, you goofed.

Few people who watched the fight contrails realized that the spent shells, the lead that went astray, and parts of aircraft came down around them. This was one of the reasons for the tin hats issued to civilians. Jettisoned bombs or out-of-control aircraft, German or British, caused the most frightful, because of its unexpectedness, havoc. Death literally, and senselessly, dropped out of the skies.

But the nature of war had changed so much in a few months and if the sky over your home became a battleground, then your back garden became a graveyard. There was always the chance of a sudden, haphazard, violent end. There were also thousands of close calls which filled the papers with human interest stories. For example, the mother at 4 Hardy Street, Maidstone, Kent, almost every day put her baby out into the garden behind the house to get the sun. On this one Thursday morning she just hadn't gotten around to it. Meanwhile the air had begun to boil over Hell's Corner. The German raiders were heading for Croydon, Biggin Hill, and Eastchurch, among other airfields. It was over Kent that most were intercepted.

Maidstone, where the main office of the *Kent Messenger* is located, afforded many a fine view of the battles. Members of the paper's staff watched from the rooftop of their building. A Spitfire had got onto the tail of a Messerschmitt 110. The battle began high and gyrated and twisted until it was barely a thousand feet over the ground. The Messerschmitt spurted smoke and fire. It lurched and,

War souvenirs in your back yard. These natives of Kent examine what remained of a German bomber after it came to earth. The "thumbs up" sign was as character-istic as Churchill's V (for Victory) sign.

(FOX PHOTOS, LTD.)

obviously in serious trouble, began to fall. As the Spitfire pulled away, a single parachute blossomed under the burning German plane. It was then only about four hundred feet up. The German landed on a rooftop in Hope Street, breaking both legs.

The burning plane continued on to Hardy Street, crashed against the corner of the house at number 4, taking a gable of one room with it, and then smashed into the garden. The baby was not there but in the kitchen and escaped injury. Many staff members of the *Messenger* ran to the scene of the crash to find the Me-110 burning fiercely in the garden. But there was an additional danger: the heat of the flames caused the machine-gun bullets still in the plane to explode, spewing them in all directions. Despite this the fire department was soon on the job to put out the fire.

III

Meanwhile, as German invasion barges began to accumulate along the coast, Fighter Command was in a seriously depleted state. And it was Park's No. 11 Group in Kent which had taken the brunt of the German attack.

"I was worried daily from July to September by a chronic shortage of trained fighter pilots and it was not until the battle was nearly lost that the Air Staff of the Air Ministry assisted by borrowing pilots from Bomber Command and from the Royal Navy," Park later recalled, not without some bitterness.

The Air Ministry, Park felt, was not attuned to the demands of a full-scale war in the air. Later, when he was relieved of his command in the post-Battle of Britain shake-up, Park learned that the

The fortunes of air war; an Me-110 has crashed into Hardy Street, Kent, after a losing battle with a Spitfire. (KENT MESSENGER)

training schools were operating only at two thirds of capacity and "following peace-time routines, being quite unaware of the grave shortage of pilots in Fighter Command." Why this should have been true is difficult to determine today. The Air Ministry viewed the Battle of Britain in long-range terms and may have been inclined to see the problems of Dowding and Park as merely parts of the total problem. It was, too, guided by political considerations which would hardly have interested the hard-pressed Park. It was not a simple situation and was crosscut by personalities and the desperation of the times.

Park recalled another difficulty: ". . . when the German Air Force concentrated on bombing my fighter aerodromes, I could get such little help from Air Ministry to repair the bomb damage that I had to borrow some thousands of troops from the British Army to fill in the bomb craters to keep the aerodromes serviceable. For doing so I was severely criticised by the Air Ministry at the time for accepting Army assistance. Had my fighter aerodromes been put out of action, the German Air Force would have won the battle by the 15th September 1940."

The pressures upon Park mounted daily—and each day, several times a day, he was summoned from his office to No. 11 Group's Operations Room

Cottages in a Kentish village after a German bombing raid. This frequently occurred when Luftwaffe crews jettisoned their bombs to escape RAF fighters.
(KENT MESSENGER)

as soon as unidentified aircraft were detected assembling over France.

"On entering the underground operations room," Park relates, "I would examine the plotting table which showed [the] enemy dispositions and [British] fighter squadrons dispatched. Before dispatching further squadrons I would have to decide whether the German aircraft were on a training flight or a reconnaissance flight or gathering for a feint attack by fighter sweep to draw my squadrons into the air and away from the direction of a coming bomb attack.

"Having decided that the radar indicated the beginning of a bomb attack I would dispatch more squadrons and bring others to a high state of readiness in preparation for takeoff." The standard daily state of readiness was: five squadrons (of No. 11 Group) were at "Stand-by," meaning that their planes could be air-borne within two minutes; ten squadrons were in "Readiness" (takeoff time five minutes); five squadrons were ready for takeoff in from ten to fifteen minutes and declared "Available." Another five squadrons were "Released," free for the day to rest the pilots and carry on maintenance on the aircraft.

As for the battle itself: "My plan was to make 'Forward Interception' as near as possible to the coast. My aim was always to intercept the German main attack with the maximum number of fighter squadrons that were available. My Spitfire squadrons were directed against the German fighter escort and the Hurricane squadrons were directed against the enemy bombers."

But Park encountered yet another trial, a theoretical disagreement as well as, perhaps, a personality clash. This was with the commander of No. 12

Air Vice-Marshal Trafford Leigh-Mallory, commander of No. 12 Group, which shared the defense of Kent and London with Park's No. 11 Group.
(IMPERIAL WAR MUSEUM, LONDON)

Group, Air Vice-Marshal Trafford Leigh-Mallory, whose command lay to the north of Park's. "Number 12 Group," Park has written, ". . . was frequently called upon to cover my fighter aerodromes around London which were quite defenceless when I had sent all my squadrons to intercept near the coast. Number 12 Group, however, always delayed dispatching its reinforcements in order to assemble wings of four to six squadrons which went off on roving sweeps from the South East of England, and on several occasions allowed my fighter aerodromes to be heavily bombed."

This disagreement between Park and Leigh-Mallory was to have its repercussions after the height of the Battle had passed. Dowding characteristically remained aloof from the argument, feeling that each group leader must be permitted to act without interference from him. Members of the Air Staff, however, upon visiting some of the fighter stations, listened to the pilots and junior officers of No. 12 Group complaining about not being permitted to take part in the battles over Kent because they were not given sufficient time in which to form. Park saw no point in calling upon No. 12

Group (although he did, of course) only to have it form into wings—"Balbos" they were called, after Italo Balbo, the Italian aviator who had led a mass flight from Italy to Chicago in 1933. By the time the wing had formed up the enemy had attacked and left. But when one of the wings, especially the Duxford wing led by Douglas Bader, did succeed in engaging the German formations, Park admitted (although not without a small barb), "that had already been attacked by 11 Group forward squadrons, they were successful." But there was a sentiment in the Air Ministry that the fighter operations over Kent were not efficiently co-ordinated (rather humanly impossible at the time) and that something must be done as soon as it was politic. The result was that in November Dowding was shunted off to an innocuous job as a British representative visiting aircraft factories in the United States. His position at the helm of Fighter Command was taken over by Sholto Douglas, who had served as a fighter pilot in the First World War and was, during the Battle of Britain, deputy Chief of the Air Staff.

Park, after only eight months, was "posted" to Flying Training Command and command of No. 11 Group was taken over by Leigh-Mallory. Evidently the latter's "big wing" theories had impressed Douglas and Archibald Sinclair, Secretary of State for Air. These changes, of which very little was made at the time, did not come about until late in November 1940. Few Britons realized that Dowding and Park had in fact won them the Battle of Britain.

IV

Sealion could not take place unless air superiority over the Channel was secured, and that was possible only by the destruction of the Royal Air Force— and by early September that seemed feasible. Not, however, to the Germans, who, though noting the claims of the Luftwaffe, were puzzled by the appearance of Spitfires and Hurricanes supposedly no longer existent according to the intelligence of Beppo Schmid. On September 3 German Intelligence Chief Schmid estimated, under pressure from Kesselring and Sperrle, that perhaps Fighter Command had only 100 fighters left—or maybe they had 350. Meanwhile hundreds of invasion barges lay in

Kent was "Hell's Corner" as much for the Luftwaffe as for the RAF. A Do-17 burns on the beach in Kent, *like the Luftwaffe its back broken in an attempt to destroy the RAF.* (FOX PHOTOS, LTD.)

French and Belgian ports in readiness for Sealion—and these were suffering under the attacks of British Bomber Command. The earliest date for the sailing of the invasion fleet, Hitler had informed them on the same day, "has been fixed for September 20, and that of the landing for September 21." The German High Command was also informed that the launching of the attack upon the British Isles (through Kent) would occur "on D-Day minus 10," presumably therefore on September 11.

But the Luftwaffe was faced with eliminating the RAF, which theoretically should have been all but wiped out. Schmid did not know that the attacks upon the forward airfields had done extensive damage to five of them and knocked out two, Manston and Lympne, so effectively that they were unusable by fighter aircraft for several days. Six out of Park's seven sector stations had also been hit, with Biggin Hill forced to evacuate two of its three squadrons. In the period from August 24 through September 6 Fighter Command had lost 295 Spitfires and Hurricanes, with 171 severely damaged. In the same period replacements (new and repaired aircraft) numbered 269. But the most serious factor was the loss of pilots: in this same two-week period 103 pilots were dead or missing and 128 were wounded

seriously enough to be taken out of the Battle. At this rate of loss—an average of 120 pilots a week—Dowding would shortly have no Fighter Command.

Inexperienced pilots were too often lost on their first patrols; veteran pilots were exhausted, jumpy, and vulnerable. The gay young fighter pilot was no more. They were raw-nerved, gray-faced, listless, filled with that hatred that Bader described: "We hated those aeroplanes with their iron crosses and their crooked swastikas flying into our English sky. . . ." Only now it was goaded by desperation. The younger pilots were shocked upon seeing their seniors shooting at Germans in parachutes. This was considered a "Hunnish trick" and not cricket. But it was done.

For all their fatigue, despite the shortage of pilots, Fighter Command continued to intercept the German formations—much to the Luftwaffe's consternation. They were being assured that there was no RAF left. They had no idea, however, how close Schmid was to the truth.

The Luftwaffe High Command then on September 3, 1940, in their conference at The Hague, came to a grand decision. They were certain it would wipe out Fighter Command completely. And as with so many of the Nazi Grand Decisions, it saved the enemy.

8

"THE GREATEST DAY"

On September 4, 1940, the day following Göring's meeting with his High Command at The Hague when he had resolved upon a change in Luftwaffe tactics, Hitler spoke on the occasion of the opening of the *Winterhilfe* ("Winter Relief") campaign at the Sportpalast. The majority of his audience consisted of nurses and social workers concerned with *Winterhilfe*.

Hitler was in a rare sardonic, threatening mood—and his audience, including the angels of mercy, responded accordingly to his outbursts.

"In England," he told them, "they're filled with curiosity and keep asking, 'Why doesn't he come?'

"Be calm," Hitler confided, mockery in his voice; the audience tittered. "He's coming! He's coming!"

Hitler's audience responded thrillingly, encouraging him to speak with his customary mastery bordering on hysteria. When his listeners, most of them women, became quiet again Hitler waxed solemn. Winston Churchill, "that noted war correspondent," was "demonstrating his new brain child, the night air raid. Mr. Churchill is carrying out these raids not because they promise to be highly effective, but because his Air Force cannot fly over Germany in daylight."

German planes flew over England every day, Hitler told them. "Whenever the Englishman sees a light, he drops a bomb . . . on residential districts, farms, and villages."

The very air was charged in the Sportpalast as Hitler came to the point of his speech. "When the British Air Force drops two or three or four thousand kilograms of bombs, then we will in one night drop a hundred and fifty, two hundred and thirty, two hundred, or four hundred thousand kilograms—"

Great waves of applause interrupted Hitler at this point.

"When they declare," he shrieked, "that they will increase their attacks on our cities, then we will raze their cities to the ground!"

The audience rose to its feet, screaming, applauding. Their dedication to mankind did not include the British, the French, the Dutch, the Poles.

"The hour will come," Hitler promised in conclusion, "when one of us will break—and it will not be National Socialist Germany!"

"Never! Never!" screamed the nurses, leaping to their feet again, shouting, nearly hysterical, approving and adoring.

Hitler was in his own way approving of the Luftwaffe's decision of the previous day. The major target of the German Air Force would be London. The fiction of "only purely military targets" was ended. The war between the soldiers was over, it would now become a war between peoples. The civilian no longer enjoyed bystander status: modern war had "officially" taken on a new, deadly posture. Perhaps it had always been there but finally no one pretended. The simple "art of war" was revealed for what it was—and is—the technology of slaughter. This great truth may very well be Hitler's contribution to mankind; he had little else to offer.

II

The fateful decision to bomb London came about by accident. On the night of August 24 (this was the day on which the British airfields first came under heavy attack also) German aircraft dispatched to bomb an aircraft factory at Rochester and oil storage tanks at Thames Haven made a slight error in navigation. As a result bombs fell upon London for the first time since 1918, when the Gotha bombers had flown over the city. Great fires were kindled in London Wall and Fore Street; other sections of the city and its outskirts received isolated bombs. In Bethnal Green about a hundred dwellings were destroyed. Militarily practically nothing was accomplished, except that the old warrior, Churchill, demanded a reprisal raid on Berlin.

Bomber Command did not view this request with equanimity. The Luftwaffe could reach London from just across the Channel, but it was a six-hundred-mile trip—one way—to Berlin. Except for psychological effect, Bomber Command saw little of value in striking the German capital. The long distance precluded heavy bomb loads, for a good deal of the weight carried by the bombers would have to include fuel. But Churchill persisted—as did public sentiment—and on the night of August 25/26 eighty-one British bombers took off for Berlin. These were the Wellingtons, Whitleys, and Hampdens of Nos. 3, 4, and 5 Groups respectively. Of these, twenty-nine aircraft (of Nos. 44, 49, 50, 58, 61, 83, and 99 Squadrons) claimed to have bombed Berlin. The operation was greatly hampered by a thick cloud down to two thousand feet. Twenty-seven other aircraft reached Berlin but, unable to identify their targets, did not bomb; of these, twenty-one returned to England with their bombs and six jettisoned them into the sea. Eighteen bombers struck at alternative targets. Seven were forced to turn back because of mechanical troubles. Five aircraft were lost—three of which were ditched in the sea and their crews rescued.

According to German sources only ten bombers actually dropped bombs in what might have been considered industrial target areas. The rest of the bombs scattered through the city. If it had proved a not very successful mission, this first attack on the German capital came as a distinct shock to Berliners. They had been promised by Göring himself that no British aircraft would ever appear over Germany. The effect was minimal, but the implications were appalling.

Three nights later the British bombers came again and for the first time in history German civilians were killed in Berlin. Ten were dead and twenty-nine injured in the very heart of the Reich. The headlines of Berlin's newspapers read: COWARDLY BRITISH ATTACK! A popular epithet for the crews of Bomber Command was "British Air Pirates." It was a curiously unrealistic reaction to the facts of war—as if Germany could rightfully anticipate half a war.

So it was with these bombings of the very heart of the Reich in mind that Hitler promised, threatened, and exhorted. When he pledged, "He's coming!" Hitler alluded to Sealion, for even as he spoke the barges and other invasion craft converged upon ports along the coast from the Netherlands to northern France.

The stimuli for the Luftwaffe's shift from the airfields to London were not simple. It would be an overstatement to say that the plain and simple motive was Hitler's mad desire (though he was capable of it) to retaliate to Churchill's retaliation. Even Hitler from time to time harkened to professional military counsel. It was goading to have the British bombers over the Reich, but they were in truth doing little real damage to the war machine. Göring believed that with Fighter Command all but finished an attack upon London and all it symbolized to the British would bring out the few remaining fighters which he was assured Dowding had pulled back out of Kent. With London just within range of the Me-109s it would be possible to lure the last Spitfires and Hurricanes into the battle and finish them off. Göring was reasonably certain—and Beppo Schmid had concurred—that most of the airfields of Kent were finished. They required no further attention.

This was the first of two misconceptions. True, Park's No. 11 Group was in poor shape, but it was still deployed throughout Kent. Another two weeks of the kind of pounding it had taken might very well have finished it off. But when the decision was made to make London the major target of the Luftwaffe Park still had his squadrons—they were under strength, they were at nerves' end, they were battle-wearied, but they were there.

The other misconception concerned the Londoners themselves. If the attack were mounted upon the densely populated capital and if it were razed, as Hitler had promised the nurses in the Sportpalast, then the "warmonger" Churchill would be forced

had ordered Paris stripped of all its finest statuary. Among these was an especially fine one of Moses which he had placed in his home. One day, so the tale went, Hitler was found on his knees before the statue of Moses saying, "Oh, Moses, tell me, tell me how you got your people over that little bit of water."

The British had no illusions—they knew that if Hitler could possibly cross, he would. Grim preparations were under way, including a fiendish de-

Lockheed Hudsons on patrol over the English Channel. The first American aircraft to go into RAF service, the Hudson was a versatile plane of all work: photog- *raphy and reconnaissance plane, fighter and bomber. British crews called it "Old Boomerang."*

(IMPERIAL WAR MUSEUM, LONDON)

by his own people to sue for a *Pax Germanica*. There would be no need for Sealion, a roseate, though nagging, consideration that Hitler nurtured. It was an idea which Admiral Raeder greatly admired. He had come to detest that English Channel, as did the pilots of the Luftwaffe, who referred to it as the *Shite Kanal*. The concept of a large-scale amphibious operation was regarded with suspicion by the landlocked Germans.

It was around this time that a revealing story was making the rounds of the English pubs, where the natives gathered to enjoy their bitters and bore each other with their bomb stories. This story, however, had to do with Hitler and his problem. He

vice which Churchill found good. Along the southern coast of England, from Beachy Head to Weymouth —the finest landing grounds—a method had been devised to pump oil and petrol into the water. As the first wave of German invasion barges approached this area a single Blackburn Skua dive bomber, piloted by one "Nobby" Clarke, was to flash over the treated waters and drop incendiaries. The invading Germans would be met by a wall of flame. Smaller aircraft, including de Havilland Tiger Moths (ordinarily used as primary trainers), would further harass the invaders with anti-personnel bombs.

It was a grand, if rather horrifying, conception

although never actually put to use—except in one practice session and in various rumors. There were other arrangements awaiting the invaders. The sea approaches were mined, the beaches bristled with barbed wire, the Home Guard was armed with everything from breech-loading rifles of First World War vintage sent by the United States to simple clubs. The doughty Islanders awaited Hitler's coming. Churchill had even prepared a slogan which, like the burning seas device, was never implemented: "You can always take one with you."

For weeks the Photographic Reconnaissance Unit, using the American-built Lockheed Hudson as well as Spitfires, kept a wary camera eye on the Channel coast. The count of invasion barges rose from day to day; to these were added motorboats and other vessels moving from the North Sea toward the Channel ports. At Ostend, for example, there were eighteen barges on August 31. By September 6 the photographs revealed no less than two hundred. The Combined Intelligence Committee in London, after assessing the portents, issued an invasion alert. GHQ, Home Forces alerted its units with the code word "Cromwell," indicating that invasion was expected imminently. In some parts of England Home Guard commanders summoned their members by ringing church bells, thus giving rise to the rumors that parachutists had begun descending upon Britain and that German invasion boats were already approaching the English coast.

That was the mood on Saturday, September 7, 1940, in Britain: some confusion but all in readiness. To Park in No. 11 Group headquarters it promised to be a day like all of the others, with his afflicted airfields heavily attacked and his pilots further taxed. Across the Channel—though Park did not know this until it was released via a radio news broadcast—Göring had arrived at the Pas de Calais. Setting up his headquarters at Cap Blanc-Nez he announced that he had "taken over personal command of the Luftwaffe in its war against England." In his private train Göring brought his personal cooks, a stock of wines, his doctor, his valet, and his nurse.

As Park braced himself for the next round of blows at his sector stations, a massive raid began forming up over Calais. But it was London which was the target and it caught Fighter Command off guard. The first full-scale bombing attack on London

began shortly after five in the afternoon: more than three hundred bombers (Ju-88s, He-111s, and Do-17s), escorted by six hundred fighters (Me-109s and 110s), almost a thousand aircraft, converged on the city.

Although there were interceptions, the change in target did confuse the controllers and the heavy fighter protection interfered with the British attack on the bombers. London's inadequate antiaircraft guns could not stop the bombers either, flying as

An He-111 hovers over the Thames, London, September 7, 1940—the day the Luftwaffe diverted its attentions from the RAF fighter stations to London.
(IMPERIAL WAR MUSEUM, LONDON)

they were at altitudes between seventeen thousand and twenty thousand feet. Tons of bombs rained down upon London—the docks, the Woolwich arsenal, the oil tanks, and other military targets were hit and raged into flame. Bombs fell also on the streets of East End, with its clutter of dwellings —now hardly better than slums—dating from the early Victorian period. The heavily populated streets filled with pitiable rubble, dazed refugees, and the dead.

The fires ignited in the first attack blazed well into the night, lighting the way for the night bombers. While the fire brigades, comprised of great numbers of auxiliaries who had never fought a fire, attempted to contend with the out-of-control conflagrations, the German bombers returned to drop additional bombs into the burning areas.

By midnight London was ablaze with nine "hundred-pump" fires (a thirty-pump fire was considered a very big fire). In the Surrey Docks there were two large fires (one 300- and the other 130-pump); there were a half-dozen hundred-pump fires at Bishopsgate Goods Yard and other points along the docks. The heat from the Quebec Yard of the Surrey Docks became so intense it set the wooden

London burns after a Luftwaffe bombing.
(NATIONAL ARCHIVES)

blocks in the roadways ablaze. Paint blistered off the fireboats three hundred yards distant in the Thames.

At the Woolwich arsenal (200-pump) the firemen fought the fires among boxes of ammunition and crates of nitroglycerin. But the docks storing more conventional stock gave the most trouble. Tea, it was soon learned, produced a blaze which was "sweet, sickly and intense"; one fireman thought it ludicrous to be pouring *cold* water on *hot* tea. Liquefied sugar burned fiercely on the surface of the water. Burning rubber released dense black smoke and asphyxiated the firemen. Cans of paint burst, spraying white-hot flame into the air, coating the fire pumps with varnish—which took weeks to clean off. From a spice storage dock fires carried

pepper into the air, making it almost impossible to breathe. To the firemen, inhaling the peppered air was almost like breathing flame itself. And great stores of rum too created difficulties: the casks themselves burst with bomblike intensity and blazing streams of grog poured out of the warehouses into the streets. Grain warehouses burned violently and filled the air with swarms of black flies; hundreds of rats ran in the street. The burned wheat left a residue—"a sticky mess that pulls your boots off."

"The fire was so huge," one of the fire fighters later recalled, "that we could do little more than make a feeble attempt to put it out. The whole of that warehouse was a raging inferno, against which were silhouetted groups of pigmy firemen directing their futile jets at the wall of flame. . . ."

A stretcher-bearer stationed at the Redriff School in the dock area (portions of which were poor residential sections) thought "it looked one flaming mass and the flames were terrifically high. To us it seemed a remarkable thing that people could get out of that area, and when we saw—when we saw the people come streaming down from dockland we were absolutely amazed. They seemed to come like an army marching and running from the area. The people coming from down town [Bermondsey, an inhabited strip between the Surrey Docks and the Thames River] looked in a very, very bad condition, they were dirty, dishevelled and hurrying to get away."

Not all got away, however, and in the attacks of September 7/8 about three hundred Londoners died and over a thousand were seriously injured. But these impressive figures, and the even more impressive fires in eastern London, were not acquired without cost to the Luftwaffe. Although Dowding's Fighter Command had been prepared for a continuation of the attacks on the airfields, it had sent fighters to intercept the mass German formations. Among the most effective was the hard-fighting No. 303 Squadron (Polish), which ripped into the German swarms with cavalrylike ferocity to get at the Dorniers. Corporal S. Wojtowicz, although he succeeded in shooting down a Dornier, found little to exult over. "I turned back from the chase but I was returning with a heavy heart, in spite of my victories, for the whole eastern suburb of London seemed to be burning." It recalled his homeland to Wojtowicz when he had left it a year before.

The switch to London brought a greater burden of responsibility to the German fighters. They were expected to furnish close escort for the bombers, but the RAF pilots avoided the German fighters to slaughter the bombers. Here the Me-109s are readied for the trip across the Channel: arming up, strapping the pilot's boots, and, finally, closing the canopy and pulling the chock from under the wheel. The "arched cat" insignia belonged to 8/JG 51. (H. J. NOWARRA)

General Wladislaw Sikorski, head of the Polish government-in-exile, visiting No. 303 Squadron (Polish). Greeting him is Squadron Commander Witold Urbanowicz, highest-scoring Polish ace of the RAF (seventeen *victories); Urbanowicz later served in the U. S. Fourteenth Air Force, brought his score up to twenty when (1944) he destroyed three Zeros.*
(EMBASSY OF THE POLISH PEOPLE'S REPUBLIC)

Douglas Bader's Duxford wing also intercepted a large formation of Dorniers with Me-110 and Me-109 escort to the east of London. Bader's No. 242 Squadron succeeded in mixing with the Germans and, though his own plane was damaged, Bader accounted for two enemy fighters. The other two squadrons of Bader's Duxford wing, Nos. 19 and 310, had not caught up with the Germans in time. They had been too low when the order to attack had come. Fighter Command lost forty-two aircraft on September 7, 1940, and fourteen pilots.

All during the day and into the night the German radio reported the progress of the battle to the Reich. In the evening a triumphant, vaunting Göring spoke of the "heavy sacrifices" of the Luftwaffe, but he crowed, "This is the historic hour when for the first time our Air Force delivered its thrust right into the enemy's heart!" The thrust had cost fifty-three aircraft, most of them fighters. It was a heavy toll, but, Göring reasoned, worth it. Even so seasoned a leader as Major Hannes Traut-

loft, of Kampfgeschwader 54, noted that they had been met only by single British fighters "which could do nothing. . . ." Perhaps Fighter Command was down to its last Spitfires.

But in turning to London the Germans afforded Fighter Command the time to put its stations back into efficient operational status. Repairs could be made to the ground installations; communications systems could be restored to normal. The Germans had, by their switch to London, unwittingly granted Fighter Command a sorely needed period of grace. The question was: Could London take it—or would London go the way of Guernica, Warsaw, and Rotterdam? Hitler and Göring were confident it would—with twinges of perplexing doubt which found expression in the vacillation with respect to Sealion.

The canny Dowding, however, had no such qualifications. In June, when he knew that the Luftwaffe had moved into the forward bases in the Low Countries and France, Dowding said, "The nearness

Arming up a Spitfire for the next round with the Luftwaffe. The advantage of fighting over one's own grounds was that during the lull in the battle, or if ammunition was expended, it was possible to land and rearm quickly. (IMPERIAL WAR MUSEUM, LONDON)

The strain of battle fatigued pilots. Sergeant G. B. Booth catches a few moments of that precious commodity sleep while awaiting the call to intercept. Booth was killed during the Battle of Britain.

(KENT MESSENGER)

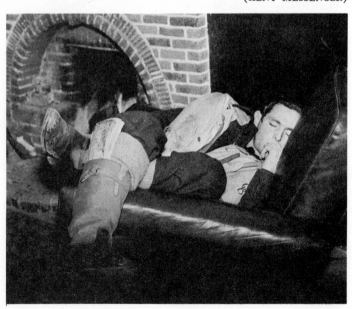

of London to German airfields will lose them the war." Not that the German shift in target concentration took all the weight off Dowding's shoulders. The daylight attacks continued, some even striking at the airfields and the radar installations. As for the night bombings, they went nearly unchallenged, for the night fighters were not yet operating with radar and had missed the German planes in the dark. The antiaircraft guns did little more than fill the air with projectiles and succeeded only in annoying the bombers a little.

On September 8, the day following the first large-scale daylight bombing of London, only minor raids ensued. On the ninth, however, Fighter Command was ready for the raids which developed in force late in the afternoon. But of the two hundred bombers dispatched against London, only ninety managed to break through the fighters sent up by Park as well as fighters from Nos. 10 and 12 Groups. Perhaps seventy bombers were diverted from their main objective and bombed secondary targets while nearly sixty German bombers were turned back and did not bomb at all or jettisoned their bombs. Some of the latter fell upon Canterbury in Kent. Thirty-seven German planes crashed to earth or into the sea and an additional seven were lost either during the Channel crossing or in landing in France. Fighter Command lost nineteen aircraft and fourteen pilots.

The fighting of September 9 gave the Luftwaffe pause. Yet there remained the hope that a few more days of heavy fighting would wipe out Fighter Command once and for all. By September 13 Hitler wistfully implied that if all went as they hoped he might never have to give the order for the launching of Sealion. He had, on September 11, postponed it once again and promised another, perhaps on the fourteenth: this would set the actual invasion date for September 24. This depended upon air superiority over southeast England and the internal collapse of England hopefully because of the London bombings. On September 14, with disconcerting regularity, Hitler postponed Sealion once again, setting the new warning date for September 17 (and D-Day, as planned, for ten days after, September 27). The unco-ordinated interceptions by Fighter Command on that day all but confirmed the German hopes. The critical moment was at hand: the moment for the Luftwaffe's *coup de grâce* to Fighter Command.

Some of Churchill's "few": a handful of pilots who took part in the Battle of Britain—Pilot Officer John L. Allen, Flight Lieutenant Robert S. Tuck (No. 92 Squadron), Flight Lieutenant Alan C. Deere, Flight Lieutenant Adolf G. Malan (No. 74 Squadron), and Squadron Leader James A. Leathart—and a bugler. *Allen, Deere, and Leathart were all members of No. 54 Squadron (of which the latter was commanding officer) and frequently flew together as a section. Allen died during the Battle. This quintet scored nearly a hundred victories against the Luftwaffe during the course of the war. (IMPERIAL WAR MUSEUM, LONDON)*

III

On the morning of Sunday, September 15, 1940, Winston Churchill, accompanied by his wife, Clementine, drove from his home at Chequers (the official country seat of Prime Ministers) to nearby Uxbridge. It was but another in Churchill's countless visits to the scenes of action. Here, at the headquarters of No. 11 Group, Churchill and his wife were taken by Keith Park down into the Operations Room, about fifty feet below ground beneath Hillingdon Golf Course. "The Group Operations Room was like a small theater," Churchill has written, "about sixty feet across, and with two storeys. We took our seats in the dress circle. Below

Spitfires in attack formation.
(IMPERIAL WAR MUSEUM, LONDON)

us was the large-scale map-table, around which perhaps twenty highly trained young men and women, with their telephone assistants, were assembled."

Opposite the Churchills, Park, and others essential to the operations was a giant blackboard covering an entire wall. This was the "tote board" on which, in a glance, Park was able to ascertain the status of each squadron in each sector of No. 11 Group. This was graphically depicted by vertical subdivisions on the tote board; colored lights indicated the state of readiness of each squadron. Those squadrons in action were indicated by red lights. Correlated with the board was a great map spread across the room, over which the plotters worked, showing the disposition of the squadrons and the plots of the incoming Germans. Officers slightly offstage, so to

speak, in a glass enclosure kept track of British antiaircraft guns. Thus the tote board reduced the three-dimensional battle in the skies to little more than a two-dimensional graph.

The atmosphere was charged with tension, although Park, drawn and tired, said to the Churchills, "I don't know whether anything will happen today."

Through the previous night the ground crews had worked on the Hurricanes and Spitfires, patching those which had been damaged in the day's action. Fourteen British fighters had been lost; the Germans too had lost fourteen aircraft, but some of them had been bombers.

By dawn of Sunday the airdromes of Kent reverberated to the sound of Merlin engines catching and the roar of their warming up. Armorers threaded ammunition belts into the wings of the fighters and petrol bowsers darted here and there among the poised aircraft, fueling them up. The tension increased with the coming light—it promised to be a fine day with some cloud patches possible.

The Churchills had barely settled themselves into "the Hole" at Uxbridge when the radar posts along the Channel reported German aircraft activity forming up over Dieppe. "Forty plus," was the estimate; the bulbs along the bottom of the tote board flashed on and Park's squadrons came to "Stand-by" status. It was now eleven o'clock in the morning and as the minutes ticked by the radar stations reported more and more enemy aircraft building up: "Forty plus, sixty plus, eighty plus . . ." Within moments Park ordered eleven of his squadrons into the air; a single squadron from No. 10 Group was requested to cover 11 Group's western boundary. To the north the five squadrons comprising the so-called Duxford wing of No. 12 Group led by Douglas Bader leaped into the air.

Park's Spitfires and Hurricanes intercepted the bomber formations—over two hundred strong with hundreds of fighters escorting—over eastern Kent. The odds, except in numbers, lay with the defenders. For a half hour the radar operators had plotted the massing of the German formations and Park, with uncanny certainty, judged the target to be London. He knew where to place his squadrons for effect. Churchill's cigar had gone dead as he concentrated upon the action unfolding before him.

The Spitfires of No. 72 and No. 92 Squadrons, meeting the Germans over Canterbury, knifed through the formations with guns hammering. It was the first blood of the day. Engines of Dorniers flickered and smoked; some fell from the formation, others broke and turned for the coast. The Me-109s whipped into the melee to protect the bombers. The battle, moving westward across Kent, swarmed in clusters and darting individual combats toward London, leaving in its wake burning aircraft, parachutes drifting through the smoke, and the dead.

The Dorniers of Kampfgeschwader 3, now decimated and with dead men at some of the gun positions, pressed on to London. The shaken crews, who had taken off certain that Fighter Command no longer existed, bombed with no accuracy. Very little of military value was hit: a number of dwellings, a couple of bridges, a suburban electrical plant; a sin-

gle bomb even fell into the grounds of Buckingham Palace, although it proved to be a dud. Sergeant Ray T. Holmes, Hurricane pilot of No. 504 Squadron, which had met the Dorniers on the outskirts of London, was certain he had brought down the plane which had bombed the palace.

Holmes was acting as rear guard for the squadron on patrol; his job was to weave around behind and above the other planes keeping an eye out for German fighters. The squadron had just met the Dornier formation and had broken it up with an attack. "By then," Holmes relates, "the Dornier formation had become ragged and was turning for home, and 504 had broken away to reform and I spotted three Dorniers blazing a lone trail toward London. No one seemed to have noticed them, so I decided to give them a little attention."

Throttling the Hurricane to speed, Holmes overtook the three German planes and then attacked from the flank. The first Dornier spurted oil just as Holmes passed underneath, blotting out his vision when the windscreen was covered. The slipstream cleared the oil away in time for Holmes to get a quick glimpse of the Dornier's tail, just inches from his Hurricane's nose. One of the German's propellers had stopped. Holmes came up from under the plane to attack the other flanking Dornier. The root of the wing caught fire and a parachute ejected from the Dornier. For a few moments the hapless German chutist draped across the wing of Holmes's Hurricane. He then was dragged off into nothingness by the twisted parachute.

Holmes then turned to the lead plane, attacking it from behind. This had little effect and Holmes found himself with only fifteen seconds of firing time left. "I thought a head-on attack might cool his ardor, and climbed up past him to his left from my last breakaway." As he readied for this attack, Holmes noted that his engine sounded rough and that oil (his own) had begun to bubble into his cockpit. As he tore in head-on, eight guns firing, Holmes ran out of ammunition. Frustrated, he simply kept going over the Dornier and "clipped one side of his fragile-looking twin tail with my port wing." The only sensation was a slight bump, and Holmes was certain that little harm could have come to his Hurricane. Then his wing dropped—the tip had been torn off—the nose dropped too, and the controls would not respond. The Hurricane snapped

Douglas Bader (center) with two members of his No. 242 Squadron, George Eric Ball (left) and William L. McKnight. Active through the Battle and the blitz,

Ball and McKnight were killed during fighter sweeps after the RAF went over to the offensive.
(IMPERIAL WAR MUSEUM, LONDON)

into a vertical spin. Holmes fought his way out of the plane and joined his opponents in floating down toward London.

He had afforded Londoners with quite an exciting spectacle, for the German bomber crashed spectacularly into Victoria Station. The surviving German crewmen landed across the Thames in the Kennington cricket oval. Holmes fared not so well: after bouncing off a rooftop in the Chelsea section of London, he came to rest in a Londoner's back-yard trash can.

Although they continued their thrust to London, the tormented German bomber crews wondered where all the Spitfires and Hurricanes had come from. The German fighters—those not tied closely to the bombers—swept in to clear the way, but not all of the British planes could be stopped. These careened through and chopped up the formations.

Adolf Galland, leading his Jagdgeschwader 26 on a forward free hunt, charged into the attacking British fighters but without, even after ten minutes of savage fighting, stopping them. Twisting in his cockpit he saw, nearly two thousand feet below him, a pair of Hurricanes. He flipped into a dive and sent one flaming into the Thames. But after the time spent in France forming up, crossing the Channel, fighting across Kent, and a few minutes of combat, it was time for Galland to streak for home unless he wanted to end up in the *Shite Kanal.*

It was over London on this Sunday, September 15, 1940, that the German bomber formations, having dropped their bombs, and after having traversed miles of smoking sky to do it, received a further shock. Where had all the Spitfires and Hurricanes—which Beppo Schmid had claimed had dwindled to the last fifty—where had they all come from? And

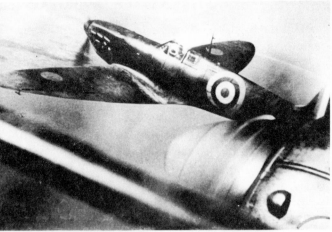

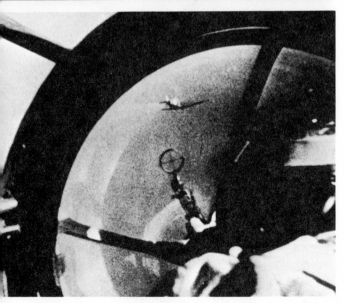

then from the north, like a biblical plague, screamed a full sixty fresh fighters led by Douglas Bader. He had led his squadrons—his own No. 224, the Czech No. 310, and the Polish No. 302 (all in Hurricanes), and the two Spitfire squadrons, Nos. 19 and 611—as high as possible to get above the Germans and into the sun. When he saw the Germans—forty or more Ju-88s and Dorniers—Bader swiftly studied the air around them for a glimpse of the escort. Then alerting the others to the telltale specks in the distance, Bader nosed into the German bomber formation, shouting, "Break 'em up!"

With his eight guns firing Bader swept into the vanguard of the German planes. He kicked the Hurricane around, pulled up and onto the tail of a Dornier. The guns shook the Hurricane as holes and sparks appeared behind the Dornier's right engine. Then a flash, black smoke—and Bader had to jerk the stick to avoid ramming the stricken German bomber. As he pulled off he saw another Dornier slipping into a cloud bank for sanctuary. Above it a lone Spitfire dived into the same cloud. The British pilot had not seen the German bomber. There was a billow of orange flame, black smoke, and with the wings of the Dornier twisted around the Spitfire, the two aircraft fell churning through the air into London.

Bader, twisting his neck, sought more targets and saw only one other plane, a Do-17 spinning and burning. A crewman managed to get out of the gyrating plane, but opened his chute too soon. The silk brushed through the flame and seared away into the clouds. The hapless German, trailing useless shrouds, plummeted straight down. Bitterly, almost without pity, Bader thought, "Now you've got a little time to think about it and there isn't any answer."

And now, except for wisps of black smoke, the curls of evaporating tracers, the sky was empty. Emotionally tired, his fuel low, Bader turned the Hurricane for Duxford.

By twelve-thirty peace had come again to the Sunday skies of England. But the day was only half

A Spitfire makes a fighter pass on an He-111 over the Channel. In these (probably in a staged action with a captured Spitfire) photographs the British fighter has come under the tail and the starboard wing, flashes by the nose gunner's position, and begins to turn for another attack. (H. J. NOWARRA)

over. The second, and heavier, round of Luftwaffe attacks began just before two-thirty in the afternoon. There had been less time to scramble the Fighter Command squadrons than in the morning. Bader, again leading the Duxford wing, was critical of this short notice, feeling that his unit could have done much better had it been given ample time to assemble and to meet the Germans head on before they reached London. When they finally met the Germans Bader's aircraft intercepted them from below—not an advantage at all. The Me-109s could bounce them before they got at the bombers.

The Germans came over in three large formations, crossing the English coast between Dungeness and Dover. Park had dispatched twelve of his squadrons in pairs to meet the Germans as they came in over Kent; soon another seven and a half squadrons took to the air. The leading German formation was intercepted over Canterbury by two squadrons from the Hornchurch sector station; soon these were joined by more Hurricanes which had been patrolling over Maidstone. The heavens, as they had two hours earlier, were racked with the sound of guns, the trail of battle and defeat: the reek of cordite and burning metal.

The radios crackled in the Operations Rooms as the controllers sent the fighters to meet the attackers. The Churchills listened as the tension mounted even more at Uxbridge. The language did not always make sense to the layman, but the urgency in the young voices conveyed the drama of the battle.

"Bullfinch patrol Maidstone, Angels twenty," the controller ordered. "Bullfinch" was the day's code name for one of the squadrons; "angels" was an altitude indication: angels twenty was twenty thousand feet.

Then the radio might come to life as the fighter pilots closed with the enemy (these are authentic transcriptions):

"109s at four o'clock above."

"Keep in, Blue 2" (elements in the squadrons were coded by color and number. Blue 2 was the second plane in blue section; Blue 1 led this section; a third plane completed the section.)

"Watch your tail, Red 3!"

"Break right, Red 3, break right!"

The people in No. 11 Group's Operations Room could hear but not see any of this, of course.

"Got the bastard!" the radio crackled. A squadron mate had come to the aid of Red 3.

"Typan [the code name for a controller] to Ferret leader. Fifty plus near Gravesend. One hundred plus approaching you from southeast. One hundred and twenty plus. Angels eighteen. North of Base 2."

"Ferret leader to Typan. Don't tell me any more, you're making me nervous."

A bomber formation is seen and the "Tally Ho!" is given.

"Black 2 to Black leader. Dorniers at twelve o'clock, just below."

"OK. Head-on attack. Break right and left, I'll break upward."

A brief silence, and an unknown voice crackles, "God, that was dangerous!"

It was dangerous for the Germans too. Again, as in the morning's confused terror, the gnawing question was: What was the source, seemingly inexhaustible, of all those British fighters? How confidently, even disdainfully, had they checked off the British airfields, the aircraft factories, as destroyed in the weeks before. That Park had committed all of his squadrons to the battle, as well as the great Duxford wing and a single squadron from No. 10 Group, might not have assured the harried Germans. To them it seemed that the British fighters materialized out of nowhere.

At the battle's climax Churchill, his eye upon the line of lighted electric bulbs on the toe board, asked, "What other reserves have we?"

"There are none," Park told him. All the squadrons of No. 11 Group were in the air and Park had drawn upon the neighboring Groups for reinforcements. Complications arose when, during the great air battles over London and its suburbs, a small bomber and fighter force slipped across the Channel in the south to bomb shipping at Portland—and perhaps to draw off some of the British fighters from the main attack upon London. A single British fighter squadron, of a possible five of the Middle Wallop sector, intercepted—but only after the German bombs had dropped. Even so, the bombing was inaccurate and little harm was done to Portland.

The day's last attack, again in the south, came shortly after six o'clock when about twenty bomb-laden Me-110s came in over the Hampshire coast.

Shot down while on a raid against London, a German crew is taken prisoner while, in the background, their Heinkel burns. (FOX PHOTOS, LTD.)

The target of Test Group 210 was the Supermarine (Spitfire) factory at Woolston. With only twenty minutes' warning, it was almost impossible for Park to get the squadrons up in time, but he did send some of his and some from No. 10 Group to intercept. Again the British fighters did not find the enemy aircraft until after they had dropped their bombs. Once again the bombing was inaccurate, thanks in this attack to the Southampton antiaircraft guns, which trained on the Me-110s on their bombing run, upsetting the aim of the bombardiers and the flying of the pilots. The bombs missed the Spitfire factory but fell into residential areas. Thus ended the last flicker, a whimper, of the daylight battles.

Churchill by this time had returned to Chequers for his afternoon nap. He had been fatigued by the strain in the Operations Room at Uxbridge. It had been a close one. Just one more sizable German attacking force and they would have had nothing with which to meet it. Having slept Churchill immediately called his secretary, John Martin, to learn the very latest news. Martin had a little good to report from Italy on the Atlantic. "However," he concluded, "all is redeemed by the air. We have shot down a hundred and eighty-three for a loss of under forty."

The evening's BBC broadcast, and the newspapers, added a couple more and proclaimed to a jubilant Britain that 185 German aircraft had been destroyed. The official Air Ministry account called it "the Greatest Day." Churchill dispatched a congratulatory message to Dowding on Monday. "Yesterday eclipsed all previous records of Fighter Command," he wrote. "Aided by squadrons of their

Battle's end: a Hurricane pilot of No. 85 Squadron wearily leaves his cockpit as the sun sets after a hard day of combat. (IMPERIAL WAR MUSEUM, LONDON)

Czech and Polish comrades, using only a small proportion of their total strength [not true, but this message was for public consumption] and under cloud conditions of some difficulty, they cut to rags and tatters three separate waves of murderous assaults upon the civil population of their native land. . . . These results exceeded all expectations and give just and sober confidence in the approaching struggle."

But in the light of postwar truth was September 15, 1940, actually "the Greatest Day"? Not if its greatness is measured by the number of enemy aircraft destroyed. The British lost 35 planes that day and 11 pilots. The Luftwaffe lost 30 Do-17s, 15 He-111s, 3 Ju-88s, 3 Me-110s, and 23 Me-109s, plus four others, a total of 78—not 185—aircraft. But of this total the greater number was bombers—fully one quarter of the total sent against England on September 15 during the daylight attacks (a force of 181 bombers came in over London that night). These were lost despite the heavy fighter protection of nearly five fighters for every bomber. But the order which tied most of the fighters tightly to the bombers, excepting the free-hunt units which generally preceded the bomber streams, crippled their fighting abilities.

The tired airmen on both sides of the Channel, hollow-eyed, nerves tingling, muscles tight, were unimpressed with "the Greatest Day" designation. They were too depleted to care. The RAF crews, however, could delight in the news of a great victory despite their exhaustion. The Luftwaffe pilots were shaken and demoralized: their High Command had, in fact, failed them. First, it had misinformed them about the strength of Fighter Command, and second, it had further handicapped the fighters with unrealistic tactics. Even so, the Luftwaffe did not consider the Battle decided, let alone lost.

Nor, in truth, did the RAF High Command, whose members were more realistic than their German counterparts, consider the Battle won. The Battle was won, however, though neither side was aware of it at the time.

The effort of RAF's Fighter Command on "the Greatest Day" contributed heavily to a decision revealed in an entry in the war diary of the German Naval Staff dated September 17, 1940:

The enemy Air Force is still by no means defeated; on the contrary, it shows increasing activity. The weather situation on the whole does not permit us to expect a period of calm. The Führer therefore decides to postpone Sealion indefinitely.

He was not coming after all; he would never come.

9

THE BLITZ

THE REPULSE of the Luftwaffe—which Göring promptly blamed on the fighters—on "the Greatest Day" neither closed the Battle of Britain nor ended the planning, however dispirited, for Sealion, despite the Führer's deferment. To remove the vessels and troops from the various ports would be an admission of defeat—and that would not do. This was neatly side-stepped by the propaganda machine. On September 18 the German-controlled Paris Radio informed the British, and the world, that "the legend of British self-control and phlegm is being destroyed. All reports from London concur in stating that the population is seized by fear—hair-raising fear. The seven million Londoners have completely lost their self-control. They run aimlessly about in the streets and are victims of bombs and bursting shells."

London, indeed, had become the target—but after the fighting of September 15 the daylight attacks dwindled significantly. On the eighteenth there was a large flurry—about seventy German bombers appeared over London and were fought off ferociously. The final weeks of September were devoted to relatively minor daylight raids upon aircraft factories. Göring's High Command recognized the urgency of denying the RAF a supply of aircraft. The end of October was characterized by a decided lack of mass raids and the introduction of wider use of fighter-bombers (Me-109s carrying thousand-pound bombs). Although these high-flying aircraft could evade the British fighters and made positive identi-

fication difficult—radar and direct observation could not discern whether the Messerschmitts were merely fighters and therefore not worth scrambling after or fighters carrying bombs—they accomplished little.

In short, though he was unaware of it at the time, Dowding had won the Battle of Britain.

But then began a new terror. For fifty-seven nights, from September 7 through November 2, not a night went by without the drone of German bombers overhead, the crash of bombs and fire in the streets of London. "None of it seems real," wrote Anthony Guthrie to Vivien Leigh and Laurence Olivier. "One can't believe that one isn't living in some highly superior Wagnerian production. The night of the big fires was utterly amazing. . . . We came out [of Sadler's Wells Theatre, London] to find the entire sky crimson from the reflected glare of the fires—you could easily read small print in the street—and on every window reflected back the dancing, terrifying glare."

It was unreal, but the rubble, the burned-out streets, and the dead and injured were undeniable fact. So were the barrage balloons which swayed dumpily over London Bridge; Londoners called these balloons, which were not especially effective except against low-flying aircraft, "our dumb friends." Although not of much use, their floating presence was comforting. The air raid warning signals—"sirens" or "Wailing Winnies"—cried out nightly for those fifty-seven nights. The average

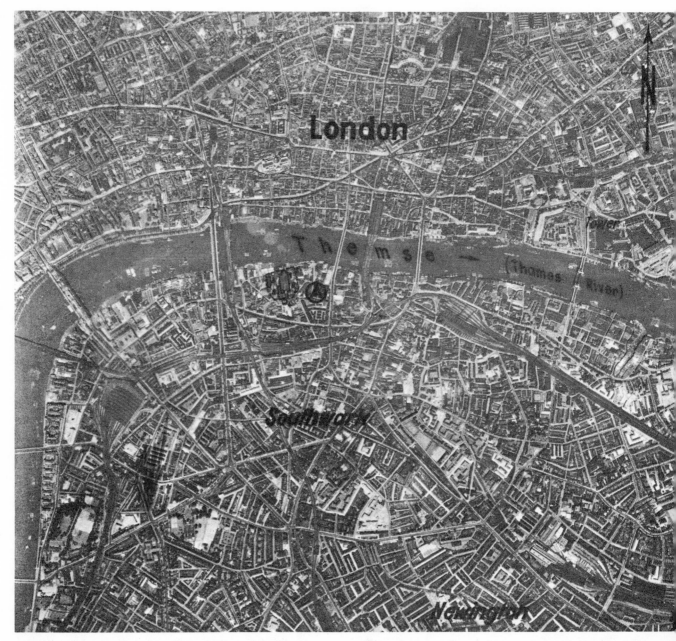

Luftwaffe target map. The circled A locates a South-wark power station on the south bank of the Thames.

Almost directly north, across the river, may be seen St. Paul's Cathedral.

(IMPERIAL WAR MUSEUM, LONDON)

nightly raiding party consisted of about 160 bombers during this period—ranging from 7 on the night of October 6, when bad weather interfered, to more than 400 on October 15. There was little the defenses could do to counter these attacks. The night fighter, equipped with radar, was but a crude idea in the early days of the blitz; antiaircraft defenses were weak and inaccurate. Like the dumb friends

the sound and flash of the guns were more inspiring than effectual. By September 10 the number of heavy antiaircraft guns protecting central London was increased from 92 to 199; restrictions forbidding gunners from firing at aircraft they could see or which were officially detected led to a massive barrage over London when next the Germans came. This, while rarely if ever accounting for downed

He-111s cross the English Channel during the winter of the blitz. (IMPERIAL WAR MUSEUM, LONDON)

An incendiary bomb burns in a London street; once burning an incendiary was difficult to control and was most responsible for the damage to London during the blitz. (IMPERIAL WAR MUSEUM, LONDON)

A German bomber after a raid on England, lucky to have made the return trip. The pilot, slightly dazed, sits atop the fuselage while others (including cameraman) study what appears to be antiaircraft shell hole behind the port engine. (H. J. NOWARRA)

German bombers, was disconcerting and did force the Luftwaffe formations to fly higher—and it did make a joyful noise for the beleaguered Londoner.

Although the Luftwaffe's objectives were primarily the docks, the railways, public utilities, as well as governmental and financial centers, the chief victims were the ordinary Londoners, generally of the poorer classes. They lost sleep, were improperly fed, lost their pitiable possessions, their homes, and their loved ones. The panic predicted by the Germans, however, did not occur. Instead a grim resolution set in, a tough, bitter humor, a deep sense of fellowship (as class lines, temporarily at least, broke down), and a determination not to be defeated by "'Itler." But they died by the hundreds on each of the fifty-seven nights as well as other nights throughout the remainder of the Second World War.

On the big night of October 15, when 410 bombers dropped 528 tons of high explosives and 177 canisters of incendiaries, 400 civilians died and 900 were seriously injured. Rail traffic between London and the cities to the north and south was disrupted or stopped. Where once fifty trains ran per day, only four were running after the raid. Hundreds of fires broke out and water mains burst, some filling the underground tube stations. While all of this was disrupting, damaging to property, and took a heavy toll of life (although never as high as had been predicted before the war), little of military import was

achieved. Neither did the railroads, docks, factories, or utilities close down, nor did the Londoner petition his government for an early armistice.

There was reason enough for fear and panic. The Germans sowed vicious fires with their incendiaries, more destructive than the high-explosive bombs. They also dropped delayed-action bombs, thus rendering streets and buildings hazardous until the bomb exploded or was dealt with by the UXB (Unexploded Bomb) Disposal Squads. Churchill, in his memoirs, recalled one of these remarkable groups, "the Holy Trinity," consisting of the Earl of Suffolk, his lady private secretary, and "his rather aged chauffeur." This unique, gallant trinity, working at a trade for which none of their previous experience had prepared them, had actually learned how to disarm the UXBs. This was a most delicate operation, calling for courage as well as skill. All the proper mechanisms inside the bomb had to be taken apart without disturbing the detonation device. "Thirty-four unexploded bombs did they tackle with urbane and smiling efficiency," Churchill reported. "But the thirty-fifth claimed its forfeit. Up went the Earl of Suffolk in his Holy Trinity. But we may be sure that, as for Greatheart [a character in *Pilgrim's Progress*], 'all the trumpets sounded for them on the other side.'"

Churchill admired such eccentric valour and while he appeared to make light of their tragic end he mordantly expressed the mood of the time, of people he termed "the grim and the gay," the unbeatable British courage which "'Itler" found so unfathomable.

II

By December 8, 1940, London was no longer the prime target of the Luftwaffe night war. On November 14 Göring had decided, since the bombing of London seemed to accomplish so little, that attention should be given the smaller industrial cities. These presented less sprawling targets than London, if more difficult to find. But with Kampfgeschwader 100 leading the way with incendiaries which were planted with the help of an electronic navigation device they called *X-Gerät* ("X-Device"), there was no problem finding the target for the 450 bombers that night. *X-Gerät* was operated on a complex system of radio beams, a main beam plus beams which intersected it.

A Luton *News* historian noted that on November 14, "just after tea German bombers flew over Luton for hour after hour on the way to the Midland city of Coventry." The Luton hat factories were spared that night, but for about ten hours wave after wave of Heinkels and Junkers dropped five hundred tons of high explosives and about nine hundred incendiaries upon the old cathedral town, which had achieved notoriety with the legend of Lady Godiva and Peeping Tom, dating from the eleventh century.

Coventry housed, besides the legend and a beautiful medieval cathedral, factories devoted to the manufacture of machine tools and parts for aircraft industries. The main target was the facilities of the Standard Motor Company; in short, Coventry, according to the "civilized rules of warfare," was a "legitimate" military target. When the last German bomber left at around six-thirty in the morning Coventry, its cathedral included, was a flaming ruin. By 3:30 A.M. at least two hundred major fires were reported in the center of the city, but hydrants were buried under the debris and many water mains were destroyed. The main railroads were blocked so that rescue teams coming from other towns could come only to Coventry's outskirts and then were forced to make their way through the rubble, flame, and danger of unexploded bombs. The once maligned Civil

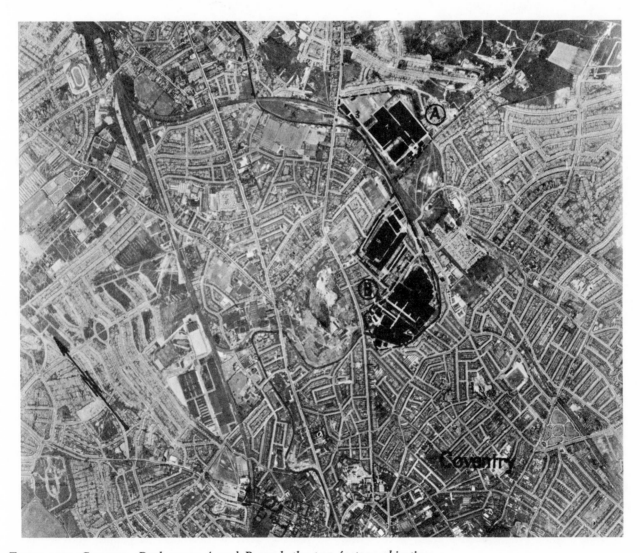

Target map, Coventry. Dark areas A and B mark the two factory objectives.

(IMPERIAL WAR MUSEUM, LONDON)

Defence workers, who had become unpopular because of their insistence upon no lights showing and who seemed to spend most of their time, with nothing to do, in the local pubs, came into their own. These anonymous heroes, who went about their work quietly and matter-of-factly, saved the lives of countless men, women, and children at the risk and at times the cost of their own lives. Ordinary citizens transformed by emergency dashed into blazing, crumbling buildings to save a life. Or they worked for hours to rescue someone trapped in the wreckage of what was once a home.

The Germans boasted later of what they had done to Coventry; they even coined a word to describe what would happen to other towns devoted to the making of arms: "Coventrated." But because of the widespread havoc, impossible to confine to the purely military targets, Coventry joined Guernica, Warsaw, and Rotterdam as a symbol of German frightfulness and thoroughness.

No less than five hundred shops in the city's shopping center were put out of business; only the spire of the cathedral remained standing; twenty-one factories essential to the aircraft industry were hit. The destroyed water and gas mains halted work in other factories not as severely hit. The death toll reached at least 554 and 865 people were seriously wounded. But despite the shattering damage and the casualties there was no panic and comparatively

London burning following a bad night blitz.
(NATIONAL ARCHIVES)

minimal work stoppage. The fires were under control by the evening of November 15. Three days later all the rail lines, except one which took an additional three days, were cleared and running.

Work was resumed at the Standard Motor Company on November 16 by half of its usual staff. Factories which suffered more severe destruction were longer in resuming production, but despite Coventration, Coventry was not knocked out of the war as Göring presumed. Other "arms towns" including Birmingham, Sheffield, Manchester, and Bristol were treated to the same near-saturation bombing during the winter weeks of November and December. So were the ports, Liverpool, Portsmouth, Southampton, but with the same inconclusive results. There were the same casualties, the same fires and rubble, and the same stiffening of the British spirit.

"Have you ever spent the night in a hole in the garden?" asked a young woman schoolteacher from Norwich. "Well, you're too damn tired to bother about the bombs. Luckily our soil is gravel so it's not as bad as it might be but dirt is dirty and full of ants . . . lift up your tin hat, as you grovel in the entrails of the earth, and see the Milky Way above you and the searchlights finding the bomber which you can hear, directly above you. Would you think you'd be scared or wonder what was going to happen—I should have thought so—but you simply try to see if you can see it and it never enters your head that you might be here, there, and everywhere in about two seconds."

In Clydebank (a shipbuilding center in Scotland) a woman made a comment that deserves preservation. She had just finished sweeping debris from her walk when she said to her neighbor, "Well, there's one thing about these raids, they do make you forget about the war."

Be grim and be gay, Churchill had asked of them. They could be practical too, as witness the statement of a lord mayor of one of the port cities which had been noted for its slums. "At least we can say that the Luftwaffe did for us in twenty seconds what we have been trying to do for twenty years," he said. "It removed the slum dwellings. . . ."

The switch to the arms towns and the ports did not mean that London had ceased to be a target completely. In fact, on the night after the Coventry attack London was the major target and Coventry received only a token visit. Had it been reversed the rapid recovery of Coventry might have been seriously cut short. But Göring was certain he had finished it. So the raids continued on through November and December, weather permitting—for the season of rain, snow, ice, and fog came to interfere with German operations. During December Britain enjoyed fifteen bomb-free nights, thanks to the weather.

On December 29, 1940, a Sunday evening at the end of Christmas week, just before seven o'clock the bombers came. They were led to their objective by ten Heinkels of the pathfinder Kampfgeschwader 100, which, in turn, was turned into the *X-Gerät* beam which was laid directly across London. It was a dark night and the winds, from the west and southwest, ranged to as high as fifty miles an hour at an altitude of six thousand feet. So it was that the incendiaries sown by the ten Heinkels drifted slightly eastward from the beam into the section of London known as The City, London's financial center, as well as Westminster, site of Buckingham Palace, No. 10 Downing Street, and other government buildings. In the center of all this stood St. Paul's Cathedral, the masterpiece of Sir Christopher Wren, which had been built 1675–1710.

The attacking force was not very large: 136 bombers, but they dropped 127 tons of high explosives and more than 600 canisters of incendiaries. The HE, with some scattering, fell mainly into the riverside boroughs of London. The incendiaries, which scattered also, very quickly ignited nearly fifteen hundred fires. Six were classified as "conflagrations," twenty-eight were "major," and fifty-two were "serious." Because it was a Sunday evening many of the buildings, even the churches, were locked, making it impossible to deal with the incendiaries which fell onto the roofs. Also, on this night the Thames was at its lowest ebb, a problem further complicated when bombs ruptured an emergency main pipe used in fighting fires. Hose pressures waxed and waned throughout the blazing nightmare.

For about three hours the German aircraft droned over London and then returned to France to reload. But luckily the bases had become weathered-in and the bombers did not return, affording the hard-pressed Londoners the time to try to save their city undisturbed by further bombing. Some fires even by then were so out of control that nothing could be done. Water evaporated in mid-air even before reaching the flames. Sections of The City were merely abandoned and cordoned off to burn out.

"For miles around the sky was a bright orange-red," one Londoner recalled; "the balloons in the barrage stood as clearly as on a sunny day. St. Paul's Cathedral was the pivot of the main fire. All around it the flames were leaping up into the sky. And there the Cathedral stood, magnificently firm, untouched in the very center of all this destruction."

Not quite untouched, for at least two dozen incendiaries struck the dome and only some bounced off into the street. The men of the St. Paul's Cathedral Watch and volunteers (many of them architects) joined forces to fight the fires. Although the water supply failed early, emergency containers of reserve water placed around the cathedral by the leaders of the watch were put to use. Those incendiaries which blazed against the structure threatening to incinerate the old, dry beams were put out with minimal damage.

But one incendiary had struck the dome and had become lodged in the outer lead shell. It protruded hundreds of feet off the ground, sputtering, melting the lead of the outer dome. Fearfully the men of the watch observed helplessly as the single in-

A Hurricane I night fighter takes off to engage the Luftwaffe during the blitz. In this period the single- *engined fighters did not prove very effective against the German bomber forces.*

cendiary seemed about to fall inside the inner dome into the dry timbers. "We knew," the dean of the cathedral said, "that once the fire got hold of the Dome timbers it would, at that high altitude, quickly be fanned into a roaring furnace."

Across London, a woman in Bethnal Green, wearing her tin hat, stood with some firemen on a roof and gazed toward The City. "And I've always remembered how I was choked," she said; "I think I was crying a little. I could see St. Paul's standing there, and the fire all around, and I just said: 'Please God, don't let it go!'"

The incendiary in the dome, now burning fiercely, moved as the lead flowed in the intense heat. Then the bomb fell away from the dome—no one knows quite how—and into the stone gallery of the cathedral, where the relieved men of the watch disposed of it.

St. Paul's was saved and became the symbol of British strength during the Battle of Britain. But other historic buildings did not escape what became known as the Second London Fire. The first, in 1666, resulted in the rebuilding of the city

Not all raids on England during the blitz were made at night. This Me-109 had made a day sortie over the London area, attacked two British trainers, misjudged their speed, and came to grief in Windsor Great Park.

by Christopher Wren. Eight of Wren's churches were consumed in the Second London Fire; so were the Guildhall, the County Hall, and portions of the Tower of London. Nine hospitals, although not targets, were hit; so were five railway stations and sixteen underground stations. The dead numbered 163 with more than 500 seriously injured. Sixteen firemen died, some of them in the crew which had successfully fought off the flames threatening the house of Dr. Samuel Johnson, just off Fleet Street, not far from St. Paul's. The small crew had just left the historic house and had lost their way in the narrow, smoke-filled streets. They had just emerged near a burning building when a member of the pump crew fighting that fire saw them.

"I thought when I saw them that they were too near," he said. "Just at that moment a wall, which looked as if it was bulging dangerously, crashed down on them. As we looked around all we could see was a heap of debris with a hose leading towards it."

Although the Sunday night raid was the last of the year, it was not the last of the fire raids of the blitz. Bad weather interfered with operations during the first two months of 1941, London and several port cities received major attacks. By March, with the coming of somewhat better weather, the raids were resumed with greater ferocity if not in number. In April some of the German bomber strength had been drawn off to assist in the Balkans. Then an even more critical withdrawal came in May as Hitler prepared for his Russian offensive.

Despite the wholesale withdrawals of the Luftwaffe, or perhaps because of them, the effort of the remaining forces was intensified. The effort devolved upon Sperrle's Luftflotte 3, which had to cover for the units which had slipped away. Between the first great fire raid in December and those later in the winter of 1941 much had been learned, at no little cost, about dealing with the night bombers. Roof watchers were stationed throughout London (and other target cities) to keep an eye out for incendiaries, and techniques were developed to deal with them most efficiently. Also, means had been developed to confute the *X-Gerät* beam, as, for example, on the night of May 8/9, when the target was the Rolls-Royce factory at Derby. The beam was detected early and deflected

electronically so that the great German bomber force dropped most of its bombs in the moors northeast of Derby. At the same time "Starfish" were lighted —these were decoy fires which appeared to be pathfinder markers. On this same night Starfish beckoned the German bombers away from Nottingham, which the German pilots mistook for a burning Derby. Consequently, the bomber stream "corrected" and bombed the Vale of Belvoir (mistaking it for Nottingham) with high explosives, an oil bomb, and incendiaries. This effort netted them a casualty toll of two cows and two chickens.

London was easier to find and during the second half of April it received two of its worst raids, so memorable that Londoners ever after referred to them by name, "the Wednesday" (April 16/17) and "the Saturday" (April 19/20). On the first 890 tons of high explosives and 4200 canisters of incendiary bombs fell; on the Saturday the weight increased: 1026 tons of HE and 4252 canisters of incendiaries rained on London.

Then on May 10/11 came another heavy blow, the last of the night offensive. On that same night deputy Führer Rudolf Hess, having stolen a Messerschmitt, flew alone from Germany and parachuted to earth near Glasgow. He was looking for Lord Steward, the Duke of Hamilton, whom Hess had met at the Olympics in Germany in 1936. Hess insisted that he had come on a peace mission; he was certain that he could convince the British with Lord Steward's help of the Führer's kindly intentions toward Britain and bring the war to an end.

Meanwhile London burned. More than 400,000 civilians were to die in the blitz, and 46,000 suffered serious injuries. A million homes were destroyed. The average Londoner was thoroughly familiar with Hitler's intentions. Out of the ruins of one of the buildings a woman emerged covered with blood and powdered brick and plaster. Her eyes were dull, her face drawn, she said nothing to her rescuers except the phrase she repeated, like a litany, over and over again: "Man's inhumanity

---

The main shelter during the blitz was the London Underground, the subway. Deep under the streets of the city, Londoners sought refuge from Hitler's bombers and proved, in the phrase at the time, "London can take it." (IMPERIAL WAR MUSEUM, LONDON)

to man, man's inhumanity to man, man's inhumanity to man . . ."

By the late spring of 1941 the blitz was over. So in fact was all planning for Sealion. But the future of the Third Reich, and its leaders, its cities, its people—innocent and guilty—was assured.

"Man's inhumanity to man . . ."

On that December night when St. Paul's stood out of the smoke and flame with an almost human British show of defiance and dignity, the newly appointed Deputy Chief of the Air Staff stood on the roof of the Air Ministry building watching the fulminating desolation. He was Arthur Harris. Moved by the fiery spectacle, he spoke to the old sentry on the roof, reminding the man that they were looking directly upon history. The old man, however, who called himself "an observer of nature," seemed more interested in the sex life of the cats on the rooftops of Whitehall.

"The last time London was burnt," Harris tried again, "if my history is right, was in 1666." But the sentry was not impressed. The conflagration was to Harris such a "fantastic sight" that he went downstairs and brought up his chief, Air Chief Marshal Sir Charles Portal, from his office to see it.

The two airmen, one of whom would in time be Chief of Bomber Command, watched the sea of flame in bitter silence. As they turned away from the awesome sight, so unreal in its magnitude, Harris said to Portal, "Well, they are sowing the wind."

For they have sown the wind, and they shall reap the whirlwind.

"Man's inhumanity to man . . ."

10

"GIVE IT 'EM BACK!"

THE pattern of modern war was unmistakably defined: Everyman had become a legitimate military target. The war of the peoples had begun.

The Germans were ill advised to expect the Londoners to panic in the street. Instead, there was fear, dread, grief, and loss, but no panic. And there was a hard mood of retribution. During the blitz the King and Churchill made visits to the hard-hit areas; the King, for example, visited Coventry immediately after its devastating attack. Churchill recalled one of his experiences at the site in the south of London where a large land mine had exploded. He was terribly moved, walking through the ruins of what had been two dozen homes of the poor in the district. As if in defiance of the Germans, the people had stuck tiny British flags in the ruins. The people crowded around the old warrior, cheering, happy just to touch him, and saw tears in Churchill's eyes.

They showed him a great crater, perhaps twenty feet deep and forty yards across, at the edge of which teetered an Anderson shelter. (This was the uncomfortable and not always effective government-issued air raid shelter widely used by the poor.) Still alive, though dazed by the miracle of their escape, were the inhabitants, a young man, his wife, and their three children. All were smiling, enjoying their celebrity. As Churchill turned to go, he sensed "a harsher mood" which animated the tattered crowd, then someone shouted, "Give it 'em back!"

"Let *them* have it too!" another shouted, and the cries followed Churchill as he left the scene. "Give it 'em back!" became a battle cry of the non-combatants who suffered under the new mode of the "art of war." And Churchill did all he could to comply with the mood of his people. "Certainly the enemy got it all back," he wrote later, "in good measure, pressed down and running over. Alas for poor humanity!"

II

The members of the Air Staff, viewing the situation more professionally, did not regard the principle of "Give it 'em back!" as militarily sound. With London as a target, it followed in popular logic that Berlin must also be a target. When the towns and cities suffered, then it was expected that the lesser German cities and towns should suffer also. Berlin, especially, as far as the average Londoner—and Winston Churchill—was concerned was a most enticing objective. Bomber Command would have preferred targets of more strategic value. In the long months of the Battle of France, the Battle of Britain, and the blitz, during which the Luftwaffe pretty much dictated the turn of events, Bomber Command operated defensively as much as offensively. Instead of concentrating upon the oil installations in Germany, as it would have wished, Bomber Command had to contend with invasion

A Coastal Command B-17 coming in over an English cottage after an over-water patrol.
(IMPERIAL WAR MUSEUM, LONDON)

barges on the coast of the North Sea and across their own Channel.

When it became reasonably obvious that the Germans had abandoned their daylight attacks and postponed their Sealion plans—toward the end of September 1940—Bomber Command hoped to resume strategic operations upon German industry crucial to the supply of the war machine. But the blitz, with its heavy London toll, plus the temper of London's population (as well as of others with even greater political influence) split the effort. Under pressure it was resolved by Bomber Command to resume the strategic offensive against the industrial complex in the Ruhr and to "Give it 'em back" in Berlin. The German capital was one of a dozen German cities (originally twenty or more) which could be attacked "to affect the morale of the German people." Among the other "morale" targets were Hamburg, Cologne, Munich, Leipzig, Essen, Dresden, Breslau, Frankfurt, Düsseldorf, and Stuttgart.

The primary objectives, now that the invasion threat had receded, were to be oil and morale. The desired emphasis would be upon the oil targets, but with the rather hazy "morale" now accepted as an objective, purely military definition of targets became academic.

Reports from inside Germany encouraged the "area bombings," that is, attacks not aimed at precise military pin points but at the general vicinity of known targets. Fire would do the rest, as successive waves of bombers disrupted the work of the fire fighters. Neutral visitors in Berlin reported that German morale had indeed suffered under the unexpected bombings of their city. Germans were shaken, but like the Londoner, the Berliner proved he could take it. In truth, the effect upon morale never approached the effect expected.

The concession to area attacks upon populated areas was not an admission of wanton British brutality. It was a recognition of a fact: not all bomber crews were so skilled that they were able to find the target area, let alone bomb it. Weather, flak, poor navigation, fear: all interfered with the performance of air crews. There were great distances to cover— the flight to Berlin traversed nearly six hundred miles, part of it over the North Sea and the rest over Germany itself. And then, there was the return trip.

Meanwhile, the Battle of the Atlantic also shunted Bomber Command from strategic targets. As it had during the First World War, the U-boat danger became critical, menacing the food supply and essential war materials, the bulk of which Britain had to import. Also there were the German battle cruisers, particularly the *Scharnhorst* and the *Gneisenau*, which aircrews readily nicknamed the "Salmon" and the "Gluckstein." The *Bismarck*, the great German battleship which had taken a terrible toll of British shipping, was sunk in a combined sea and air battle late in May 1941. But Hitler continued to promise

RAF Coastal Command "Fortress I" (the B-17C) over a British Atlantic convoy on watch for German submarines. (IMPERIAL WAR MUSEUM, LONDON)

to starve the British in their island and to cut off war supplies by sinking their ships from under the sea, on the surface, and from the air.

To fight this Battle the aircraft of both Bomber Command and Coastal Command were confronted with an area of roughly ten and a half million square miles of sea. Not only the U-boat and the battleship must be found in this great expanse but also the Luftwaffe reconnaissance planes and bombers. The British employed not only their own aircraft, such as the Short Sunderland, a giant flying boat, but also American-made Lockheed Hudsons and Consolidated Catalinas. In time, by 1942, the Boeing B-17 Flying Fortress, which Bomber Command had not been able to use effectively for various reasons, was employed by Coastal Command in sea reconnaissance and long-range convoy patrol. Later another heavy American bomber, the Consolidated

The U-boat's friend, the Focke-Wulf Condor, the Luftwaffe's only long-range four-engined aircraft during the Battle of the Atlantic.

(IMPERIAL WAR MUSEUM, LONDON)

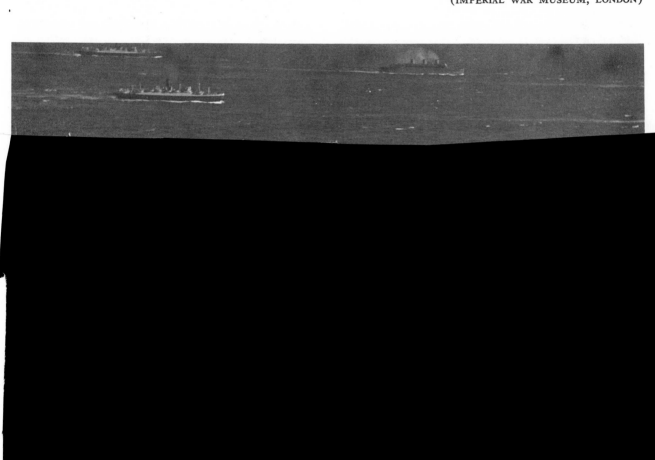

B-24 Liberator, joined the B-17 as a reconnaissance aircraft.

Long over-water flights, beset by sudden Atlantic squalls, fog, and the perils of icing, were as hazardous as they were boring, with an occasional spurt of action to relieve the monotony. The quarry was the U-boat or German aircraft which were capable of bombing British convoys or spying them out and radioing their positions to U-boat packs. Thanks to the Luftwaffe's dedication to the close-support concept, no long-range heavy bomber was available for such missions. Pressed into service was the Focke-Wulf 200 Condor, a four-engined transport, late of Lufthansa. Modified, the Condor, despite an impressive range, was still not a true bomber; even the addition of guns—a 20-mm. cannon in a top turret, plus twin machine guns in a forward firing position and another covering the tail—did not complete the conversion. The added weight and protuberances served to decrease the speed of the Condor, rendering it vulnerable to fighter attack. With all its deficiencies as a battle plane, the Condor was the best the Luftwaffe could muster in the Battle of the Atlantic.

With its range of nearly fourteen hundred miles (remaining air-borne for sixteen hours) the Condors,

chant ships beyond the range of protecting aircraft. The greater part of the fighting was a matter of ship against U-boat, or U-boat against aircraft—rarely did the classic dogfight occur over the Atlantic. The larger reconnaissance-bomber aircraft were not suited to such actions—and fighter aircraft did not have the range to venture far out to sea.

The work was monotonous and grueling for both German and British crews, what with the erratic weather and the tedium. The pilot of a Lockheed Hudson, one Pilot Officer Down, described how he and his crew longed "for some real liveliness" following a typical escort patrol.

"We did our usual stuff over them for more than a couple of hours, circling round and round in wide sweeps looking for possible danger. There wasn't a sign of anything in the air or on the sea. . . ."

Knowing that his relief was flying out and that his fuel was getting low, Down signaled "Goodbye and good luck" to the convoys and turned for home. But just for good measure he decided to make another circuit of the convoy. Half through the maneuver, Down spotted one of the escort ships signaling "Suspicious aircraft to starboard."

Down was all but certain that the plane was in fact a Coastal Command Wellington also on convoy

A German U-boat under attack by a Sunderland in the Atlantic. (IMPERIAL WAR MUSEUM, LONDON)

craft also lost altitude until Down and his crew saw the German plane splash into the sea. As he flew over the Condor, Down saw that "its wing tips were just awash—and Ernie photographed [it]. Four of the crew were in the water, hanging on to their rubber dinghy. . . . A fifth man was scrambling along the fuselage. We learned afterwards that a Met. man [weather observer] who had been aboard had been shot through the heart. The others were all right."

II

Sinking a submarine or shooting down a German plane was gratifying to air crews, but it was not quite giving it 'em back. Keeping the supply lines open was essential, but that could be left to the convoys themselves with their depth charges and massive antiaircraft gun concentrations. But striking at Germany and at the Luftwaffe: that, it was believed, should be the main concern of the Royal Air Force and especially Bomber Command.

Gradually, as the force of Bomber Command increased and as its units were released from the Battle of the Atlantic, it could be brought to bear di-

Night attack on a German submarine by a Coastal Command plane. Three flares illuminate the scene as a depth bomb explodes to the right of the U-boat.

(U. S. AIR FORCE)

A Condor down in the Atlantic after an encounter with a Coastal Command Hudson.

(IMPERIAL WAR MUSEUM, LONDON)

rectly upon Germany. But with a difference, for as had been learned during the Battle of Britain by the Luftwaffe and by Bomber Command in its initial operations, bombing heavily defended targets by day was suicidal. Bomber Command would bring the war to Germany and to the occupied countries primarily at night. The concept of pin-point precision upon absolute military targets, subsequently, diminished in favor of "area" attacks.

By the summer of 1941 a change came into the policy of Bomber Command. Bombing accuracy had not been good (after the war it was learned that of the total number of bombs dropped on southwestern Germany from May 1940 to May 1941 nearly half fell in open country). Hitting factories in the Ruhr, heavily ringed with flak, was extremely difficult and costly. On July 9, 1941, Air Marshal Sir Richard Peirse, Commander in Chief, Bomber Command, was instructed by the Air Staff to "direct the main effort of the bomber force, until further instructions, towards dislocating the German transportation system, and to destroying the morale of the civil population as a whole, and of the industrial workers in particular."

In effect, this was a concession to the "Give it 'em back" advocates, but it was also an admission of the failure of the daylight missions and the night missions against small targets, such as factories or

oil installations. It was, at the same time, a turn in the direction of taking the offensive; it boded ill for the German civilian.

Nor was it "a piece of cake" (or what the Americans were to call "milk runs") for bomber crews. Missions were long and tiring, formations were small —so were bomb loads consequently—as individual aircraft carried their lonely crews to the target and, if lucky, back. The same determination, courage, and defiant invincibility that characterized the civilian of the blitz was exhibited by the bomber crews. Weather made the flights to and from the German targets a nightmare of navigation, and flak, if not always accurate, did fill the night sky with bursting shells. And there was always the chance that on the return home, as light began to break, German fighters based in France might intercept the strays and the crippled.

This occurred in the early morning of July 7, 1941, in the early phase of the "area bombings," when a Wellington bomber of No. 75 (New Zealand) Squadron was intercepted by a Me-110. The Wellington had just successfully dropped its bombs on Münster, a comparatively small city but an important traffic junction in the Ruhr. Except for the distraction of searchlights and light flak over the city, the Wellington ran into no trouble until after it had left Germany and headed for home over the Zuider Zee in Holland.

Before it could be driven off by the Wellington's tail gunner, Sergeant A. J. R. Box, the Messerschmitt had succeeded in hitting the British bomber with cannon fire and incendiaries. The pilot, Squadron Leader R. P. Widdowson, nosed the Wellington into a dive in an attempt to elude the attacker. As the Messerschmitt dropped out of the fight, apparently hit by Box's guns, Sergeant James Ward, exschoolmaster and the plane's copilot, was thrust into the cockpit by the Wellington's dive. Ward had been in the astrodome on lookout for German interceptors, and after seeing the Me-110, learned that radio communications inside the plane were out. As he approached the cockpit to inform Widdowson of the problem, Ward was thrown forward by the dive.

The two men, relieved to see the Messerschmitt leave, soon found much to concern them. Ward peered out of the cockpit toward the right wing. "The starboard engine had been hit and the hydraulic system had been put out of action, with the

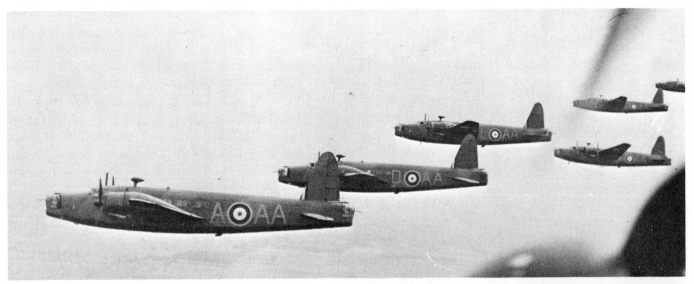

Wellingtons of No. 75 Squadron (New Zealand) setting out on mission to Germany.
(IMPERIAL WAR MUSEUM, LONDON)

result that the undercarriage fell half down, which meant, of course, that it would be useless for landing. . . . The bomb doors fell open, too, the wireless sets were not working and the front gunner was wounded in the foot.

"Worst of all, fire was burning up through the upper surface of the starboard wing where the petrol feed pipe had been split open."

Attempts to reach the fire with fire extinguishers, even coffee from flasks, were useless, for the flame was too far from the fuselage. The prospect of taking to their parachutes seemed equally hopeless.

The burning Wellington approached the Dutch coast. Before attempting to cross the North Sea Widdowson flew parallel with the shore while he and the crew discussed their next move. "I think," he said, "we'd prefer a night in the dinghy in the North Sea to ending up in a German prison camp." All agreed—they should attempt to get as close to England as possible. The flame was now steady on the wing and did not seem to be spreading. The lattice-like structure of the aircraft (technically known as geodetic) stood out in skeletal relief where the fabric had been burned away. The geodetic method of structure of the Wellington, a kind of loose basket weave, afforded it great strength without adding weight. But to copilot Ward it suggested a kind of askew ladder. It was his idea to get out of the

Sergeant James Allen Ward, V.C.
(IMPERIAL WAR MUSEUM, LONDON)

plane through the astrodome, crawl along the wing (wearing a parachute, of course, and tied to the Wellington by a rope), and put out the fire.

To Ward it seemed to be a better alternative to the possibility of freezing in the North Sea. After a brief argument the crew agreed to participate in the attempt. As the fire grew hotter, the crazy scheme of Ward's seemed less impossible. Widdowson throttled down the Wellington as much as possible and still keep it air-borne, so that the rush of air against Ward would be at a minimum. Ward then crawled through the astrodome. "Then I reached out with one foot and kicked a hole in the fabric so that I could get my foot into the framework of the plane, and then I punched another hole through the fabric in front of me to get a hand-hold, after which I made further holes and went down the side of the fuselage on to the wing. Joe [the navigator] was holding on to the rope so that I wouldn't sort of drop straight off."

Inching along, Ward moved along the wing, on which he gouged and kicked holes for his hands and feet. "Once I could not get enough hold and the wind lifted me partly off the wing and sent me against the fuselage again . . . it was like a terrific gale, only worse than any gale I've ever known."

Ward persisted until he reached the burning area. He had brought along a canvas cockpit cover to stuff into the hole, hoping to smother the fire with it. The cockpit cover, catching the wind, nearly took Ward with it. But he continued to stuff it into the wing—and, before the cover blew into the slipstream, the fire went out. Ward had cut off the supply of fuel long enough to extinguish the flames. It flared up again after Ward returned to the plane so exhausted that he could not remember how he got back. Seeing the flames he could only think, "This is pretty hard, after having got as far as this."

But it was a mere flare-up of fuel which had collected in the fabric and had been ignited by the heat of the exhaust. The fire went out and Widdowson brought the Wellington down "beautifully," as Ward described it, after the crew pumped the wheels down by hand. The only mishap was that the Wellington ended up in a barbed-wire entanglement. "Fortunately nobody was hurt though, and that was the end of the trip."

For his exploit over the North Sea Ward was given the Victoria Cross; Widdowson received the Distinguished Flying Cross and rear gunner Box the Distinguished Flying Medal. Ward died in action within two months of receiving his decoration.

If the British could bomb Germany by night, so could the Germans bomb Britain. Early attempts to deal with the German night raiders were not very successful. Defiants and Blenheims, which were no match for German fighters, were pressed into service as night fighters. Spitfires and Hurricanes were also

The Boulton Paul "Defiant," showing its rear gun turret, which deceived the Luftwaffe briefly (mistaking it for a Hurricane), but which proved to be inferior as a fighter. Mauled during the Battle of Britain, it was converted to a night fighter by the end of the summer of 1940. (U. S. AIR FORCE)

The Bristol "Beaufighter," deadliest of the two-man night fighters introduced into the blitz in the winter of 1940. (U. S. AIR FORCE)

used, but pilots were not properly trained for night fighting nor were fighter bases equipped for night flights. And air-borne radar was crude and inefficient. Consequently, interceptions by British night fighters were rare; claims for enemy aircraft destroyed were even rarer.

By late 1940, as the blitz diminished, certain advances were made in technology and aircraft. The former was the Mark IV AI (Air Interception) set and the latter the twin-engined Bristol Beaufighter. The plane was the first designed which was capable of carrying the added weight of the radar equipment without sacrifice of performance and firepower. With a two-man crew (one to operate the AI set) and generally in co-operation with a ground-controlled radar (GCI, Ground Controlled Interception), the Beaufighter proved a scourge to German night bombers.

The Mark IV AI had a range of about four miles so that the Beaufighter was guided to an enemy plane by ground control. The set also cut off at six hundred feet; by the time the Beaufighter was within that range, the enemy aircraft was generally under visual observation by the pilot. With the enemy plane in his sights, the Beaufighter pilot

One of Britain's outstanding night fighter teams: Wing Commander John Cunningham (left) and Flight Lieu- *tenant C. F. Rawnsley; the former was the Beaufighter pilot and gunner, the latter radar operator.*

(IMPERIAL WAR MUSEUM, LONDON)

was capable of bringing it under massive fire: four 20-mm. cannons were mounted in the nose and six .30-caliber machine guns were set in the leading edges of the wings.

The first squadrons began receiving the Mark IV-equipped Beaufighters in September of 1940. One of these was No. 29 Squadron, to which a young Bomber Command pilot, Guy Gibson, had been assigned as a flight commander. This assignment was regarded as a rest tour at the time, the action in night fighter units till then having proved rather tepid. While "resting" with No. 29 Squadron, however, young Gibson accounted for three enemy aircraft. Obviously the new system worked.

Number 604 Squadron was issued its first Beaufighter in October. Originally flying Blenheims in convoy protection and escort patrols, the squadron's pilots complained of never seeing one enemy aircraft. And then, with the switch to night fighting it was, apparently, more of the same: they rarely saw the German raiders and, if they did, the slow Blenheims were unable to overtake them.

Then came the Beaufighter; within a month No. 604 Squadron had scored its first victory. This had been accomplished by ex-test pilot John Cunningham and radar operator Warrant Officer J. R. Phillipson. By war's end Cunningham was the second highest-scoring night fighter pilot, with twenty victories. (Bransome Burbridge, a conscientious objector when the war began, had the highest score, twenty-one.)

In April 1941 Cunningham formed a deadly partnership with Sergeant C. F. "Jimmy" Rawnsley (as radar operator). One of their early missions, that of the night of April 12, 1941, is typical of a night fighter action. Already air-borne in their Beaufighter they were ordered by GCI to intercept a northbound raid at thirteen thousand feet. Cunningham throttled the Beaufighter to "buster" (full speed), flying due north into the dark night. Rawnsley was ordered after a short while to "flash" his AI set, but he did not pick up the enemy plane.

Ground control then suggested that Cunningham bring the plane down 2000 feet on a course of 350 degrees. During the descent Rawnsley flashed again, picked up a "blip" on the set. Whatever it was was four miles away. With Rawnsley guiding, Cunningham closed in on the blip source. Suddenly out of the misty night, above and about 2500 feet away,

Cunningham recognized the familiar outline of an He-111. Apparently unaware of the approaching Beaufighter, the pilot of the German plane continued in steady flight.

Cunningham brought the Beaufighter within eighty yards of the German bomber before opening fire. "Immediately there was a big white flash in the fuselage centre section and black pieces flew off the fuselage," Cunningham wrote in his report. "E/A went into a vertical dive to the right and about half a minute later the sky all around me was lit up by an enormous orange flash and glow. Bits of E/A were seen to be burning on the ground."

Three nights later, Cunningham and Rawnsley destroyed three Heinkels—the first time a night fighter team had scored a triple victory. (The entire night fighter toll for the month of the previous January had totaled three.) Obviously the Beaufighter and Mark IV, plus the pilot-radar operator teams (Cunningham and Rawnsley, Burbridge and F. S. Skelton, J. R. D. Braham and W. J. Gregory, and others), had proved most formidable against the German night bombers; when the Beaufighter was joined by the de Havilland Mosquito night-bombing became an extremely hazardous undertaking for the Luftwaffe.

Not all effective night fighters were teams. An extraordinary pilot was Richard Playne Stevens, who had been a civil pilot before the war. Stevens enlisted in the RAF at a rather "advanced" age—thirty-two, the maximum limit for enlistment. Stevens, who had not participated in the Battle of Britain, enlisted in the RAF with an especially poignant compulsion to give it 'em back. His wife and children had been killed in a German night raid on Manchester.

Stevens was an exceptionally well-equipped pilot with hundreds of hours of night flying (between London and Paris) to his credit. Using a non-radar-equipped Hurricane Stevens flew with a legendary abandon. Some even hinted that when he attacked a German bomber formation he screamed like a man gone mad. Without ground radar control Stevens found the enemy aircraft by flying into British antiaircraft bursts. He was certain he would find his quarry there.

During the year in which he was active Stevens shot down fourteen German bombers. His score for some time exceeded that of the two-man, radar-

Opponents in the phase of the war that followed the blitz when the RAF turned to offensive "sweeps": the

Me-109E (top left), the newer 109F (top right), the Hurricane Mark II-B (armed with bombs), and the Spitfire Mark V-B. (H. J. NOWARRA/U. S. AIR FORCE)

equipped Beaufighters. Finally, one night in December 1941, Stevens took off to harass an enemy airfield across the Channel in France and never returned. The demon which had driven him had ultimately brought him peace.

III

Stevens had been killed while on an early intruder mission—sudden night attacks on enemy air-

fields. The tide was changing by the end of 1940: even Fighter Command was operating offensively. Intruder missions and their daytime counterpart, the fighter sweep, were designed to keep the Luftwaffe busy in the west, thus affecting the campaigns in the east, to which Hitler had ordered the bulk of the air forces for his Russian gamble. To contend with the growing RAF forces, the Germans mustered only two *Geschwader,* JG 2 and JG 26, consisting of about two hundred fighters, most of them

RAF armorers belting ammunition in preparation for a Spitfire fighter sweep.
(IMPERIAL WAR MUSEUM, LONDON)

Me-109Es with a sprinkling of the newer Me-109Fs. The Spitfire Mark V was a decided match for the Messerschmitt.

The secondary objective of the sweeps and intrusions was to destroy enemy equipment, aircraft, and installations. The initial "rhubarb," as the smaller (generally two aircraft) fighter assaults were called, occurred on December 20, 1940. Two pilots, G. P. Christie and C. A. Brodie of No. 66 Squadron, took off from Biggin Hill and, after crossing the French coast at Dieppe, pounced upon a German field at Le Touquet, strafed it, and returned to England without opposition.

About two weeks later, weather permitting, two formations of fighters—five squadrons in all—crossed the Channel and wheeled over the German-occupied coast of France. As before, there was no challenge from the Luftwaffe. The next day, January 10, 1941, the first "circus" took place: this was a large aggregation of aircraft, a squadron of Blen-

Spitfire Vs of No. 122 Squadron in various stages of multiple takeoff. Formed after the Battle of Britain, the squadron was very active during the fighter sweep phase. (IMPERIAL WAR MUSEUM, LONDON)

Group Captain Adolf Gysbert "Sailor" Malan of Wellington, South Africa. An exceptional commander, Malan's final victory score totaled thirty-five. He survived the war but died of sclerosis in 1964.

(IMPERIAL WAR MUSEUM, LONDON)

Merchant Navy before he enlisted in the RAF in 1935. Malan's nickname, "Sailor," was a reminder of his nautical days. At Dunkirk Malan scored his first two victories and by the time the evacuation was over was unofficially an ace.

At thirty Malan was just about a decade older than the average fighter pilot. He seemed aloof to the younger men, matter-of-fact, blunt in speech, and not given over to the usual boyish high jinks. In the air Malan was methodical and ruthless. Killing in the air to Malan was simply that: killing and not a sport. He was the author of the RAF's *Ten Rules for Air Fighting,* in which he expounded his

heims with a six-squadron escort of fighters. The objective was a Luftwaffe airfield near Calais. This time there was a flurry of opposition, costing Fighter Command a Hurricane and two Spitfires, the latter two crashing while landing in England. One pilot died in one of the crashes.

The rhubarbs and circuses were not in fact very decisive as far as "getting on with the war" went, but were good for the morale of pilots, who had for so long been on the defensive. The sweeps were also good preparation for operating in large formations (for future escort missions when the air war would become predominantly a matter of heavy bombardment); at the same time great leaders to lead such formations were developed.

Perhaps the greatest of these new leaders, some of them survivors of "the Battle," was Adolf Gysbert Malan, a South African who had served in the

Wing Commander Douglas Bader. Bader best summed up the mood of the British fighter pilot during the Battle of Britain when he said, "We hated those aeroplanes with their iron crosses and their crooked swastikas flying into our English sky and dropping bombs indiscriminately on our English towns."

(IMPERIAL WAR MUSEUM, LONDON)

method of survival for the benefit of others. Malan survived the war, a living exemplification of his own theories, ending his combat tour with a score of thirty-two (some sources credit him with thirty-five), before being taken out of battle to instruct and command.

Malan was a superb commander, fearing neither friend nor foe. During the height of the Battle of Britain Churchill visited No. 74 Squadron, then commanded by Malan. The inquiring Churchill asked Malan what might be done to improve operations.

"Send me more bloody petrol bowsers," Malan blurted. These were the little trucks which darted across airdromes to refuel fighters during combat. It is said that within the hour Malan had his bowsers. Churchill greatly admired Malan for his directness and ability and later became the god-father of Malan's son.

By May of 1941 Malan was commander of the Biggin Hill wing. To the north, based at Tangmere, was another wing commander, Douglas Bader, who also led his squadrons over the Channel on sweeps. The long-time advocate of the "big wing" tactic, so controversial during the Battle of Britain, had also evolved another technique, which was called "finger four" formation. The larger formation broke up into units of four planes, rather loosely formed (like the fingertips of one's hand, thus the name). This supplanted the old World War I "vic" or V-formation which had proved so ineffective in the early months of the war. The loose finger four formation permitted the mutual protection of the vulnerable tails of one's squadron mates. The day of the "Hun in the sun" was just about finished.

Wing commanders, almost by virtue of their administrative position, did not always accumulate spectacular victory scores. By the summer of 1941 Bader had taken a toll of more than twenty German aircraft when his colorful fighting career came to an end. Leading a large formation in a sweep over France, Bader, in company with three other Spitfires, bounced a formation of Messerschmitt 109s. In the melee, after accounting for two 109s, Bader collided with another enemy plane. The collision tore the aft half of the Spitfire's fuselage away. Pinned into the wreckage by centrifugal force, Bader fell twenty thousand feet before he was able to tear himself out of the cockpit. And he nearly did

Pilot Officers Eugene Tobin, Vernon Keogh, and Andrew Mamedoff, three of the seven Americans who took part in the Battle of Britain. Following the Battle they transferred into the all-American "Eagle" squadron, No. 71. (IMPERIAL WAR MUSEUM, LONDON)

not make that, for as he attempted to jump from the plane his artificial leg caught in the cockpit.

All but resigned to death, Bader continued to struggle half in and half out of the cockpit when a strong lunge snapped the leg away and he fell free of the shattered Spitfire. As Bader floated earthward an Me-109 approached head on. Whether the German had intended to fire upon the British pilot dangling helplessly under his parachute or not, Bader could never say. The plane loomed closer as Bader stared, wondering what would happen. Then the German pilot flipped away and was soon out of sight. It must have been unnerving to see a fellow airman—even an enemy—falling out of the sky with only one leg.

No. 71 Squadron, February 1941 (from left): William Nichols, Ed Bateman, Stanley Kolendorski (Polish), W. E. G. Taylor, Andrew Mamedoff, Eugene Tobin, Nat Maranz, Luke Allen, Peter Provenzano, K. S. Taylor, R. Tongue (British), Gregory Daymond, and Samuel Muriello. By the time this photograph was taken Keogh had been killed in an accident; Mamedoff and Tobin, also of the original Battle of Britain trio, were later killed in action.

(IMPERIAL WAR MUSEUM, LONDON)

Flight Lieutenant Chesley Peterson and Flight Officer Gregory Augustus Daymond, Americans who served with distinction in No. 71 "Eagle" Squadron.

(IMPERIAL WAR MUSEUM, LONDON)

Eagle Squadron (No. 71) Hurricanes "beat up" the field in traditional RAF style.

(IMPERIAL WAR MUSEUM, LONDON)

Genesis of a "sweep": pilots of No. 340 Squadron ("
de France"), composed of Free French personnel, le
an RAF briefing (upper left), study their maps—
their own homeland generally—while waiting for

*...der to take off (upper right). The word comes
...rough to man their Spitfires in cockpit readiness
...ower left); and finally, "En l'air!"*

(FRENCH EMBASSY)

Bader was taken prisoner, treated with respect by Adolf Galland, who also arranged for the delivery by the British for a replacement of the broken artificial limb. (The British complied although to the Germans the delivery lacked somewhat in sportsmanship: a box containing the artificial leg was dropped immediately after a regular bombing raid.) Meanwhile, also, the leg which had been abandoned in the Spitfire was recovered and carefully repaired by the Germans and presented to Bader. From then on he never gave his captors a moment's peace, for true to form Bader spent the rest of the war attempting to escape. He became so difficult that he was finally shipped to the practically escapeproof prison at Colditz Castle, from which he was freed after the end of the war.

Better known in the United States than even the redoubtable Bader during those days of the sweeps were the so-called "Eagle Squadrons," whose members consisted of Americans. These were, initially, No. 71 Squadron, followed by No. 133 Squadron and finally by No. 121 Squadron.

The Eagle Squadrons were the brain children of a soldier of fortune, Charles Sweeny, who originally had hoped to form a kind of Lafayette Escadrille to fight the Russians in Finland. Among Sweeny's first recruits were Eugene Tobin, Andrew Mamedoff, and Vernon Keogh (who eventually ended up in the RAF and participated in the Battle of Britain). Sweeny had about thirty young men willing to fight in the air, but the fall of Finland closed that avenue of adventure. Sweeny then got them into France, from which they were driven by the victorious Germans. Most of the pilots landed in England, where for various reasons—the most important of which was the pilot shortage—they were permitted, along with other aliens, to enlist in the RAF.

Another American, artist Clayton Knight, assisted in enlisting Americans for the RAF, although he was not associated with Sweeny. In time enough Americans had gathered in England, despite official American declarations of neutrality, to warrant the formation of an all-American unit. Thus did Tobin, Mamedoff, and Keogh transfer from No. 609 Squadron to No. 71 Squadron in September 1940.

The Yanks did not get off to a very good beginning. The squadron by the following spring, although in constant training, had seen no action. The Americans did not take too gracefully to the British conception of discipline; Sholto Douglas complained to Henry Arnold that No. 71 Squadron in his opinion suffered from "too many prima donnas." Two months later, when No. 71 Squadron participated in one of its first sweeps over Calais (May 15, 1941), Section Leader John Alexander shot up the Hurricane of his wingman while attempting to get a Messerschmitt which had jumped the wingman. With disconcerting impartiality Alexander fired into both aircraft and succeeded in driving off the Messerschmitt. His wingman barely made it back to England.

In the nine months of the squadron's existence its only score was one scrapped Hurricane. In addition, it had lost pilots in training accidents, among them the veteran Keogh. And when No. 121 Squadron was formed, the day after the shooting up of Alexander's wingman, the situation worsened because of the rivalry between the two units and jealousy over publicity.

It appeared that the Eagle Squadrons were more trouble than they were worth, but again, leadership made the difference. Under the command of Walter Churchill (not related to the Prime Minister) and later H. de C. A. Woodhouse the American units became fine combat units. From among their own members too came such outstanding pilot-leaders as Gregory Augustus Daymond, late of Hollywood and only twenty when he became a full-fledged fighter pilot; another great Eagle leader was Chesley Peterson, who had been rejected by the U. S. Army Air Force because of an "inherent lack of flying ability." Both men in time won the Distinguished Flying Cross and in turn commanded No. 71 Squadron.

The Eagles proved themselves during the period of the fighter sweeps and received credit for destroying more than seventy German aircraft— enough planes to outfit six German squadrons. Besides the sweeps, the Eagles participated in less exciting, but no less essential, convoy patrols—this duty generally fell to No. 133 Squadron.

With the entry of the United States into the war the survivors of all three Eagle Squadrons were absorbed into the U. S. Air Force as the 4th Fighter Group. They would be heard from again.

Brenden "Paddy" Finucane, Irish poet of the air, leader of fighter sweeps, whose final words when he fell into the Channel were, "This is it, chaps."

(IMPERIAL WAR MUSEUM, LONDON)

IV

But until England could depend upon massive aid from America the Channel sweeps continued. No longer did anyone speak of the Battle of Britain, nor even the blitz; the fight was being taken back to the enemy, by the bombers at night and the fighters by day. A new spirit of hope had begun to glimmer. The mood was once again more gay than grim.

This was expressed by Brenden Finucane, better known as "Paddy," an outstanding pilot and wing commander by the summer of 1942. "It's a grand life," he said, "and I know I'm lucky to be among the squadrons that are carrying out the sweeps."

Finucane loved flying and the sky. "Sure," he once said, "the queen of heaven tonight has more stars than she knows what to do with. Often and often I'm put to it not to collide with the stars up there, and me dodging in and out the clouds. Stars now, have a great hold over me."

It was Finucane's dream that he might destroy twenty-one enemy aircraft by October 14, 1941, his twenty-first birthday. Poet he may have been, and a dreamer, but by that date he had shot down two dozen German planes and had been awarded the Distinguished Service Order. Finucane had one great hatred—the English Channel, which he called "demented."

The Channel persisted as a formidable ditch and mercilessly swallowed up Bomber Command planes returning from German raids and fighter pilots after sweeps, despite the brilliant rescue work of the RAF's Sea Rescue launches and planes.

The frightful Channel weather was greatly responsible for the success of the famous Channel Dash (February 11–13, 1942), when the battle cruisers *Scharnhorst* and *Gneisenau,* plus the cruiser *Prinz Eugen,* broke out of the French port of Brest, slipped through the English Channel, and returned to ports in the fatherland. The success of the operation was also due to unusually close cooperation between German naval and air forces. Adolf Galland's units, some flying the new Focke-Wulf 190 fighters, participated in the action. Despite heroic attempts by British fighters and bombers under poor weather conditions the German ships actually made it through "their" Channel to the shocked dismay of England.

That the German ships had had to flee French waters was an indication of the turn of battle, the true and conclusive end of the Battle of Britain.

It was in the summer of 1942, long after the German ships had fled, that Paddy Finucane took his last flight. Having completed a sweep, Finucane, accompanied by his wingman, a Canadian, Pilot Officer Alan Aikman, had swooped down for some strafing on the way home. Hidden among the sand dunes near Le Touquet was a machine-gun nest which opened fire on the lead Spitfire as it passed over. Finucane's plane shuddered momentarily and then continued toward England. Aikman, meanwhile, dropped down, strafed the gun position, then swung out over the Channel to overtake Finucane.

Pulling up alongside the Spitfire, Aikman radioed, "You've had it, sir, in your radiator."

"I thought so," Finucane replied; "my engine's running a temperature. I shall have to get out of this." The Spitfire had lost altitude and was too low for Finucane to parachute; he would have to ditch in the "demented" Channel. As his plane splashed into the water Finucane said, "This is it, chaps." The Spitfire fell tail first and sank immediately. Aikman circled the spot in vain, for Finucane never came to the surface. The twenty-two-year-old wing commander drowned in the waters he never loved.

The ascendancy of such leaders as Malan, Bader, and Finucane marked the official close of the Battle of Britain, of the transition from the dogfighting, exciting days of the Battle to the more deadly, businesslike making of war. Although Britain was hard pressed by a lack of supplies and men, this lack was inadvertently to be provided for by a handful of warlike men in Tokyo.

Index

Note: References to illustrations are in italics

d.once if

I GREW UP WITH A FAMOUS FATHER.

My name is Martin Luther King III. But when I was a kid, my friends and family called me Marty so no one would confuse me with my father, the Reverend Martin Luther King, Jr.

When I was five years old, my dad gave one of his most famous speeches. "I have a dream that one day this nation will rise up and live out the true meaning of its creed . . . that all men are created equal," he declared. "I have a dream that my four little children will one day live in a nation where they will not be judged by the color of their skin, but by the content of their character."

I am the second of those four children he spoke about.

There have been a lot of books written about my father. But not a whole lot has been written about my dad. This book is about my daddy, what it was like to live with him, and how much I loved him.

My sister Yolanda, who we called Yoki, and I wanted to go to Funtown more than anything. "Well, kids, you know Daddy is working very hard so that you and all children can go to Funtown, but it's not possible today," Daddy would say. "Maybe next week." But that week never came.

"You just don't want to take us!" Yoki wailed. And finally my mother explained. We were not allowed in Funtown. The rides and the roller coasters were for white people only. That's how it was when I was growing up. My dad fought to change that.

At home, though, my father was just Dad. He tossed the football with me, taught me how to shoot hoops, teased me, and played with me. He would lift me up and put me on top of the refrigerator. I imagined swinging from the ceiling fan as if I were flying in my own airplane. Then I would let Daddy catch me as I fell into his arms.

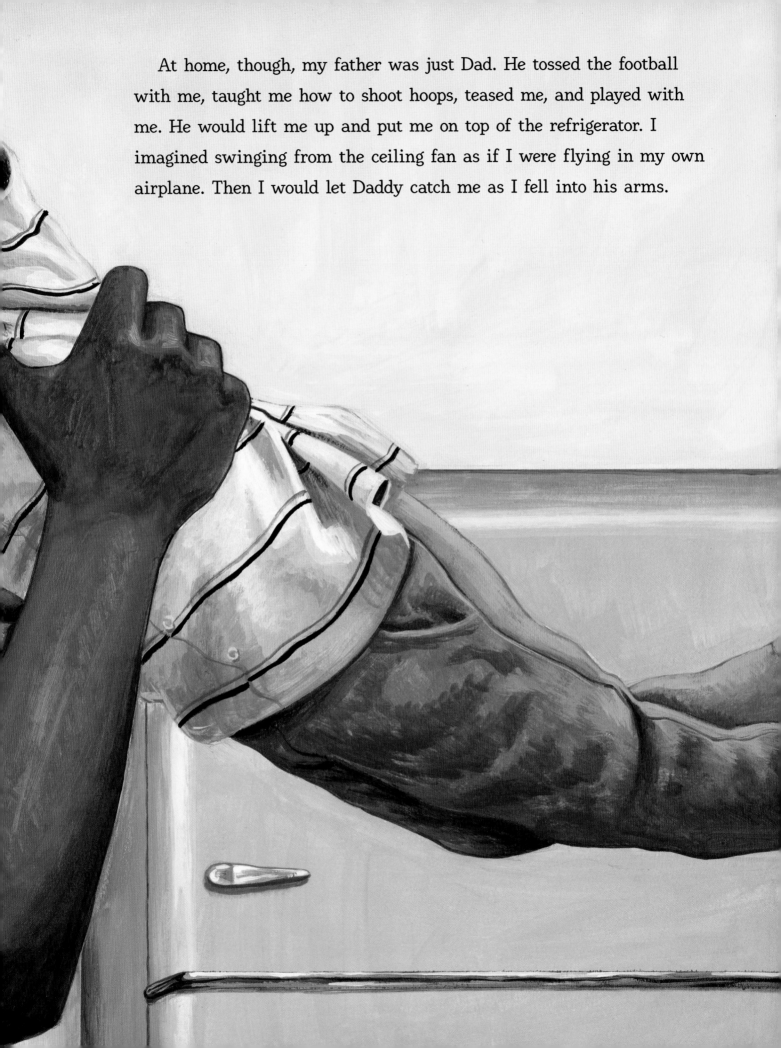

Away from home, things were different. It wasn't always easy being the son of Martin Luther King, Jr.

"What's your name?" the two older boys asked.

"I don't remember," I said. "I forgot."

I knew it was wrong to lie.

"Why'd you say that, Marty?" my mother asked later.
"You know your name. It's your father's name." I knew. And
I knew why I hadn't said my name—because I was afraid.

Some people didn't like my father's work. He was "stirring up trouble," they said. My father never stole anything or hurt anyone. Even so, he was thrown in jail more than thirty times. He had the courage to stand up and say "This law is unfair," and sometimes he was arrested for that.

Once, a neighbor was driving me home from school. On the radio we heard that the Reverend Martin Luther King and about eighty other people had been thrown in jail. I was terrified. I ran inside my house crying and asked my mother, "Why did Daddy go to jail? What did he do wrong?"

My mother hugged me. "Your dad went to jail to help people," she told me. "Some people don't have enough to eat, or comfortable homes, or clothes to wear. They are not as fortunate as we are. Daddy went to jail to make it possible for all people to have these things. Don't worry, Daddy will be coming back."

I carried her words close to my heart. A year later, when Daddy was arrested again, Yoki was afraid that he wouldn't be back for Christmas.

This time, I was the one who consoled her. "Don't cry, Yoki. Daddy will be back. He has to help the people. He has already helped some people, but he has to help some more, and when he finishes, he'll be back."

My father was not the only one in danger. Many people were hurt or even killed as they tried to change unfair laws.

Once, as I marched in a protest, I saw a pretty lady with a bandage over her nose. My mother explained that she'd been attacked by a police officer. The marchers were peaceful. But that didn't stop people from trying to hurt them. Even police officers sprayed marchers with fire hoses or turned dogs on them.

Later, a police officer came up to us with a huge dog that growled at me. I was terrified. "It's okay, Marty," my dad told me as he took my hand.

And I felt safe. My dad was not a tall man, but he always made me feel like he was a giant. I was never afraid when I was with him.

No matter how bad it got, my dad never fought back. "We must meet violence with nonviolence. We must meet hate with love," he always said.

Nonviolence wasn't just for marches and protests. It was for home as well. One Christmas, my brother, Dexter, and I got toy guns for presents. Most of the other boys in the neighborhood played with guns, and we wanted to be just like them.

But we knew that guns were wrong. They were not toys—they were machines made to hurt and kill. Together the whole family took the guns outside, made a bonfire, and destroyed them.

That night, as my brother and I watched our gifts burn,
we believed we were destroying all the hate in the world.

One bonfire couldn't fix everything. But some things *were* getting better—like the law that kept black and white children from going to the same school. When I was in third grade, that law was finally changed. My mother told Yoki and me that we'd be going to a new school in September.

I didn't want to be the new kid who sat alone. Yoki felt the same way. "We don't want to go," we complained. "We don't want to be the only black kids at the school."

My mother said she'd see what she could do. The day before school started, we found out that our three friends, the Abernathys, would be going with us to Spring Street School.

I was glad to have my friends and my sister with me, because when we got to the school, there were flashbulbs going off and TV cameras everywhere. Why did reporters want to talk to us? We were just kids going to school like everybody else.